Young People, Popular Culture and Education

Other titles in the Contemporary Issues in Education Studies series include:

Changing Urban Education – Simon Pratt-Adams, Meg Maguire and
    Elizabeth Burn
Education and Constructions of Childhood – David Blundell
Multiculturalism and Education – Richard Race

Also available from Continuum:

Exploring Key Issues in Education – Derek Kassem and Dean Garratt
Introduction to Education Studies – Sue Warren
Rethinking Childhood – Phil Jones
Rethinking Children and Research – Mary Kellett
Rethinking Children and Families – Nick Frost
Rethinking Children's Rights – Sue Welch and Phil Jones

Young People, Popular Culture and Education

Chris Richards

Contemporary Issues in Education Studies

continuum

Continuum International Publishing Group

The Tower Building	80 Maiden Lane
11 York Road	Suite 704
London SE1 7NX	New York, NY 10038

www.continuumbooks.com

British Library Cataloguing-in-Publication Data
A catalogue record for this book is available from the British Library.

ISBN: 978-1-8470-6544-5 (paperback)
       978-1-4411-0735-0 (hardcover)

Library of Congress Cataloging-in-Publication Data
Richards, Chris, 1952–
Young people, popular culture, and education / Chris Richards.
   p. cm. – (Contemporary issues in education studies)
Includes bibliographical references and index.
ISBN 978-1-84706-544-5 (pbk.)
1. Education–Social aspects–Great Britain. 2. Popular culture–Great Britain. 3. Mass media and teenagers–Great Britain. 4. Teenagers–Great Britain–Social conditions. I. Title.

LC191.8.G7R53 2011
306.43'20941–dc22

                                                      2010020311

Typeset by Newgen Imaging Systems Pvt Ltd, Chennai, India
Printed and bound in India by Replika Press Pvt Ltd

Contents

Series Editors' Preface

The series *Contemporary Issues in Education Studies* is timely for its critical exploration of education in this period of accelerating change. Responding to this challenge, the books in the series have titles which correspond closely to the needs of students taking a wide range of courses and modules within Education Studies and related fields such as teacher education. Education Studies is an important subject area and should be at the heart of many faculties of education. There is a need for relevant, core texts within Education Studies, which explore and critique contemporary issues across the discipline and challenge prevailing discourses of what education is about. We also need to provide students with strong theoretical perspectives and frameworks, focusing on relevant literature in an accessible and readable format.

We set the authors of this series a number of challenges in terms of what to include in their text. Therefore, each book addresses a contemporary issue in education and has an international rather than just an English focus. The texts are structured to provide a clear grasp of the topic and to provide an overview of research, current debates and perspectives. Contextualized extracts from important primary texts ensure readers' exposure to dominant contemporary theories in the field of education, by demystifying essential vocabulary and educational discourse, enabling the education student to engage with these texts in a meaningful way. The extensive and appropriate literature review in each text gives a firm base for contextualizing the subject and promoting understanding at multiple levels.

This series is grounded in a strong conceptual, theoretical framework and is presented in an accessible way. Each book uses features such as case studies, reflective exercises and activities that encourage and support student learning. Key relevant and contemporary questions are inserted throughout each chapter to extend the readers' thinking and understanding. Furthermore, additional material is also provided in the companion website to each book.

Chris Richards writes with the perceptiveness gained from his extensive experience and knowledge of working as a secondary school teacher and university lecturer and researching young people and popular culture in urban schools and more recently in higher education. Young People, Popular Culture and Education will be of particular interest to Education Studies students; indeed for many years, the author was the course leader on the BA Education Studies degree at London Metropolitan University. However, readers from a range of subject areas will also benefit from the author's observations, reflections and analysis of the cultural study of youth in different educational settings.

The work draws on historical and contemporary contexts as both are important in discussing young people, popular culture and education. By contextualizing the significance of the concept of Cultural Studies within an examination of the subject area, historical perspectives are highlighted and used to inform contemporary developments in the cultural study of youth and popular culture. As with all of the texts in this series, we have encouraged the authors to challenge the readers to think critically and differently about educational issues. Young People, Popular Culture and Education makes an authoritative and constructive contribution to ongoing debates. Challenging previous constructions in which young people and popular culture have been understood in multidisciplinary contexts, it will become a major resource for all those who care about the changing nature of youth, culture and education.

Simon Pratt-Adams and Richard Race
Series Editors
London and Athens, July 2010

Acknowledgements

I first started teaching in London when I was 22. It was November 1974 and, working with Waltham Forest's West Indian Supplementary Service, I was placed, initially, in Downsell Junior School. I was not entirely serious about teaching, had not trained to do it, and got the job just a couple of months after finishing an MA in American Studies. I stayed for a little more than a year, then took off, as I had intended, to travel to Japan by way of the Trans-Siberian Railway and to stay there for some months. Back in London, in the Autumn of 1976, I commuted to the Centre for Contemporary Cultural Studies at Birmingham University. I had a troubled and unhappy two years there. I gave up on Cultural Studies physically, by no longer going to the Centre, in the early summer of 1978. But as I embarked on postgraduate teacher training at Goldsmiths College, it was to the recently published work of Paul Willis – both *Learning to Labour* (1977) and *Profane Culture* (1978) that I turned. And as the year (1978–1979) went on, I read more and more into Cultural Studies, finding it persuasive and illuminating.

I taught English and Media Studies in inner London secondary schools for a little more than five years (1979–1984) and also worked with the magazine *Teaching London Kids*. I taught for a further five years in further education in Harrow (1985–1989). I got involved with the British Film Institute and, belatedly, should thank David Lusted for supporting me at that time. I also joined the Media Teachers' Research Group, led by David Buckingham, at the Institute of Education. He too was immensely supportive and contributed, probably more than anyone else, to the more focused writing that I did through 1988–1998. From 1989, I taught at the Institute of Education, University of London for about six years. After that, I was busy with teaching, developing and often running the Education Studies degree programme both at the University of North London and its successor, London Metropolitan University. Still carrying my past engagements with American Studies, Cultural Studies and Media Studies, I devoted much of my time to writing and teaching 'modules' representing those interests. Through more than 13 years of such teaching, some hundreds of mainly Education Studies students have had the sometimes unexpected and perhaps challenging experience of taking on the work of Cultural Studies authors such as Stuart Hall, Angela McRobbie, Paul Gilroy, David Morley, Paul Willis, Richard Dyer and, indeed, others such as Pierre Bourdieu, Simon Frith and bell hooks. I want to thank all my students both for their tolerance and their enthusiasm.

As I finish writing this book, in the Autumn of 2009, I am no longer teaching. But I am regularly visiting a London primary school where, instead of spending my time in the classroom, I am out in the playground 'doing research'.

Through all of this, there are also personal acknowledgements that I want to make. Elizabeth Rouse, with whom I spent those months in Japan, and many years since, continues to live with my sometimes obsessive and frequently nocturnal working habits. Her own working life, as Deputy Rector of the University of the Arts, London, is busy, to say the least. Both our daughters – still students, one doing an MA in American Studies, the other completing postgraduate training in paediatric nursing – remain mostly politely interested in what I do. So big thanks to Elizabeth, Fay and Francesca.

London, November 2009/March 2010

Part 1
Culture, Youth and Education

The first part of this book introduces the idea of culture and the field that, at least in its formative years, defined its concerns around such a pivotal concept – Cultural Studies. For many years, Cultural Studies was mainly identified with Birmingham University's Centre for Contemporary Cultural Studies, often also known as the 'Birmingham School' and as the pre-eminent source of 'British Cultural Studies'. Though the Centre's title included the word 'contemporary', a great deal of historical work, some of it reaching back into the nineteenth century and earlier, was pursued there. Even when the focus was on the 'contemporary' in the sense of the present time, historical analyses were important. In both parts of this book, historical perspectives inform the discussion of young people, popular culture and education. The opening chapters here look back to developments from the late 1950s through to the first decade of the twenty-first century. Significant publications, and their authors, are introduced with their full titles and names. Often the titles evoke the character of intellectual debate and political commitment in the period of their first publication. Full names help to establish the reality (and sometimes the gender) of writers too often depersonalized through conventions of academic referencing. Later in the book, titles are used less and authors, if already introduced, are referred to by their last names. The third chapter outlines more recent and emergent developments in the cultural study of youth, shifting from the contemporary towards the future.

Culture and Youth

The idea of culture

This chapter reviews the concept of 'culture' and shows how it has been debated in the cultural study of youth, especially in the work of Birmingham University's Centre for Contemporary Cultural Studies (1964–2002). Its value and relevance for continuing work in youth cultural studies and in Education Studies are explained and illustrated.

'Culture is one of the two or three most complicated words in the English language' (Williams, 1976: 76). There's no way around this. The words that seem so familiar and that are used daily without much pause for thought carry layers of meaning and histories of dispute that need to be recovered. This chapter will begin the work of reflection on the language that we use, recalling moments when particular words appeared new, sharp challenges to the authority of official discourse. Culture is, of course, the root term for Cultural Studies, the field or discipline to which this book will refer most often and in which many of those I discuss have made their careers. Raymond Williams, opening this first chapter, though a Professor of Drama at Cambridge, was the author of, among many books, *Culture and Society 1780–1950* (Williams, 1958), *Television: Technology and Cultural Form* (Williams, 1974) and *Problems in Materialism and Culture* (Williams, 1980). *Keywords: A Vocabulary of Culture and Society* (Williams, 1976), from which the assertion of the complexity of culture is taken, was originally an appendix to the draft of *Culture and Society* Williams completed in 1956. These years of publication, and of first writing, do matter. They point to the histories of the words that now routinely shape the way we think and talk about the social worlds in which we live. And arguments about culture have been critical to thinking about the education of young people not just in the past half century of Cultural Studies but earlier in the 1800s too (see, for example, Matthew Arnold's *Culture and Anarchy* 1869/2009).

The main focus of this chapter is on the middle years of the twentieth century and the subsequent emergence of Cultural Studies. Some of those who contributed to the early formation of Cultural Studies were trained in the study of literature and were, therefore, preoccupied with the analysis and evaluation of texts. In one of the definitions of culture, only a small selection of highly distinctive texts would be regarded as worth the kind of detailed, intense and sustained attention such literary analysts were accustomed to. This idea of culture can be traced back to Arnold, a Victorian cultural critic and Inspector of Schools, and involves asserting that only a small fraction of what people read, or even of what they don't read, has any cultural value at all. Judgements about what counts as culture were very much in the hands of specialized intellectuals – university-based academics, critics, reviewers and, perhaps, teachers. At its most restricted, this could mean that even most recent and contemporary novels and poetry and plays would be eliminated from serious consideration just because they had yet to endure and accumulate the value recognizable in texts from past centuries.

This elite view of culture has had a profound and continuing influence in education. The school curriculum has been shaped by the establishment of subjects such as English which, having displaced the study of Greek and Latin, became, through much of the twentieth century, the secure home of the particular, and elevated, cultural value both of some kinds of texts (novels, plays and poetry) and of some authors (Shakespeare, most obviously). More broadly, the school curriculum has involved judgements about what constitutes worthwhile and legitimate knowledge and continues to do so. One insistent criticism of this, in part from early proponents of Cultural Studies (Williams, 1961/1965, 1977), was that such judgements, and the idea of culture they assumed, were representative of class interests. In the classic Marxist sense, this was an instance of the *particular* interest being misrepresented as of *universal* value. Of course, the mistake that might follow from this involved arguing that what was valued in these terms should therefore be rejected – crudely, this could result in throwing out Shakespeare altogether!

Another way of conceptualizing the field of culture involved a loosening of the boundaries so that all sorts of writing, and eventually visual media too, could be admitted as worthy of study (Williams, 1976). Such an extension would therefore include newspapers and advertisements and all the fiction (in print and, logically, in film and on TV too) that, often, was described as 'popular'. Though the concern with value, and with discrimination in exercising judgements of value, appeared to recede, the relationship to these other cultural materials was still most often shaped by earlier attachments to the practice of selection and elevation. Richard Hoggart's *The Uses of Literacy: Aspects of Working-Class Life with Special Reference to Publications and Entertainments* (1957) and Stuart Hall and Paddy Whannel's *The Popular Arts* (1964) illustrate this both in the range of their concerns and in the occasional expressions of distaste at what they find. Hoggart went on to be the first Director of the Centre for Contemporary Cultural Studies at Birmingham University. Stuart Hall succeeded him and became the most well-known and influential figure in British Cultural Studies. This is an important strand in the history both of English and of the Cultural Studies that emerged and ultimately broke from it. In this version of the idea of culture, the objects of study were, still, texts, and the ways of studying them were substantially inherited from the practices of literary criticism formed in previous decades.

A third way of thinking about culture, crucial to the direction taken by Cultural Studies from the later 1960s and since, distances itself from both the central preoccupation with texts and, apparently, the issue of value (Williams, 1976). This is culture as a whole way of life. Defining culture as about how people live can seem to be so all encompassing that it allows no focus. But this approach to culture had important precedents in social anthropology in which a tradition of studying very small-scale communities (for example, a village) produced accounts seeking to describe all aspects of life in the chosen 'field'. Work and education, religion and family life, sex and the weather, might all figure in an integrated study (Gray, 2003). The urge to document and describe, to detail and to map, had an ambiguous history in anthropology's close involvement with colonial administration. Such meticulous efforts to portray the lives of others were implicated in strategies of surveillance and control (Evans-Pritchard, 1940; Asad, 1973). But they also tended towards a liberal cultural relativism, acknowledging, it seemed, the validity, rationality and coherence of life perceived as alien to that of late nineteenth- and twentieth-century Europe and America. In this respect, culture as a whole way of life was more than a value-neutral category. To acknowledge that a particular practice, eating raw fish or decapitating your enemies, for example, was a feature of a culture, was to allow a degree of value (Rosaldo, 1993). Typically, such cultural value lies in the meanings of these activities for those who were 'native' participants in a particular cultural setting. The great strength of this much-expanded concept of culture was that it insisted on giving attention to the full breadth of social life and therefore to lives very different from those of literary intellectuals. This idea of culture moved Cultural Studies into somewhat the same 'territory' as sociology and the more urban-orientated developments in social and cultural anthropology. But for Cultural Studies, in the 1960s and 1970s, the new 'discipline' was also a challenge to these older social sciences and, in some respects, seemed to carry forward aspects of the new Left and of the counterculture. Sociology was about social order; Cultural Studies was about change, political upheaval, and social revolution, persistent themes in the decades of its emergence.

E. P. Thompson, the Marxist historian and author of *The Making of the English Working-Class* (1963), questioned the adequacy of conceptualizing culture as a whole way of life, preferring the formula 'a whole way of struggle'. His point was that culture could be used to make a way of life seem settled, unchanging and uncontested. In his view, that was never the case. Not an anthropologist preoccupied with the internal logic of a relatively isolated social entity, his field was the longer history of conflict in relations between social classes in British society. This historical perspective gradually entered into Cultural Studies, at least as it developed in Birmingham where the historian Richard Johnson eventually replaced Stuart Hall as the Director of the Centre for Contemporary Cultural Studies at the end of the 1970s. Out of this historical inflection of Cultural Studies, two books, *Unpopular Education: Schooling and Social Democracy in England since 1944* (1981) and *Education Limited: Schooling, Training and the New Right in England since 1979* (1991), aimed to review and intervene in contemporary debates around the organization of state schooling. For reasons to be considered later, these historical initiatives have not, on the whole, been regarded as central to, and often do not figure in, the more internationalized profile of Cultural Studies prevalent in the 1990s and since. Indeed, when Cultural Studies is conjoined with Media Studies, it tends to loop back to the earlier emphasis on texts, if with an increased interest in questions of production and consumption.

But the study of a culture, as if it could be isolated or at least literally located in a relatively bounded geographical setting (like a village, miles from anywhere else), was never quite imported into Cultural Studies in those terms. Paul Willis's widely influential *Learning to Labour: How Working-Class Kids Get Working-Class Jobs* (1977), though gaining some notoriety for focusing on just a dozen truculent and foul-mouthed 'lads', was actually attentive to much wider contextual issues, both historical, such as the formation of working-class culture, and more contemporary matters of educational policy and economic change. More recently, American inheritors of British Cultural Studies have argued that the concept of culture as defined within a circumscribed physical place is now, if it ever was, entirely inappropriate to any adequate understanding of how people live their lives. Shirley Brice Heath, in her 1996 epilogue to *Ways with Words: Language, Life, and Work in Communities and Classrooms* (originally published in 1983), stresses the mobile, disparate and technologically mediated character of everyday life among the people, and particularly young people, in the apparently long familiar region of the Piedmont Carolinas where she conducted her fieldwork through the late 1960s and 1970s (Heath, 1996: 370–6). Nadine Dolby, investigating a single school in Durban, South Africa, rejects the idea of culture as tied to 'geography' and 'territory', insisting by contrast, on less circumscribed processes of identification enacted in the context of globalization (Dolby, 2001: 16). Her book, *Constructing Race: Youth, Identity, and Popular Culture in South Africa,* is an important example of what Cultural Studies research can do in the circumstances described, perhaps with just a hint of lament, by Shirley Brice Heath (1983/1996).

So, it is worth asking, what is a viable, working definition of culture? Probably, the most sustained and constructive emphasis is on 'meaning'. In other words, by approaching the study of any aspect of social life with culture as a central concern, the meanings of the various aspects of that life are highlighted. Provided that such an emphasis does not exclude the need for a critical debate about aspects of the social life in question, it is a useful approach. Suppose, for example, that we wanted to know why young people go out and get drunk, often so drunk that they throw up, or get into fights. It should be possible to ask questions and construct an account that gives space to the meaning of this behaviour for those involved. But this shouldn't then collapse into the kind of cultural relativism that so reveres meaning that questions of social consequences – basically damage and dismay – are then ruled out of consideration (see Willis et al., 1990: 100–9).

One well-known statement of the importance of working with a concept of culture comes from the American anthropologist Clifford Geertz. It is included in the first essay of a collection, *The Interpretation of Cultures*, published in 1973. The essay is about how anthropologists study the social world, typically by doing ethnography; it is called, memorably, 'Thick description: toward an interpretive theory of culture'. He comments:

> The concept of culture I espouse . . . is essentially a semiotic one. Believing, with Max Weber, that man is an animal suspended in webs of significance he himself has spun, I take culture to be those webs, and the analysis of it to be therefore not an experimental science in search of law but an interpretive one in search of meaning. It is explication I am after, construing social expressions on their surface enigmatical. (Geertz, 1973: 5)

Another definition, but from those working within Cultural Studies in the 1970s, includes a similar emphasis on the active production of meaning, though drawing more explicitly on Marx than Weber, it also emphasizes the constraining 'circumstances' of such production:

> A culture includes the 'maps of meaning' which make things intelligible to its members. These 'maps of meaning' are not simply carried around in the head: they are objectivated in the patterns of social organisation and relationship through which the individual becomes a 'social individual'. Culture is the way the social relations of a group are structured and shaped: but it is also the way those shapes are experienced, understood and interpreted. (Clarke et al., 1975: 10–11)

This, from 'Subcultures, Cultures and Class', in *Resistance through Rituals* (1975), has lingered in the debates around culture and youth for many years. This publication became a key point of reference for debates between youth researchers then and since. It is at this point that the question of why Cultural Studies should have been, apparently, so especially concerned with youth needs to be posed.

Youth

The authors of *Resistance through Rituals* (Clarke et al., 1975), in common with E. P. Thompson, were not happy with culture in the singular. They too wanted to insist that the more concrete social reality was composed of cultures in relations of conflict and dissonance, not a whole way of life in any stable and unified sense. Social class and the differentiation of culture associated with class conflict and division was one enduring preoccupation but so too was the formation of differences between generations and, in particular, the emergence in the 1950s and since of youth cultures. In 'Subcultures, Cultures and Class' (Clarke et al., 1975), there is a deep scepticism towards the notion of 'Youth Culture', and much of the work of that long essay is directed towards dismantling what the authors regard as a simplistic figure emerging from journalism. Despite their subsequent reputation for their attention to 'spectacular' youth subcultures, their discussion is more cautious and more measured: 'For the majority, school and work are more structurally significant – even at the level of consciousness – than style and music.' (Clarke et al., 1975: 16) Their rejection of 'Youth Culture' is followed by an exploration of various youth subcultures and of the more diffuse 'counterculture', each characterized in terms of class histories and of the larger economic and political contexts of their formation. The essay is seminal, and many of the issues debated through the following years are raised already in this discussion from the mid 1970s. For example, the contribution of middle-class counterculture (hippies and others) to the formation of a new middle-class and to more flexible, and commercially profitable, 'lifestyles' is recognized long before these trends were confirmed in the events of subsequent decades (Hall, 1969, reprinted in Gray et al., 2007; Frank, 1997). But, to repeat the point, the importance of their approach is that culture is not treated as a singular and cohesive way of life, and it is the variety of class-located cultures lived and reworked in shifting historical circumstances that occupy their attention.

Youth should not be separated out and elevated to the mythical status of a culture (Connell et al., 1982). Even within the idea of a 'generation', all those who live through youth in the same few years, the divisions and contradictions between the more particular class-cultural locations of its members are likely to be of greater importance than the rather bland generalizations about 'young people', of then or now, that so routinely fill public journalistic discourse. But there are of course distinctive characteristics of particular periods that do produce a degree of generational commonality. The organization of state education after the 1944 Education Act is one significant strand in shaping young people's experience through the 1950s and 1960s. The division of secondary education into academic and vocational routes had profound consequences (Centre for Contemporary Cultural Studies, 1981; Richards, 1992; Jones, 2003). So too is the development of a youth-orientated popular media, music, film and television, especially from the mid-1950s onwards. In combination with the proliferation of youth-orientated leisure institutions – clubs and discos for example – this formation of a market in which young people could spend and spend their time was significantly different from that experienced by the parental generation (those who were adults in the 1940s). The broader pattern of the availability of employment, and of particular types of work, was also a condition defining differences between generations (Clarke et al., 1975: 49–52).

In this period – the 1950s and 1960s – and arguably ever since, youth has also been a focus of widespread concern, sometimes panic but often in combination with fascination and sometimes envy. Youth as a powerful symbol of the new, of change and of the future, has become a recurring feature of public discourse. In this sense, the young become the bearers of the larger society's debate about its own difficulties and its possible futures. This pattern of displacement of wider anxieties onto young people has been discussed by many authors, but especially Griffin (1993) and Buckingham (2000a).

It may seem as if the idea of culture has begun to slide away in the past few paragraphs. But 'culture' is actually quite crucial to critical thinking about young people's lives. An emphasis on culture encourages attention to the meanings given by people to their own lives. It is especially appropriate to the task of understanding the positions occupied by young people and, from those positions, how and why they act as they do. This, a core concern of Cultural Studies, makes such an approach particularly important for those adults who work with young people, not only in youth work but also in education. 'Youth' may be a complex, unpredictable and unstable category but, with a sufficiently concrete and differentiated grasp of cultures, or subcultures, the specific circumstances of particular young people can be rendered meaningful in terms that go beyond the accumulation of reductive and simplistic banalities such as 'raging hormones', 'boys will be boys' or 'it's the company she keeps'. Back in the mid-1970s, Paul Willis' study of working-class boys in a West Midlands secondary school explored the logic of apparently foolish and often offensive behaviour in terms of the longer histories of working-class labour, the related formations of masculinity and the realistic pessimism informing working-class families in their encounters with state education. Though his work has been criticized for attributing rather too much insight to the boys in question (Willis, 2000), it remains, in its key argument, a landmark study in the application of cultural theories to the detail of an empirically researched case. In particular, it showed that the failure of working-class boys in school was the outcome of sustained and meaningful action rather than evidence of a lack of intelligence, aspiration or diligence.

Valerie Hey's (1997) study of teenage girls, *The Company She Keeps: An Ethnography of Girls' Friendship*, though less focused on the educational implications of girls' actions, is a similarly detailed study of girls in everyday life in and around school. In this case, the study directly questions assumptions about just how friendly and 'nice' girls may be in their relations with each other. Though not written in a Cultural Studies department, Hey's book (based on a PhD in sociology) well illustrates the uses of ethnographic methods derived from anthropology in the detailed study of apparently familiar and ordinary features of young people's lives. Separated from the preoccupation with exotic, 'other' people, ethnography becomes a method of study applicable to the social settings in which the ethnographer may herself have been formed (see also Heath, 1983/1996).

However, even ethnographers working within social worlds to which they may feel they belong (Heath, 1983/1996) are inevitably involved in attributing meanings to what *other* people do. If the idea of culture is reduced solely to a concern with meaning, studies limited by that concern might produce an interesting and speculative map of the subjective dimension of people's lives. But ethnography is properly orientated to achieving rather more than that. The emphasis of ethnography has been on constructing holistic accounts. In other words, the relationships between all the components of a social setting are supposed to be specified and explained. Such an aspiration to examine the whole social entity may not ever be realizable, but it keeps questions of explanation in play. For example, Willis's *Learning to Labour* does not settle for telling us what it means to the lads to swear at and wind up teachers. Such actions are explained in relation to a much wider mapping of class histories and of the social relations of work in a post-industrial capitalist society.

Resistance through Rituals and its legacy

Some influential studies of young people have been introduced briefly in the preceding pages. It is now the work of this introductory chapter to provide an outline of the broader growth of youth cultural studies over the past decades. Many examples do not focus at all on educational settings but this illustrates one important tendency in Cultural Studies: to locate the really dynamic and 'self-defining' features of young people's lives in the sphere of leisure and not in the life of families, or in work and, often, not in education. The double issue of the journal *Cultural Studies* (7/8) published in 1975 as *Resistance through Rituals* launched the kind of youth studies that became so integral to the reputation of Cultural Studies at Birmingham University and beyond. Some of the studies had already been made available in more ephemeral form as cheaply reproduced papers, typed and stapled, and distributed direct from the Centre for Contemporary Cultural Studies. But full publication of many of them came in the years after 1975 (Gray et al., 2007).

The *Resistance through Rituals* collection included two studies by Dick Hebdige, 'The meaning of mod' and 'Reggae, rastas and rudies'. These foreshadowed the publication of Hebdige's *Subculture—The Meaning of Style* in 1979. This was the book that made Hebdige *almost* famous (academic fame is after all relatively modest). Long since settled in California (where he has taught at the University of California, Santa Barbara, CA), Hebdige's (1979) innovative reading of subcultural styles of dress went far beyond the accounts that participants in these subcultures might themselves have articulated. Drawing on literary, semiotic and aesthetic theory, he did rather more than elucidate the meanings of parkas and scooters or dreadlocks for those that displayed them. Situating these, and many other, signs of rupture and affiliation in the whorl of 1970s cultural theory produced a subtle, complex and exhilarating study floating free of the 'lived reality' of young people's lives. The problem of the relationship between the academic interpretation and the insiders' own self-understandings was not exactly explored, though it was, unambiguously, conceded:

> It is highly unlikely . . . that the members of any of the subcultures described in this book would recognize themselves reflected here. They are still less likely to welcome any efforts on our part to understand them . . . We are in society but not inside it, producing analyses of popular culture which are themselves anything but popular. (Hebdige, 1979: 139–40)

In a sense, the book, and the project which it represented, is a very personal one. It brings Hebdige's own aesthetic preoccupations into the encounter with young people's styles on terms that are really non-negotiable. This is Hebdige's intellectual journey, not one to be impeded by the words and thoughts of young people themselves. In this respect, his work, among Cultural Studies writers, is furthest from the kind of encounters with young people that arise through the more sustained contact allowed by teaching – in which young people themselves may directly contest what adults think of them. Hebdige's work, though vivid and precise, is most obviously implicated in the reputation of Cultural Studies for neglecting the ordinary, mundane and unspectacular lives of the young. This may not be fair because Hebdige was exploring just how youth subcultures struggled to defy boredom but, as many have argued since, he did privilege a radical aesthetics over more cautious empirical enquiry into how the larger majority of young people live their youth. Perhaps inevitably therefore his interests did not turn to the lives of young people in school.

But several of the other contributors to *Resistance through Rituals* did engage with educational settings. Paul Corrigan, whose book *Schooling the Smash Street Kids* was also published in 1979, wrote a short piece bluntly asserting that the 'the main action of British subculture is, in fact, "doing nothing".' (Corrigan, 1975: 103) In reading Corrigan, the really striking difference from Hebdige is that there is so much quoted speech from young people themselves: it is in their words that, at least initially, Corrigan's interpretation is grounded. Actually, all the essays that do touch on education, though in more broadly historical terms than in Corrigan's observations on 'doing nothing', come from figures somewhat outside the main core group of Birmingham-based 'subculturalists': Graham Murdock and Robin McCron ('Consciousness of class and consciousness of generation'), Paul Corrigan (again) and Simon Frith ('The politics of youth culture'). Paul Willis, whose *Learning to Labour* was in preparation, contributed an article on 'The cultural meaning of drug use'. The origins of this collection in a critical engagement with the sociology of deviance did not, on the whole, favour attention to schooling. Indeed, the main, though not exclusive, preoccupation was with white male working-class youth subcultures of the kind often defined as troublesome in public space and therefore likely to be in conflict with, among others, the police.

Perhaps one of the best known and most frequently cited essays from *Resistance through Rituals*, 'Girls and subcultures: an exploration', by Angela McRobbie and Jenny Garber, initiated a continuing critique of the male dominated field of youth research and was the first published challenge from feminism to the largely masculine agenda of Cultural Studies. 'Youth' had been construed as meaning boys and young men, and as a result, girls were not visible. This can also be explained by the inherited focus on male behaviour in the sociology of deviance, though the neglect was also compounded by the assumption that innovations in style were exclusively driven by male youth – teddy boys, motor-bike gangs, skinheads and even mods. The lingering influence of McRobbie and Garber's essay is most often evident in the use of just one phrase – 'the culture of the bedroom' (McRobbie and Garber, 1975: 213) or, later, 'bedroom culture'. Here, the idea of culture is yoked to another kind of territory, not out on the street but right inside the home, where girls could, it was argued, more securely conduct their engagements both with each other and with youth-orientated popular culture. In a way, this idea also launched McRobbie's long career in the feminist reconstruction of youth cultural studies.

She subsequently contributed to the Birmingham Centre's first Women's Studies working papers *Women Take Issue: Aspects of Women's Subordination* (1978). This title was more than a casual pun; it was a double challenge. Taking issue with Cultural Studies and its predominantly masculine preoccupations and taking over the whole issue of the Centre's journal for Women's Studies work was a painful achievement. The mood and the difficulty of the period are recalled both in Stuart Hall's (Hall, 1992: 278) recollections (of 'bad feeling, argument, unstable anxieties and angry silences') and Charlotte Brunsdon's (1996) further engagement both with his account and her own reflections on participating in Women's Studies at the time. Perhaps the point to underline here is that these 'intellectual' developments were not achieved in a happy, harmonious and always mutually supportive setting. There is little point in looking back at Cultural Studies in the 1970s with nostalgia, as if it was all much more exciting, and even convivial, then. It wasn't. There were casualties. There were survivors, Angela McRobbie among them.

Feminism and Youth Culture: From Jackie *to* Just Seventeen (1991) collects McRobbie's work from the mid-1970s onwards. Many other collections followed, some her own essays, notably *Postmodernism and Popular Culture* (1994) and *In the Culture Society: Art, Fashion and Popular Music* (1999), and some edited assemblies of others' writing, for example *Zoot Suits and Second-Hand Dresses* (1989) and *Back to Reality? Social Experience and*

Cultural Studies (1997). Since the mid-1970s, many important studies of girls and young women, drawing on Cultural Studies, have followed, among them Christine Griffin (1985) *Typical Girls?*, Sue Lees (1986) *Losing Out*, Valerie Hey (1997) *The Company She Keeps*, Beverley Skeggs (1997b) *Formations of Class and Gender* and Maria Pini (2001) *Club Cultures and Female Subjectivity: The Move from Home to House*. Despite the recurring, and somewhat inflated, fuss about 'failing boys', these authors have effectively undermined the assumption that a 'youth' is always a boy.

Until the latter part of the 1970s, the cultural study of youth was not only mainly about boys and young men, it was about *white* boys and young men. Dick Hebdige's highly innovative MA thesis did include work on black styles (see 'Reggae, rastas and rudies' in *Resistance through Rituals* or Chapter 3 in Hebdige, 1979) but really the primary focus was on white youth, if often in relation to black, especially Jamaican, working-class culture. Later, Hebdige (1987) published a very informative study of, again, mainly Jamaican music, *Cut 'n' Mix: Culture, Identity and Caribbean Music*. Iain Chambers, who contributed 'A strategy for living: black music and white subcultures' to *Resistance through Rituals*, revisits the white appropriation of black American music in 1950s rock 'n' roll and, as he concludes his essay, gestures towards the issue of how white youth in Britain 'adopted and adapted' black, music. Further, more extensive, reflections on these issues appeared in *Urban Rhythms: Pop Music and Popular Culture* and *Popular Culture: The Metropolitan Experience* (Chambers, 1985, 1986).

However, the most substantial turn to matters of 'race' surfaced in Cultural Studies at the end of the 1970s, partly in *Policing the Crisis: Mugging, the State and Law and Order* (1978) but also in *The Empire Strikes Back: Race and Racism in 70s Britain* (1982), a collection introducing new authors, among them Hazel Carby, Paul Gilroy, Pratibha Parmar, Errol Lawrence and Simon Jones. The centrality of white working-class male experience was, at last, questioned by a slightly younger and more 'ethnically' diverse group, all students in the Birmingham Centre for Contemporary Cultural Studies three or four years after *Resistance through Rituals* (1975). Simon Jones subsequently published *Black Culture, White Youth: The Reggae Tradition from JA to UK* (1988), and Paul Gilroy (1987, 1993a, b, 2004a, b) has published many, often theoretically eclectic, studies of 'race' and ethnicity (see Chapter 5). Given these, and other related publications, it is perhaps difficult to grasp how central to Cultural Studies white cultures were in the 1970s.

Nevertheless, in terms of the Gramscian (Gramsci, 1971) theoretical project realized in *Resistance through Rituals,* it can be argued that the more diverse and flexible studies that followed were facilitated by the earlier move beyond simplistic, rigid and reductive models of binary class conflict (most often, the working class vs. middle class – imagined as somewhat fixed and monolithic blocs). Stuart Hall has observed:

> *Resistance through Rituals* actively distanced itself from the classical metaphors of 'revolutionary struggle' and the reform/revolution antinomies by offering in their place an *expanded* definition of social rupture. In place of the simple binaries of 'the class struggle', it substituted the Gramscian notion of 'repertoires of resistance' which, it insisted, were always conjuncturally defined and historically specific . . . (Hall, 1996a: 294)

Clearly, in Hall's vocabulary, 'culture' is not obviously any longer a central term, displaced somewhat by questions of power, discourse and ideology (see also Hall and Jefferson, 2006). But, to put it another way, it's not so much that 'culture' is displaced and perhaps more that it is one element in the kind of discursive struggles that became the focus of Hall's work through the later 1970s and into the 1980s. 'Culture' is contested, its meanings and value constantly shifting between the widely differing social interests of those who lay claim to it. The complexity attributed to 'culture' by Williams (1976) might be recast as an unending 'multiaccentuality' (Volosinov, 1929/1973), the meanings of 'culture' never being settled, there never being a point at which we can say, finally, so this is what 'culture' means, this is what it is. Hall's observations on the persistence of the high and low culture distinction may clarify what is at issue here:

> The classification of cultural domains into the self-sufficient and apparently transcendental distinctions of high and low is . . . an exercise in cultural regulation, designed to make cultural practices into a *formation* which can then be sustained in a binary form by strategies of cultural power. The fact that the cultural field cannot be stabilized in this way does not prevent the exercise in boundary construction being attempted again, in another place, for another time. Cultural practices are never outside the play of power. And one way in which power operates in the apparently decentred sphere of culture is through the struggle to harness it, to superimpose on it, to regulate and enclose its diverse and trans-gressive forms and energies, within the structure and logic of a normative or canonical binary. (Hall, 1996a: 302)

In this perspective, 'culture' is a component of that regulatory mechanism which distinguishes between and attributes, or denies, value to those things or practices classified as belonging to a higher or lower category (Stallybrass and White, 1986). Though the language is different, this is not so far from Williams' (1976, 1977) concern to unravel and usurp the operation of elite concepts of culture most evident in the study of literature.

The ambitions of *Resistance through Rituals* were considerable. Though clearly starting with what particular youth subcultural ways of life mean, the project was not confined to discrete studies of such subcultures. The aspiration was to connect such studies to a much wider and more complex analysis on several levels, working towards a more elaborate understanding of the social formation in a particular historical conjuncture (Hall and Jefferson, 2006). *Policing the Crisis* (Hall et al., 1978) pursued this project further with a sustained 'multilevel' analysis of youth, crime and media and political discourse in the years immediately preceding the election of the first Thatcher government (1979). If *Resistance through Rituals* 'was first taken up within education, as a set text on E202, the Open University course on *Schooling and Society*' (Hall and Jefferson, 2006: xi), it may be that *Policing the Crisis* (Hall et al., 1978) did not cross into debates around schooling in any substantial way. However, it certainly informed discussions among teachers working in Media Studies. It provided the background to an article focused on teaching about the youth 'riots' of the early 1980s ('Media-Race-Riots') that I wrote while teaching at a secondary school in north London (Richards, 1983) and that I introduce, at length, into Chapter 5 of this book.

Though work in Cultural Studies did migrate to education, informing debates and, to some extent, developments in practice in the 1980s and since, any movement in the other direction, of research in education into Cultural Studies, seems relatively rare. Looking through the lengthy, revised and updated, bibliography to the 2006 edition of *Resistance through Rituals*, it is hard to find any titles from the field of education at all, except where the authors are well-established insiders to the Cultural Studies scene: for example, Paul Willis, Richard Johnson and Beverley Skeggs. But the precedents are there, in those brief contributions to *Resistance through Rituals* that do comment on education and do so from outside the Cultural Studies centre itself.

The 'culture' discourse

To bring this introductory mapping of developments in the cultural study of youth to a provisional conclusion, it is necessary to go back to the word 'culture'. Just a few words from Raymond Williams (1976) opened the chapter. In the discussion of 'culture' in Cultural Studies that followed, it has been possible to keep one broad definition of culture, that of culture as a whole way of life, as the most consistent point of reference. But it has been qualified and modified repeatedly in the preceding pages. 'Culture' is contested, argued over, disputed, and will go on being so (see Bennett et al., 2005: 63–9).

Of course, it is possible to use such terms descriptively, to explain how cultural products are ordered and positioned, without actually supporting the hierarchy of value that the distinction between high and low reiterates. Where the concern is with texts and other aesthetic objects, traditional critics may still wish to sustain a distinction between high culture and low culture. But 'high culture' is not what it was. It is more confined than in previous decades, the authority of its judgements and its selections not extending much beyond those involved with or closely allied to traditional arts disciplines in universities. The work of John Frow, more a theorist of literature than of youth, offers a helpful reframing of these issues. He observes:

> High culture . . . is no longer 'the dominant culture' but is rather a *pocket* within commodity culture. Its primary relationship is not to the ruling class but to the intelligentsia, and to the education system which is the locus of their power and the generative point for most high-cultural practices. (Frow, 1995: 86)

Though popular cultural texts were once mostly positioned as 'low', relative to 'high' culture, 'popular' now designates a field of shared interests and pleasures among large numbers of people, also including many among the 'intelligentsia'. For the great majority of people, the high/low distinction is irrelevant to watching *Friends* (1994–2004) or *Sex and City* (1998–2004). There is a great deal of widely enjoyed 'popular' television, film and music. Nevertheless, the negative positioning of some cultural products as 'low' is still available in the 'culture' discourses and is frequently brought into play. *Big Brother* (2000–2010), for example, is often judged both popular and low. In this case, 'popular' is perhaps inflected by the negative dynamic through which white working-class people are made the object of contempt (see Skeggs, 1997a, b, 2004). Sometimes, debates around such 'low' television recall the notion of mass culture, much less current than 'popular' in the past 30 years, pointing back to anxieties about the emergence of a mass society in which whole populations might be swayed by, for example, fascist propaganda. But generally, popular culture, even if also low, is seen as less manipulative and somewhat more participatory than 'mass' culture.

So what now becomes of 'subcultures'? The use of subcultures has followed the use of culture as a way of life rather than culture as cultural products, texts and aesthetics. Nevertheless, particular material objects, clothing especially, are a part of subcultural styles, and there is thus an intersection of culture in these two broad senses. But subcultures are not likely to be thought of as either mass or popular, though, again, they may well be associated with 'low' culture. Subcultures, as the ways of life of those often excluded from power, are not usually associated with the 'high' – because what they consume, in terms of cultural products, are located lower in the hierarchy. The contributors to *Resistance through Rituals* (1975) reserve 'subcultures' for those groups associated with working-class life. For them, *middle-class* youth cultures are not subcultures but countercultures. From hippies to riot grrrls (see Kearney, 2006), these middle-class groups are placed, as they place themselves, as oppositional to the culture defined as 'dominant' – which might well include much of what is meant by *both* high and low culture. In these oppositional youth cultures, youth is not to be lived as transition but as the founding phase of lives of defiant criticism of the ordinary, the normal and the mainstream.

But 'subcultures' may be more usefully reworked to refer not only to working-class groups but also to relatively small-scale and strongly defined networks of identification located within, or across, a variety of classes. Even some social networks primarily focused on high-cultural products may be sustained in ways that, in their small scale, their intensity and their exclusiveness, resemble subcultures lived in very different social settings. Among studies that do approach middle-class youth with a revived form of subcultural analysis, Paul Hodkinson's book *Goth: Identity, Style and Subculture* (2002) is a theoretically articulate study from someone who identifies himself as an insider to the subculture in question. Such examples take us beyond the separation of culture as texts on the one hand and culture as a way of life on the other. Texts (music and fanzines), material culture (clothes), sites (both virtual and real) and social practices (visiting clubs, for example) are interrelated elements in living through a Goth identity.

Frow examines the work of Michel de Certeau (1988) for its rethinking of culture as practices – so that, following the example of subcultures, consuming texts (however placed in terms of 'high' or 'low') is not conceptualized in terms of reception as a process of ingesting predetermined meanings but rather as itself a productive practice. He suggests that rather than seeing popular culture 'as a domain of texts or of artefacts' Certeau 'understands it as a set of practices or operations performed on textual or text-like structures' (Frow 1995: 47).

This approach, emphasising cultural practice, is especially appealing to those concerned with subcultures because, in its focus on what people do with the texts they consume, it favours a view of cultural production as within 'the practice of everyday life' (the title of Certeau's best known book) rather than confined only to the 'official' producers of cultural commodities (de Certeau, 1988). Ultimately, Frow has significant criticisms of Certeau, but these are beyond the scope of this chapter (see Frow, 1995: 55–9).

Here, the concept of the 'popular' needs further discussion. The 'popular' in its simplest sense means 'of the people'. But this is deceptively straightforward. Frow's critique of the concept of the 'people' is important:

> One way of undermining the expressive unity of the concept while still recogniz-ing its continuing discursive force as a vehicle for the self-recognition and self-identification of diverse social groups is to argue that 'the people' is not a given entity which precedes cultural forms, but is rather entirely the product of cultural forms: that it is a fact of representation rather than an external cause of representation. (Frow, 1995: 84)

Frow is arguing here that *the* 'people' is a somewhat imaginary *unity*, an idea of social agency and of belonging rather than an actual, cohesive, social force somehow able to act to express its feelings and beliefs. Turning things around, he suggests that the unitary, singular, 'people' is constructed through representational practices, to which, of course, actual people do respond and with which they may identify as, indeed, one of the 'people'. In this sense, the 'people' and the 'popular' are constructed in discourse, rather than being expressions of already formed social entities. This kind of analysis is helpfully explained, at length, in Burr (2003), an excellent introduction to social constructionism and especially to the use of the concept of 'discourse'. It provides an informed background to the kind of argument made in the final pages of this chapter.

The critique of the simplistic equation of the popular with the notion of 'the people' pursued here is also instructive for thinking about 'youth' and 'youth culture'. It can be argued that 'youth' is similarly a product of those cultural forms claiming to address and to represent 'youth'. Of course, there is always a real population of people living through the years defined as between childhood and adulthood but these are not, other than in that most ephemeral and limited sense defined by age, a unified social group. 'Their' existence as such is a sustained construction of the young in commercial media. Or so, at least, might be the case, in part. But 'youth' is subject to legal definition, to educational compulsion and regulation and to economic dependence. Moreover, particular youth cohorts, those born within particular years (for example, in the years following the second world war or following the 'collapse' of Communism in 1989), are also defined by their generational location in particular historical circumstances. It might then be more precise to argue that young people are often called upon to experience themselves as young in terms of a unified 'youth culture' and that it is at this level of possible participation in an 'imaginary community' (Anderson, 1991) that some similarity to the constitution of 'the people' can be suggested.

Frow's (1995) discussion is also centrally concerned with the relation between intellectuals, among which he locates himself as a cultural intellectual, and those they construct and interpret or on whose behalf they claim to speak. The detail of his argument cannot be fully summarized here. However, just as 'the people' can be seen as a construction to which intellectuals sometimes 'dedicate' their efforts, so 'youth' or 'youth culture' can be understood as an 'other' to which cultural intellectuals devote themselves – variously in defence, in explanation, in celebration and in apology. Moreover, cultural intellectuals, again himself included, are not independent of what he calls 'regimes of value' (Frow, 1995: 145). Such regimes are not tied specifically and neatly to particular social groups but are characterized by more loosely defined ways of 'reading' and evaluating formed at an institutional level not directly expressive of, for example, class interests. He comments:

> Regimes of value are . . . relatively autonomous of and have no directly expressive relation to social groups. In the case of 'high'-cultural regimes, this relative autonomy is an effect of historical survivals and of the relative autonomy of the modern educational apparatus, both of which then give rise to interpretative and evaluative traditions that do not directly reflect class interests; in the case of 'popular' regimes, their relative autonomy has less to do with the historical persistence of codes of value (although this is still a factor) than with the way the mass media work to form audiences that cross the borders of classes, ethnic groups, genders, and indeed nations. The concept of regime expresses one of the fundamental theses of work in cultural studies: that no object, no text, no cultural practice has an intrinsic or necessary meaning or value or function; and that meaning, value, and function are always the effect of specific (and changing, changeable) social relations and mechanisms of signification. (Frow, 1995: 145)

Reading texts of whatever kind or, indeed, interpreting young people's lives and actions is always conducted from within specific regimes of value. Frow uses graffiti as an example, drawing on the work of Susan Stewart, whose essay 'Ceci Tuera Cela: Graffiti as Crime and Art' discusses young people's graffiti writing in New York, Philadelphia and Los Angeles. Frow (1995) draws attention to the differing regimes of value through which, in Stewart's (1988) account, graffiti are interpreted. For those writing the graffiti (mainly boys between nine and sixteen years of age), there is an assertion of the individual and personal through the repeated and stylized elaboration of the handwritten name on the anonymous surfaces of public space. But the meanings and value of the signature in the writers' regime of value are in conflict with its meaning in the regime of value of officialdom. Indeed, for city officials, graffiti is perceived more as a lack of meaning, 'outside the realm of the cultural' (Frow, 1995: 148). Graffiti is treated like dirt to be cleaned from the defiled properties. Stewart comments:

> It is easy to see how graffiti becomes dirt once we consider, in the mode of much recent cognitive anthropology, dirt to be something in the wrong place or wrong time and consequently something ranked at the bottom of a hierarchical scale of values . . . graffiti can be seen as a *permanent* soiling of the environment simply in its constant replicability, its emphasis upon repetition and replacement. Graffiti is widely considered to be a *defacement*: an application that destroys the significance of its material base . . . This is graffiti as non-culture. Linked to the dirty, the animal, the uncivilized, and the profane, contemporary urban graffiti signifies an interruption of the boundaries of public and private space, an eruption of creativity and movement outside and through the claims of street, façade, exterior, and interior by which the city is articulated. (Stewart, 1988: 167–8)

But if graffiti is crime, it is also, in the 1980s and since, art. This further aestheticizing regime of value is evident in the reproduction of graffiti in art galleries and books. Stewart suggests that, within this field of aesthetic practice, there is a further subdivision in interpretation. There is a tension between a liberal valuation of the graffiti writer's skill and creativity, often associated with a wish to redirect this into more properly schooled forms of artistic practice, and an avant-garde orientation in which graffiti is valued as a folk variant of abstract expressionism. Less visibly, as Frow notes, there is also the regime of value from within which Stewart writes, a regime dependent on considerable cultural capital and appearing to stand above the social interests of those regimes of value more directly in conflict with each other.

The example of graffiti is an important one for work at the intersection of Cultural Studies with education. It is not difficult to see that in schools, the meanings attributed to graffiti are very likely to be drawn from all of these regimes of value. From art teachers to school heads, from parents to school care takers and from in-school graffiti writers to non-graffiti writing school students, the reading and evaluation of graffiti on the school walls will inevitably produce disparate and incompatible judgements. The work of Cultural Studies does not provide any secure vantage point from which to adjudicate between such judgements, or any means of reconciling differing interpretations, but it does open up some ways of understanding the strength of feeling and likely bewilderment arising between these various participants in the life of the school.

Conclusion

Though Cultural Studies has expanded into an international network of theoretical exchange, only rarely connecting in any detailed way with the concerns of those working outside higher education, and relatively infrequently with those working in schools, there is every reason to bring its perspectives into both Education Studies and educational practice. This chapter has outlined some of the perspectives on culture and youth associated with Cultural Studies in Britain through the last 50 years. Inevitably, this is an introductory commentary. In later chapters, detail and further illustration will add to the sketch given here. However, to gain some familiarity with cultural studies of youth, the best way to proceed will be to seek out and read at least some of the books cited in this chapter, some of which will be discussed further in what follows.

Points for reflection

When you hear the word 'culture', ask yourself – what is the context of its use and what does it mean?

What does the speaker use the word 'culture' to achieve?

What do you think are the strengths, and the limitations, of using 'culture' in thinking about how people live?

2 Cultural Studies and Education Studies

Introduction

This chapter examines the tension between Education Studies as defined by established disciplines and as a less-bounded area, open to a variety of less 'traditional' disciplines, including Cultural Studies, Women's Studies and Psychoanalysis.

By comparison with the apparently frenetic pace and wide-ranging theoretical eclecticism of Cultural Studies (Barker, 2007), the field of Education Studies can appear very slow moving indeed. Typically, Education Studies is defined by four or five disciplines: History, Sociology, Psychology and Philosophy and sometimes Economics or, perhaps especially where American influences are evident, Anthropology. Though Cultural Studies has sometimes defined itself as an anti-discipline, and is certainly always critical of the dominant formation of traditional disciplines, Education Studies has often appeared content to rest on its disciplinary pillars, confident that they will bear its weight.

There are problems with this. To assume that any one of these 'contributing' disciplines is a unitary and coherent domain is at odds with the reality of quite fundamental rifts, rows and separations characterizing any one of them. It would be difficult to represent or adopt a sociological or psychological perspective without having to acknowledge, eventually, that the choice is partisan and that its secure principles are in fact contested. Which sociological tradition or which psychological perspective should represent each of those disciplines? Much the same would apply to philosophy or to history. These are strongly institutionalized fields of enquiry, for sure, but they are not therefore singular, coherent disciplines. The intellectual history of the past 50 years alone has been so volatile, so complex, and so driven by critique and counter-critique, that to persist in defining Education Studies by these core disciplines is curiously blinkered.

In 2000, in its first subject benchmark statement for Education Studies, the Quality Assurance Agency for Higher Education (http://www.qaa.ac.uk), makes little explicit reference to the core discipline model. Defining the nature of the subject, it states:

> Education Studies is concerned with understanding how people develop and learn throughout their lives. It facilitates a study of the nature of knowledge, and a critical engagement with a variety of perspectives, and ways of knowing and understanding, drawn from a range of appropriate disciplines. There is diversity in Education Studies courses at undergraduate level but all involve the intellectually rigorous study of educational processes, systems and approaches, and the cultural, societal, political and historical contexts within which they are embedded.
>
> Following the satisfactory completion of courses in Education Studies, students will be able to participate effectively in a number of constantly changing discourses which are exemplified by reference to debate about values, personal and social engagement, and how these relate to communities and societies.

By contrast, in 2007, the Quality Assurance Agency's (QAA) definitive statement, though acknowledging 'differing theoretical models', does go on to state:

> It can be seen as a 'subject' defined by its curriculum content and drawing selectively upon the methods of the contributory disciplines of psychology, sociology, philosophy, history and economics. Others regard education studies as

a 'discipline' with its own academic community, its own distinctive discourse and methods of enquiry.

The earlier emphasis on 'constantly changing discourses' has been displaced by this stronger emphasis on stability, either that derived from the disciplinary foundations laid for the study of education some decades ago or that claimed by its particular academic community. Though the foreword to the June 2007 revision notes that only minor changes to the 2000 benchmarks were required, the reintroduction of named disciplines implies a more significant change of emphasis. In particular, by not naming Cultural Studies, or some of its associated fields such as social semiotics, discourse theory, gender studies or psychoanalysis, there is a risk that they are rendered invisible.

The 2007 QAA panel was chaired by Professor Stephen Bartlett and included Professor Stephen Ward, both also authors of well-known undergraduate Education Studies textbooks (Bartlett and Burton, 2007; Ward, 2008). In Bartlett and Burton (2007), the field is largely defined in relation to the disciplines of sociology, psychology, history and philosophy. Two of 11 chapters are devoted to psychology; others deal with sociological perspectives, with the history of schooling, with curriculum and pedagogy, with research, and with policy. There is also quite a strong emphasis on comparative education. Stephen Ward's (2008) edited collection, with 18 chapters by as many authors, is considerably more diverse, giving attention to issues such as religion and sustainability, favouring ecological, economic and historical perspectives. These are important initiatives. But, in these versions of Education Studies, with very few exceptions (Downes and Haywood, 2008; Bianchi, 2008), there is still a significant neglect of the cultures of children and young people. In part, an answer to this criticism may be that, for these authors, Education Studies is not necessarily about the education of young people. Education, they argue, is lifelong and far exceeds the framework of assumptions associated with schooling from five to nineteen years. However, as so much of education is in fact 'addressed' to young people, it is essential to consider their experience and to do so in ways informed by research, both in the past and continuing (see Mayall, 2002; Kassem et al., 2010).

'Student power' – the 1960s and since

Naming contributory disciplines is a problematic conceptual route into Education Studies. So much intellectual innovation takes place across or in between disciplines and sometimes in areas that lie beyond current disciplinary naming altogether. For example, the emergence of 'second wave' feminism in the late 1960s and its subsequent productivity both in theory and in empirical research cannot be located in a 'discipline' (Mitchell, 1971; Firestone, 1972; Rowbotham, 1973; Rowbotham, 2000). The constraints and dubious relevance of disciplinary boundaries were clearly questioned in the 1970s formation of Women's Studies (Centre for Contemporary Cultural Studies, 1978) and in other fields to some extent representing wider social movements and proposing new forms of knowledge. Of course, Education Studies must retain a focus on its core concerns – especially questions of learning and of the social organization of knowledge. But the history of the formation of disciplines, of challenges to them and of attempts to introduce new fields of knowledge are clearly salient to a broader account of what Education Studies has become.

One somewhat submerged strand in the formation of some Education Studies courses can be traced back to the later 1960s. In the years through 1967–1970, and to some extent continuing into the 1970s, there were worldwide challenges to the authority of universities by the students who attended them (see Rowbotham, 2000). Sometimes these challenges focused on the form of assessment – typically a series of three-hour-timed examinations – or on the imposition of assessment in any form. Confrontations also arose when university resources were identified as lending support to, for example, military operations or otherwise unethical research (see Morse, 1973). Challenges were made to traditional forms of teaching and to the content of courses. There was an animated and persistent questioning of what higher education was for and whose interests it served. In the introduction to *Student Power* (1969), Alexander Cockburn asserts:

> In most of the advanced countries of the capitalist world students have already posed the demand for student power: for control by the students of the organization and content of the education they receive. On the whole this demand has not just taken the form of resolutions or appeals to the authorities. Instead it has been embodied in acts of occupation, during which students elaborate the nature of the counter-institutions they wish to create. (Cockburn and Blackburn, 1969: 7)

In the same book, the historian Gareth Stedman Jones (then 25) argues that:

> . . . students must demand democratic control over the content of education. This means conflict with teaching staff over course patterns, reading lists, syllabuses

and above all methods of assessment . . . students are not mentally enclosed within the prevailing intellectual orthodoxy of their disciplines, by years of acceptance and transmission . . . They are thus much more given to question orthodox ideas and doubt standard answers. Such open and critical questioning is an absolute condition of all cultural progress. It is, in fact, essential for the teachers themselves to be challenged in novel and unexpected forms by their students. (Jones, 1969: 49–51)

This highly politicized educational world may now seem historically remote. But some of what students encounter in Education Studies, and of course in other degree programmes, is a product of this recent history.

In the late 1960s and early 1970s, such concerns were not confined to students alone, and in some universities (in London, Paris and Berkeley, CA), academics conducted their own arguments with the institutions for which they worked. The case for changes to the organization of university education was also made, for example, at Sussex University in the early 1970s. In the 1960s and early 1970s, Sussex was widely regarded as an innovative and progressive university with a reputation for interdisciplinary work, tutorial-based teaching (often just two undergraduate students being taught for an hour each week, sometimes more, with one lecturer) and academic flexibility. But it was also well known to recruit somewhat more than half its students from private schools and from the affluent south of England. If the university encouraged and supported innovation and critical thinking, to whom was such support extended?

Published by the Information Office at the University of Sussex, and rather ironically carrying the routine identification 'intended for members of the University of Sussex', *Socialist Education and the University* (*Focus* 30, May 1973) contained repeated exhortations to 'open' the university, to end its isolation from and exclusion of those who, living in the Brighton area, were *not* 'members' of the university. This 'guest edition' was produced by the Radical Faculty Action Group and offered 'a radical critique of the university and its place in society'. In the introductory article – 'Beyond the constraints' – Rod Kedward (*Focus*, 1973) argued that the university has 'left the inequalities and injustices of our society virtually intact' and the following priorities were proposed:

An open university – lectures, library, arts centre, sports facilities, faculty time to be open to the community. The whole university, not just part of it, to be a centre for continuing education.

Positive discrimination in student admissions in favour of schools and people in deprived areas. A decisive move towards more adult entrants. Percentage of public [private] school entrants to be drastically cut.

No compulsory or competitive exams – no classification in other forms of assessment. More collective and co-operative work.

More interdisciplinary courses, growing organically out of problems and interests and crossing traditional arts/science boundaries.

No status distinctions (i.e. lecturer, reader, professor and their parallels) among faculty and administration.

All university employees, academic, clerical, manual, administrative, technical, to be paid according to the same criteria of need.

Some of these concerns, interdisciplinary work and forms of widening participation for example, have been sustained in higher education, and elsewhere, ever since. Others, such as the abolition of academic status distinctions, clearly, have not.

Among the priorities set out by Kedward in *Focus* (1973), this book's central preoccupation is with the relationship between academic knowledge and expertise and the wider constituency of people for whom 'university' was, and for many still is, something of a mystery. Two members of the Radical Faculty Action Group, David Morse (see Morse, 1971) and Cora Lushington (now Kaplan; see Kaplan, 1985), both teachers of American literature, made observations on this issue. Writing separately, they posed critical questions for an exploration of the social relations of knowledge production. Morse's essay 'Knowledge and Impotence' (1973) focused on the tension between the apparent esotericism of academic knowledge and educational practices seeking to engage an increasingly broad constituency. Morse lamented that 'most people's education should be of so little use to them and offer so little scope for consideration of the nature of contemporary society and the role they are – destined? – to play in it'. He added:

> . . . criticism is construed as a privilege for the elite – a kind of conspicuous intellectual consumption that can sample the most exotic and unorthodox intellectual dishes in a spirit of disinterested curiosity, while leaving the structure of society completely intact. (Morse, 1973: 14)

This can be read as an argument *both* for the sense of social and political engagement evident in the work of the Centre for Contemporary Cultural

Studies (see Chapter 1) and as a prescient comment on what has become somewhat too characteristic of Cultural Studies internationally in the decades since. Of course, this criticism of elite knowledge is a lament common to many academic intellectuals whose work appears to have so little consequence for the wider social world and even sometimes for their own students. But the need to consider what is worth studying, teaching, or researching and why, if often very uncomfortable, is also a necessary element of a reflexive practice. It is a matter of knowing why, and with what justification, we take a particular intellectual direction, thus giving time and attention to some issues and problems rather than others.

Morse underlined this by recalling his experience of teaching in the United States:

> . . . at the University of Pennsylvania when I was there, as part of the variegated texture of life in the modern multiversity, some may be researching into the development of new or more lethal kinds of gas, while others may be studying American literature. The danger of the ideal of academic freedom . . . is that it tends to imply the right of the individual to pursue any line of research without due regard for its wider implications, its future uses, its general morality or the nature of the priorities it represents . . . (Morse, 1973: 14)

Academic freedom was questioned here as an evasion of social responsibility. The call for an explicit politics of academic knowledge, both in teaching and in research, suggested a need to specify a productive, and ethical, relationship to the contemporary context, to the present world in which people live their lives.

Cora Lushington (Kaplan), in her reflections on 'The Idea of an Open University' proposed that 'to counteract the isolation of the University and its members, geographic, social and psychological, the opening of doors must be part of a two-way traffic' (Lushington, 1973: 35). Commenting ruefully on what it might mean to invite in local people (and, consistent with this 1973 publication as a whole, with male pronouns as generic), she wrote, emphasizing the relatively rural isolation of the Sussex campus:

> To come to my university the public will have to make an effort of will and a considerable outlay of cash fares in order to sit passively in front of an informant whose whole education and experience have worked to alienate him from the experience and educational needs of his new audience . . . Let us encourage more

voluntary groups to hold their meetings in Brighton and advertise them widely. At the same time as we lobby vigorously for opening the facilities at Falmer to all residents of the surrounding towns and villages without cost, let us at least begin by offering our skills without cost in the towns and villages . . . For students and faculty in Berkeley, California and New York City's Columbia University crises developing around the use of University-owned property in the urban areas have had an educational impact on the University communities. By a wise isolation the founders of Sussex have avoided such crises. (Lushington, 1973: 35)

Again these are anxieties that may be characteristic of many whose working lives appear to be strongly separated from those of the people they live among. But the preoccupation with physical geography, though broadly literal and accurate, was emblematic of the social distance between academic life and its concerns and the lives of people with little access to higher education. Lushington's gestural solutions to the irony of 'wise isolation', though unlikely to have been translated into any sustained practice, were at least alert to the question of the social responsibility of intellectuals. For Morse and Lushington, and for a majority of the other contributors to *Socialist Education and the University*, the sense of confinement to an exclusive institution serving the interests of a social elite (both staff and students) was understood to compromise the value of the knowledge they produced and pursued, but also to impede the production of knowledge *formed* in a more active relationship with a wider constituency.

It could be suggested that higher education in the first decade of the twenty-first century, in Britain, has some of the characteristics for which these authors argued. But it seems doubtful that many of them would recognize these as a fulfilment of their aims. As noted in Chapter 1, fields of knowledge such as Cultural Studies and Media Studies have grown very significantly since the 1970s. Perhaps more importantly, students in higher education come from a far wider social range than in the 1960s and 1970s. If these changes can be seen as the partial completion of a project dating back to the left-wing radicalism of that period, they also define the twenty-first century context within which many of the same issues need to be re-engaged. In the context of widening participation in further and higher education, the hierarchy of universities and their sharply discrepant levels of prestige – and of resources – profoundly shape students' experiences.

In this 'new' context, however, it could be argued that Education departments, and Education Studies, have been better placed than other 'subject' fields to conduct teaching and assessment in ways that do connect with and further the interests of a much wider student constituency. Education Studies should address students as already knowledgeable, as experienced in earlier phases of education, not as newcomers to education and not as complete outsiders to a specialized body of knowledge.

Education Studies in the 1990s

The introduction of Education Studies at the University of North London provides an interesting example of a degree programme intended to be sympathetic to its particular student constituency. The curriculum of the degree was both consistent with the convention that four or five established disciplines are named as contributing to it and, perhaps, unusual in specifying *fields of study* that were 'to be visited on an interdisciplinary basis'. But, in addition to interdisciplinarity, the position accorded *non-traditional* students in this course document is especially significant:

> In recent years Education Studies has developed as a distinct academic area, with strong interdisciplinary links with the social sciences and humanities . . . The diverse range of cultural and social experiences of the student body that will be recruited to the subject will allow the course to use and reflect upon the educational and other related experiences brought to the course in a programme of learning that uses and builds upon such diversity.

> This subject particularly offers mature students and those with a diverse range of social and cultural experiences an opportunity to use their experience in a coherent academic and experientially-based programme of study . . .

> . . . there is a large group of people, not having Higher Education as part of their background, who wish to undertake studies in the area of humanities and social sciences at degree level. This non-traditional group, who may be mature, women, from ethnic minorities, or any combination of these, seek degree courses which also have potential for subsequent employment. (*Education Studies Definitive Course Document*, July 1993)

In this, an Education Studies conceived in the inner urban setting of north London, degree level study for those likely to be excluded from traditional subjects, or in whose life projects study of such subjects could not be easily justified, is made central. Though the interdisciplinary orientation of the degree is important, it is in its engagement with the students, with who they are and what they know, that the subject is to be negotiated.

In some respects, this degree programme appears to satisfy some of the aspirations identified by Sussex's Radical Faculty Action Group document from 20 years earlier. Some of those involved in developing Education Studies at the University of North London were students in higher education in the late 1960s and early 1970s when radical challenges to the organization and purpose of universities were widely debated. There is thus some continuity in the extension of such 'radical' concerns into course innovation through subsequent decades. But it is worth noting that in the 'colleges of education' of the 1960s there was *already* a greater flexibility in assessment than in most universities. Tinkham (1969) argued that 'The one advantage that college of education students have over their fellows in the university is the more enlightened examination system . . .' (Tinkham, 1969: 92).

With interdisciplinary flexibility and recognition of student interests, those participating in the degree were crucial to the negotiation of what, in practice, Education Studies would be. The case made by this book is that to do this well, Education Studies needs to acknowledge and make space for the exploration of the cultural experience of children and young people, and particularly those children and young people that students taking Education Studies once were. Or, as the age profile of the student cohort has dropped from the 'mature' to the 'traditional' (18–22) in recent years, this might also be a matter of engaging the young people that students taking Education Studies are still. The importance, and relevance, of Cultural Studies, in this respect, is that it provides several decades of youth research, a great deal of sophisticated theory, and a refusal of conventional disciplinary thinking. Such resources, in reflecting upon how childhood and youth are lived, are an essential complement to more specifically educational studies. Further revisions to the north London degree, in the later 1990s, included, as an aim, furthering 'student's knowledge of the history and sociology of childhood and of the contemporary cultural contexts of childhood and youth' and, as a learning outcome, 'a theoretically informed and empirically focused interest in the cultures of children and young people'. To some extent, these revisions were informed by earlier developments in media education in schools. The relationship between the cultural study of youth and educational practice was explored by secondary school Media Studies teachers researching and developing classroom practice in London during the 1980s and 1990s (see Moss, 1989; Buckingham, 1990; Richards, 1992; Buckingham, 1993a, 1993b; Sefton-Green, 1993, 1998; Buckingham and Sefton-Green, 1994; Buckingham, 1998; Richards, 1998b; Sefton-Green and Sinker, 2000; Buckingham, 2003).

International perspectives on cultural studies and education

Internationally, the relationship between work in Cultural Studies and Education has received some significant attention from a number of authors with enduring educational interests. In the United States, Henry Giroux has most explicitly pursued the scope for a more active engagement with Cultural Studies. Giroux (1997) posed the question 'Is There a Place for Cultural Studies in Colleges of Education?' and made a strong case in its favour, declaring:

> Traditionally, schools and colleges of education in the United States have been organized around either conventional subject-based studies (e.g., math education) or disciplinary/administrative categories (curriculum and instruction). Within this type of intellectual division of labor, students generally have few opportunities to study larger social issues through a multi-disciplinary perspective. This slavish adherence to structuring the curriculum around disciplines is at odds with the field of cultural studies, whose theoretical energies are largely focused on issues regarding gender, class, sexuality, national identity, colonialism, race, ethnicity, cultural popularism, textuality, and critical pedagogy. The resistance to cultural studies may also arise from its emphasis on understanding schooling as a mechanism of politics embedded in relations of power, negotiation, and contestation. (Giroux, 1997: 233)

He outlines the 'space' of Cultural Studies, characterized by (at least) three areas of concern:

> . . . the spread of electronically mediated culture to all spheres of everyday intellectual and artistic life has shifted the ground of scholarship away from the traditional disciplines . . . to the more hybridized fields of comparative and world literature, media studies, ecology, society and technology, and popular culture.

> By analyzing the full range of assorted and densely layered sites of learning such as the media, popular culture, film, advertising, mass communications, and religious organizations, among others, cultural studies expands our understanding of the pedagogical and its role outside of school as the traditional site of learning. (Giroux, 1997: 235)

> . . . teachers must be accountable in their teaching to the ways in which they take up and respond to the problems of history, human agency, and the renewal of democratic public life. Cultural studies strongly rejects the assumption that teachers are simply transmitters of existing configurations of knowledge. Academics are always implicated in the dynamics of social power and knowledge that they produce, mediate, and legitimate in their classrooms. (Giroux, 1997: 236–7)

Giroux's case is made from a position of sharply political critique of American education. For him, Cultural Studies makes education a site for democratic struggle and the pursuit of human rights and social justice. Despite the rather generalized rhetoric of his argument, his engagement with Cultural Studies reaches back to the more visible political imperatives of its formation in the later 1960s and 1970s.

Many others working in the North American educational context have turned to Cultural Studies as a political resource in questioning the administrative, managerial and instrumental discourses that might otherwise prevail in educational debate. Dennis Carlson and Greg Dimitriadis, in their introduction to *Promises to Keep: Cultural Studies, Democratic Education, and Public Life*, argue:

> At this new intersection of curriculum theory, critical pedagogy, and the cultural foundations of education is a hybrid and interdisciplinary or even post-disciplinary space, one that falls under the useful rubric of 'the cultural studies of education'. This is a space that gets us closer and closer to our constituencies where they live their lives – a particularly important gesture at this moment when we seem uncertain about what exactly 'education' does and can mean. Such a space is necessary if we in education are going to rearticulate a relationship with young people and their ever more complex lives, and if we are to imagine, with them, a more democratic future. (Dimitriadis and Carlson, 2003: 31)

Like Giroux, they negotiate the concerns of education with Cultural Studies but without assimilating their work to Cultural Studies as such. Dimitriadis and Carlson stress 'intersections', areas of exchange among fields led by an overarching concern with democratic education. There is a tendency in this developing 'alliance' with Cultural Studies to construct the case, often rather repetitively, through rhetorical gestures to the future and in terms of relatively unspecified notions of the 'critical', of 'renewal' and of 'progress'. However, there are also detailed research studies worth reading for their more specific and situated accounts of educational settings. These counter the abstraction and generality of the wider arguments: Ellsworth (1997a, 1997b, 2004), Fine and Weiss (1998), McCarthy et al. (1999), Yon (2000), Dimitriadis (2001, 2003), Dolby (2001), Perry (2002) and Hoechsmann and Low (2008).

In Australia, though also working in the United States in the 1990s, Bob Connell has pursued a practically engaged critique of education, making social justice the core concern of his research. *Making the Difference: Schools, Families and Social Division* (1982), written collaboratively with several others, is an especially valuable empirical study. Though by no means dependent on Cultural Studies, it is appropriate to see the path taken by Connell here, and subsequently, as an engagement with both an eclectic, cross-disciplinary, theoretical repertoire and a concern for the extension of socialist political practice. In these respects, his work has been informed by British Cultural Studies. In *Making the Difference,* some specific Cultural Studies sources include Willis's *Learning to Labour* (1977) and Richard Johnson's essay 'Really useful knowledge – radical education and working-class culture 1790–1848' (1979). But Corrigan's *Schooling the Smash Street Kids* (1979) and, in particular, Dave Robins and Phil Cohen's *Knuckle Sandwich* (1978), studies associated with Cultural Studies, but not from Birmingham, are also cited as influential in his thinking about class.

A short, key statement of Connell's political case for egalitarian education can be found in *Schools and Social Justice* (1993). An important strand in his argument involves a version of 'standpoint epistemology'. He takes the view that knowledge is differently constituted from particular social positions and that, for example, an understanding of racism is best achieved by taking the point of view of those who are its victims. He suggests that the position of those who carry 'the burdens of social inequality is a better starting-point for understanding the totality of the social world than is the position of those who enjoy its advantages' (Connell, 1993: 39). Much of Connell's best known work explores the formation of gender identities, and in further explaining his emphasis on the standpoint of the disadvantaged, he points to the productivity of feminist theory, partly arising from the foregrounding of 'experiences that had been little discussed before' (Connell, 1993: 40). He adds:

> If the necessary intellectual work is done, the point of view of the least advantaged becomes the basis of a program for the organization and transmission of knowledge, which provides a common learnings [sic] agenda for all schools . . . It

> is then possible, in principle, to construct a comprehensive educational program, whose claim to preference over the existing academic curriculum is twofold. First, it follows the principle of social justice in education by embodying the interests of the least advantaged. Second, it is intellectually better than other ways of organizing knowledge. (Connell, 1993: 41)

If grounds for claiming that such an approach is 'intellectually better' are not fully explored in *Schools and Social Justice,* the substance of Connell's argument is best grasped by returning to *Gender and Power* (1987), his wide-ranging theoretical case for a 'progressive sexual politics'. In the preface, he notes that he has been 'uneasy with conventional masculinity almost as long as I can remember, certainly since I was a teenager' (Connell, 1987: xi), briefly tracing his engagement with feminism and socialist politics back to his involvement in student activism in the 1960s. In common with several other authors cited in this chapter, his own experience of studying at university coincided with the political unrest, and sense of 'rebellion', emerging in the mid-1960s and continuing into the 1970s.

The range of *Gender and Power* is formidable. Connell deals with theories of gender, the social structure of gender relations, forms of femininity and masculinity, and with sexual politics. Of course, since 1987, major texts theorizing gender have been published (for example, Butler, 1990, 1993; Haraway, 1991, 1992). But Connell remains a significant figure because he consistently relates his wider concerns to educational contexts. Brief case studies from *Making the Difference* (1982) are inserted into *Gender and Power* (1987), beginning with a girl who wants to be a vet:

> Delia told us she wanted to be a veterinarian. Her parents knew of this and were willing to bear the cost of her training, not a small matter for them. When we returned to that school several years later to report back and follow up, we learnt how things had turned out. Delia had left school at sixteen, as she had predicted; and she had found a job. It was a notable one both in terms of the general sexual division of labour and the specific history of her parents' marriage. She was not a veterinarian but a veterinary nurse. (Connell, 1987: 17)

Of course, such an outcome will seem commonplace and predictable, but the importance of Connell's approach is that he makes the ordinary and everyday a matter for careful, theoretically guided, enquiry. The question about, and for, Delia is why couldn't she become a vet, and what kind of change is necessary to make such an ambition more likely to be realized for a working-class girl?

Connell has important things to say about the body in social theory, especially as the proliferation of discourse analysis and of various versions of social constructionism often results in an elimination of the body from the analyses it favours. He concludes his chapter on 'The body and social practice' with these words:

> Symbolically, 'nature' may be opposed to 'culture', the body (fixed) opposed to history (moving). But in the reality of practice the body is never outside history, and history never free of bodily presence and effects on the body. The traditional dichotomies underlying reductionism now have to be replaced by a more adequate and complex account of the social relations in which this incorporation and interplay occur. (Connell, 1987: 87)

Connell's argument is with bodily determinism of the kind, for example, that explains social practices and identities as consequences of bodily differences between men and women. But he does not deny bodies and bodily differences. On the contrary, he emphasizes that they are 'carried forward' into social processes. And their characteristics are, in part, socially selected and high-lighted – so, for example, in some social circumstances bodily differences between men and women are emphasized and made to seem critical to their social identities (and often to how much they get paid). Connell's point is to question those interests that, adversely for women, highlight differences rather than similarities.

A further strand in Connell's work, of continuing importance, is the space given to psychoanalysis in understanding people's lives. He provides an important example of how issues in education, in this case educational life histories, are most effectively addressed through the practice of inter or transdisciplinary thinking. Both *Gender and Power* (1987) and *Masculinities* (1995) are, in their discussions of psychoanalysis, helpful illustrations of how to engage with fields of knowledge that inhabit the cracks between Education Studies' disciplinary building blocks.

But Connell is not alone in engaging with psychoanalysis. Of course, there are those who may regard it as no more credible than astrology or alchemy. Indeed psychoanalysis *is* often excluded from 'mainstream' academic disciplines, but innovative thinkers in many of them have made significant, if selective, use of psychoanalytic concepts. For example, in sociology, there is a long history of thoughtful engagement. C. Wright Mills, in *The Sociological Imagination* (1959), for example, turned to psychoanalysis in a chapter on 'Uses of History'.

Two decades later, Anthony Giddens drew on Freud and Lacan in *Central Problems in Social Theory* (1979). Stuart Hall, who left the Birmingham Centre for Contemporary Cultural Studies to be Professor of Sociology at the Open University, used psychoanalytic concepts in essays published in the 1990s (1996b, 1997). In France, perhaps rather unexpectedly, Pierre Bourdieu, a sociologist of education and culture, also turned to psychoanalysis in his theoretical contributions to *The Weight of the World* (1999), focusing on the emotional complexities of aspiration and failure. Psychoanalysis has also had a major influence in discourses around childhood (see Parker, 1997; Phillips, 1998) and has the potential to further understanding of the complexities of learning and teaching (Donald, 1991, 1992; Britzman, 1998). Deborah Britzman's work is thoroughly psychoanalytic in its orientation, difficult to read and sometimes uncompromisingly abstract. But her starting point is important, arguing that both psychoanalysis and education 'begin with notions of childhood, learning, and sociality' (Britzman, 1998: 8).

Intersections: Women's Studies, Cultural Studies and Education Studies

Among those who have made significant efforts to work through psychoanalytic ideas, several are located at a point of intersection and exchange between Cultural Studies, Women's Studies and Education. Debbie Epstein, variously a teacher of Cultural Studies, Women's Studies and Education, comments early in her mapping out of the ground for *Changing Classroom Cultures: Anti-racism, Politics and Schools* (1993), that:

> The development of subjective identities is both complex and important, and identities themselves are multi-faceted and contradictory. They are formed through a combination of available discourses, personal experience and material existence. Psychoanalysis has a major contribution to make to our understanding of this, since it explores subjectivity and the importance of the unconscious construction of the 'Other' in the formation of identity. (Epstein, 1993: 18)

In her work, educational practice is informed by theory without regard for disciplinary affiliation. Elsewhere, Epstein (1997: 179) comments that Cultural Studies is 'at root, a political project for the subversion of dominant meanings and the empowerment of the marginalised' and that both Cultural Studies and Women's Studies are 'anti-disciplinary/inter-disciplinary disciplines'. She collaborated with Richard Johnson (successor to Stuart Hall as Director of the Centre for Contemporary Cultural Studies) in writing *Schooling Sexualities* (Epstein and Johnson, 1998). She has also worked with Deborah Lynn Steinberg, coediting, again with Richard Johnson, a volume of essays and poetry entitled *Border Patrols: Policing the Boundaries of Heterosexuality* (Steinberg, Epstein and Johnson, 1997). In this body of work, Epstein has brought educational concerns together with a Cultural Studies approach to gender politics.

Like Epstein, Steinberg's stance reiterates the commitment to 'counter-hegemonic politics' (Steinberg, 1997: 194–5) and the logic of thus refusing to work within conventional disciplinary frames. For her, Women's Studies is especially productive in bringing questions of pedagogy into focus:

> As a feminist Cultural Studies teacher I have a working definition of interdisciplinarity. I hold this as a political and moral obligation to challenge the dominant paradigms of scholarship, to design a curriculum and approach to pedagogy which challenges social inequalities as well as conventions of teaching style and assessment, to challenge the boundaries of disciplinarity and the normalising, hierarchising processes of disciplinary power, and to create a framework which fosters critical thinking, self-expression – conscientisation, in a word, for myself and my students. (Steinberg, 1997: 200)

Psychoanalysis may not be the most important or the most productive means of furthering 'critical thinking' and 'self-expression', but where the confinement implicit in disciplinary study is refused, its capacity for posing difficult questions is often also more fully acknowledged. In Britain, the careers of three key figures may illustrate how and why psychoanalysis has figured in educational thought. There are others, James Donald (1991, 1992) and Phil Cohen (1997), for example. But Annette Kuhn (born 1945), Valerie Walkerdine (born 1947) and Carolyn Steedman (born 1947) each provide accessible studies crossing the boundaries of education, cultural studies, women's studies, psychoanalysis and autobiography.

Annette Kuhn, a Professor of Film Studies, has written very vividly about her own childhood and in particular the emotional complexities of 'passing' the eleven-plus selection exam and moving on to attend a girls' grammar school. In *Family Secrets: Acts of Memory and Imagination* (1995), she reflects on the tensions between herself and her working-class mother as she became a successful secondary school student, not only fulfilling her mother's aspirations for her but also, in doing so, eliciting resentment and a growing sense of estrangement. Her account is not weighted with psychoanalytic terms and only occasionally draws on a noticeably sociological vocabulary. Nevertheless, it is a theoretically informed interpretation of her childhood and education and is both distinctively individual and resonant with wider social issues. The subtlety of her descriptions of feeling out of place and ill-at-ease (for example, in her uniform) invites readers to recall and re-examine their own experiences of educational transition. As autobiography, it may not be taken seriously as educational research. But autobiography of this kind offers more than a story and, through its analytical poise, suggests the potential for further similarly focused and questioning studies by others (see, for example, Skeggs, 1997b). Kuhn has subsequently explored memory in relation to photography, coediting *Locating Memory: Photographic Acts* (2006), thus taking further an important aspect of *Family Secrets* (1995).

Valerie Walkerdine has published extensively in the fields of visual media and psychosocial theory (Walkerdine, 1990, 1997, 2007; Walkerdine et al., 2001). A consistent and continuing strand in her work gives attention to girls and, from time to time, includes reflection on her own formation. Perhaps one of the most striking early examples of this appeared in a collection entitled *Formations of Fantasy* (Burgin, Donald and Kaplan [formerly Lushington], 1986). Reprinted in Walkerdine (1990), the main focus of her essay is a young girl in a working-class family or, at least, so it begins. Her research was concerned with 'the education of six-year old girls' (Walkerdine, 1990: 195). But attention shifts somewhat as, during a visit to the girl's home, Walkerdine witnesses the family watching *Rocky II* on television. She becomes fascinated with the social dynamics of the family's encounter with the film and attempts to identify its meanings, especially for the girl's father. What emerges is an emphasis on fighting or, more broadly, 'standing up for yourself'. Working through considerable feelings of revulsion at the male enjoyment of the spectacle of physical violence, she seeks to identify meanings that, in terms of the father's class location, suggest the enduring sense of struggle for dignity and respect:

> Fighting is a key term in a discourse of powerlessness, of a constant struggle not to sink, to get rights, not to be pushed out. It is quite unlike the pathological object of a liberal anti-sexist discourse which would understand fighting as 'simply' macho violence and would substitute covert regulation and reasoning in language as less sexist. (Walkerdine, 1990: 187)

She goes on to complicate this, adding layers of meaning to her analysis and suggesting that the insistence on fighting also conceals a fear of cowardice and femininity. And, yet further, following the logic of psychoanalytic enquiry, she explores her own feelings and fantasies, examining her 'multiple positioning as both middle-class academic *and* working-class child' (Walkerdine, 1990: 196). Such writing, though sometimes risking the accusation of 'self-indulgence', is an important challenge to the spurious detachment and objectivity claimed by some research (and researchers) in education. She shows how her personal history informs her intellectual choices and commitments. In this respect, and especially in relation to the education of girls, Walkerdine's work is an extremely valuable resource.

Carolyn Steedman is a historian but worked as a primary school teacher for eight years in the 1970s. *The Tidy House: Little Girls Writing* (1982) begins:

> In the summer of 1976, three working-class eight-year-old girls, Melissa, Carla and Lindie, wrote a story about romantic love, marriage and sexual relations, the desire of mothers for children and their resentment of them, and the means by which those children are brought up to inhabit a social world. (Steedman, 1982: 1)

Steedman offers a substantial venture into the social history of working-class childhood, extending her account far beyond the confines of her classroom in that exceptionally hot summer in the mid-1970s. But she also returns to the writing that the girls produced and repeatedly engages its possible meanings, tracing themes that, as the paragraph above might suggest, may seem surprising in the story telling of such young children. Psychoanalytic approaches to the discussion of the girls' story ('The Tidy House') are considered but remain relatively slight by comparison with the range and density of historical reference and comparison. Nevertheless, the work of interpretation in its detailed, meticulous, reflexive and sustained attention is not unlike that of psychoanalysis in practice, where a story told may be revisited many times, angles of interpretation tried out, reconsidered, their implications explored. Giving such scrupulous attention to a single story contrasts starkly with the necessary habits of attention adopted by teachers. Loaded with many children's pieces of writing, teachers are likely to read just once, and quickly, correcting, assessing and grading. Steedman's reading is slow and expansive.

In *Landscape for a Good Woman: A Story of Two Lives* (1986), Steedman writes both autobiography and theory, reflecting on her own life and that of her mother and engaging critically, as historians often do, with the universalizing tendencies of psychoanalysis. It is an extraordinarily intense meditation on memory and interpretation. Part 1 begins:

> This book is about lives lived out on the borderlands, lives for which the central interpretative devices of the culture don't quite work. It has a childhood at its centre – my childhood, a personal past – and it is about the disruption of that fifties childhood by the one my mother had lived out before me, and the stories she told about it. Now, the narrative of both these childhoods can be elaborated by the marginal and secret stories that other working-class girls and women from a recent historical past have to tell. (Steedman, 1986: 5)

The pages that follow elaborate a complex and subtle account; this is an incisive exercise in writing the cultural history of childhood. Like Kuhn's autobiography or Walkerdine's seeming digressions into self-analysis, Steedman's writing invites re-engagement in our own efforts to articulate and understand both our own childhood and the wider meanings of childhood in the context of current debates (see also Steedman, 1990, 1992, 1995). Each of these three authors, Kuhn, Walkerdine and Steedman, traces a personal history through working-class childhoods in Britain in the late 1940s and 1950s. Their accounts are particular and, of course, are written by highly successful academics, each well known and influential in quite specific fields of expertise (see Richards, 2005b). But in their writing, they draw from theory and research generated in a range of disciplines and in 'non-disciplinary' locations, exemplifying the cross-disciplinary production of knowledge.

Conclusion

This chapter has argued that Education Studies does not benefit from a close adherence to the framework of discrete disciplines and that it can be most productive, and most interesting, when work is developed across traditional boundaries. It has also argued that too much is neglected if only the relatively traditional disciplines are acknowledged. Most obviously, the scope of both Cultural Studies and Women's Studies may be neglected if the primary concern is to work from psychology, sociology, history and philosophy. A further, related, issue is that of the political motivation for pursuing academic study, both in teaching and research. In some versions of Cultural Studies, and in Women's Studies (see Lumby, 1997; Whelehan, 2000), challenges to existing authorities in the academic domain and to the credibility of some forms of established knowledge are central to the formation of these 'inter' or 'anti' disciplines. Finally, the strength of Education Studies should be found, in part, in its negotiation of knowledge with those students who participate in it.

Points for reflection

What are the principles at work in the Education Studies degree of which you have experience?

To what extent do you think higher education has made constructive changes in its curriculum and its teaching methods?

How should student experience inform Education Studies?

New Youth Research

Introduction

This chapter outlines recent developments in the cultural study of youth and the wider potential for new youth research in relation to education.

The preceding chapters have traced histories of work in Cultural Studies and in related fields. This chapter looks forward. But any book, however much it may claim to be authoritative or even definitive, has to be written at a particular time and in circumstances that will change. Writing in late 2009, it seems likely that significant political shifts will emerge in and follow from the 2010 General Election. With a currently 'unpopular' Labour government, apparently widespread public mistrust of politicians, an enquiry into the invasion of Iraq, a continuing war in Afghanistan and, in education, a recent critical report on the consequences of relentless testing in primary schools (http://www.primaryreview.org.uk/ and see Alexander, 2009), the 'progress' of New Labour may be subject to some complicated reappraisals. Looking forward, in this short review, will mean identifying some of the more recent, and emergent, developments in youth research of interest to students of and practitioners in education. Of course, it is not possible to discuss the future course of youth research with any guarantee that those lines of enquiry that I select for comment will turn out to be the most important and influential.

But the purpose of this chapter is to highlight those areas that look like they should be significant for education through the next decade.

Rather than presuming that the only responsibility of this book is to inform readers of what is going on in the world of academic research and debate, it is important now to say that research, and especially youth research, should not be confined to a world of experts and professionals. Readers of this book should consider doing their own youth research, however modest it may be (Gray, 2003). Such research has a potential for enquiry and diversity that should not be defined, and limited, by this book's account of past agendas. Indeed, it's not possible to know what social and educational interests readers of this book may bring to it. But among the concerns that might be common to many such readers may be some scope for reflection on 'being a student', a social position marked by significant change in recent decades. In particular, being a student in Education is of obvious importance for readers of this book, and it is probably worth noting and reflecting on the gender composition of the course group to which you belong. Often, Education Studies students are predominantly women. Where the expected careers of graduates in Education Studies may lie in primary education, it is likely that the continuing association of women with such work presumes characteristics of traditional femininity such as patience, caring, gentleness and responsibility. Looking back to the 1960s, students taking 'teacher training' courses were also often young women and, by comparison with those pursuing honours degree courses in universities, were judged, and may have judged themselves, to be less 'academic', less interested in, and less able to conduct, critical intellectual enquiry (see Tinkham, 1969). It might be worth considering to what extent such a division persists more than 50 years later and how you might relate your own experience as a student to such a division. Of course, it is one intention of this book, and others in the series, to contest such a division by connecting debates outside education to those working in Education Studies and related fields. Education always has a particular practice, teaching, at its core, but teaching is far from being just a 'practical' matter. It demands serious thought, informed by a wide range of theory and debate across disciplines (Schon, 1991; hooks, 1994b).

New youth research

One site of significant initiatives informed by cultural studies of childhood and youth is the Centre for the Study of Children, Youth and Media, located in the London Knowledge Lab at the Institute of Education, University of London

(IOE, 2010). For example, a project begun in 2006, and running for some three years, looks at 'the potential contribution of the Internet to promoting civic engagement and participation among young people (aged 15–25)' (IOE, 2010). The project, CIVICWEB: Young People, the Internet and Civic Participation, explored 'youth-orientated civic sites' in terms of informal learning, a major preoccupation of the Centre. A further project conducted through several years in the mid-decade investigated 'Camcorder Cultures: Media Technologies and Everyday Creativity' (IOE, 2010). Though not confined to children and young people, the site of main interest was the domestic. The research considered the 'processes and products of amateur camcorder use, ranging from parents' recordings of family celebrations, to children's horror film spoofs, to semi-professionals' self-consciously 'artistic' shorts' (IOE, 2010). Reporting on the research project, Buckingham and Willett (2009) do discuss young people's involvement with camcorders and related technologies, notably in skate-boarders' videos and in parodies displayed on video-sharing sites. Also, Buckingham and Willett (2006) and Carr et al. (2006) map out substantial areas of work both already established and emergent and variously exploring informal learning in engagements with new media forms. Of particular relevance to the concerns of this book are the papers collected in *Youth, Identity, and Digital Media* (Buckingham, 2008; see, for example, the chapter by Herring).

Several other strands of research often specifically assessing and furthering approaches to teaching new media are represented by Buckingham (2007), Burn and Durran (2007), Allen et al. (2007), Burn and Durrant (2008), Willett et al. (2008; see also Carrington and Robinson, 2009) and, with a broader theoretical sweep, Burn (2009). Various alliances between emergent fields (digital literacies), older practices (media education) and the cultural study of childhood and youth have effectively supported a new wave of research and publication likely to grow ever greater in the next few years. The studies cited here are, on the whole, just those associated with one research centre at the Institute of Education, University of London. Many more have been published by others elsewhere in the United Kingdom, in Canada and the United States and in Australia, and no doubt in other countries too, in and out of the Anglophone world (see, for example, the MacArthur Foundation Series on Digital Media Learning 2005, continuing; Livingstone, 2009; Livingstone and Haddon, 2009).

Through 2008–2010, the Centre for the Study of Children, Youth and Media, in collaboration with the Open University, organized a series of seminars entitled 'Rethinking Youth Culture in the Age of Global Media'. The series, supported by the Economic and Social Research Council (ESRC), concentrated its attention on 'young people's consumption, use and production of media and popular cultural forms (including audio-visual, digital and online media, popular music and fashion) in the context of cultural and economic globalization'. Though struggling, initially, to move beyond the familiar ground of British-based youth studies, it did provide a platform for reports on, for example, Citizenship and Dissent: South Asian Muslim Youth in the United States after 9/11 (see Maira, 2009; and also Maira, 2002; Maira and Soep, 2004) and from Pilkington (Pilkington, 1996, 2010) 'Skinhead is a movement of action': Local, national and global tropes in contemporary skinhead 'ideology'. The problematic legacy of Cultural Studies preoccupations long regarded as insular was thus acknowledged and challenged in questioning, for example, how new media might support the creation of transnational or global youth cultures (for earlier research in this area, see Banaji, 2006 and de Block and Buckingham, 2007).

Such efforts to give youth cultural studies a more transnational impetus are, however, by no means new. Though not primarily a youth researcher, Paul Gilroy's work has consistently refused to be bounded by national perspectives (Gilroy, 1987, 1993a, b, 2004a, b). As I have noted, from within British Cultural Studies, even in the 1970s, a critique of its limitations and exclusions in relation to 'race' and ethnicity was made and, if not always with as much empirical research as might have been wanted, pursued through the subsequent decade (for example, Jones, 1988). Somewhat outside the field of Cultural Studies, Hewitt's *White Talk Black Talk: Inter-racial Friendship and Communication Amongst Adolescents* (1986) is an important analysis of 'cross-ethnic' identifications, based on research in south London (see also Hewitt, 2005). Also conducting research in south London, but a decade later, Les Back (1996) pursued the example of intercultural youth research, set by Hebdige (1979), Hewitt (1986) and Jones (1988), with his *New Ethnicities and Urban Culture: Racisms and Multiculture in Young Lives*. More recently, Back has offered further, often semi-autobiographical reflections on 'race' and ethnicity, again with a recurrent focus on south London, in the enigmatically titled *The Art of Listening* (2007).

A very good example of 'new' empirical research focusing on youth and ethnicity but also engaging centrally with everyday uses of the media was pursued by Marie Gillespie in Southall in the early 1990s (Gillespie, 1995). Her study, *Television, Ethnicity and Cultural Change*, is an important example of an ethnography attentive both to the position of young people in relation to parental cultures and to popular television and film. Its emphasis on newly emergent identities is taken up and explored, with a more central focus on language use, in Roxy Harris's (2005) study of British Asian (Brasian) young people. It is a central claim of Harris's analysis that the young people he talked to should be described as Brasian – though, some years on from first publication, it's not clear that the term is at all widely used. He comments:

> The bold use of this term challenges the diffidence of the increasing number of observers and commentators who use binary expressions such as British Asian. Terms like British Asian, in my view, continue an entrenched mindset which envisages two entirely separate, strongly bounded and homogeneous cultures which individuals need to negotiate by jumping from one to the other alternately as if inhabiting one sealed world and then the other. *Brasian,* on the other hand, suggests a continuous flow of everyday life and cultural practices in which, at any given moment, both British and particular South Asian derived elements are always co-present. (Harris, 2005: 1–2)

Both taking issue with and borrowing from British Cultural Studies, Harris seeks to show how, in their use of language and in how they represent it, ordinary young people from South Asian families construct 'new ethnicities'. On the basis of research in the late 1990s, in west London, Harris aims to provide empirical detail of the claims made by authors such as Stuart Hall (see Morley and Chen, 1996), Paul Gilroy (2004a, b) and Kobena Mercer (1994) for the emergence of cultures of hybridity in the lives of young people (see also Nilan and Feixa, 2006).

Somewhat unusually in the context of discussions of ethnicity, Harris also borrows quite substantially from the work of Raymond Williams (1961, 1977). He draws on Williams's concept of the structure of feeling to justify his presentation to readers of the perhaps messy detail of his data – the stuff of hybridity as it is lived. He also makes some use of Williams's conceptualization of 'cultures' as residual, dominant and emergent – to show how elements from different locations and times coexist in the present time of people's lives and are not separated simply into what is old (and finished) and what is new (and of the future). Whether or not the word 'Brasian' has any currency, the argument that young people's lives need to be understood in terms of 'openness, variability and unpredictability' (Harris, 2005: 13) is a warning against theoretical tidiness of continuing relevance.

With a more clearly marked emphasis on a return to, and revival of, class analysis, a number of ambitious and wide-ranging sociological projects have been pursued by the Centre for Research on Socio-Cultural Change, located at the Open University, working in collaboration with the University of Manchester (and funded by a major research funding body, the ESRC). In particular, a project conducted through 2003–2006, 'Cultural Capital and Social Exclusion: Culture and Inequality in Contemporary Britain', follows, and develops, the work of Pierre Bourdieu in investigating 'cultural capital in relation to social classes, gender, and ethnicity' (CRESC, 2010). Not addressing education explicitly, and with no specific focus on young people and children, much of its research may seem distant from the concerns of this book. But it is a significant source of enquiry and debate illuminating the wider 'cultural economy' of Britain. The research contributes to an understanding of the context in which educational questions can be posed, identifying trends in the interrelationship between cultural, social and economic capital.

Often, and perhaps especially in relation to youth, the funding that allows research to be pursued is associated with areas of public debate and anxiety. For example, young people's involvement in drinking alcohol, a matter of considerable and persistent concern, is likely to be a topic given funding fairly consistently in the present and foreseeable future. Among the most interesting of enquiries in this area is that led by Chris Griffin (formerly of the Birmingham Centre for Contemporary Cultural Studies), funded by the ESRC and entitled *Branded Consumption and Social Identification: Young People and Alcohol* (2008) (see also Willis et al., 1990 and the comments in Chapter 1).

Knowledge about young people's lives is produced through complex networks of institutional support, public debate and, often, interdisciplinary cooperation. The *Branded Consumption* project is undoubtedly worthwhile, rigorous and informative, but it is worth considering what kinds of questions have not yet been asked and investigated. In this respect, it is also important to recognize that knowledge about young people is very much an adult matter and that, on the whole, young people themselves are excluded from the processes through which research enquiries are conceived and conducted (see Boyden and Ennew, 1997). Perhaps the tendency of adult concerns – to target youth as agents of excess – excessive in consumption of alcohol, of sex or of new media – might be challenged, as Griffin's (2008) research suggests, by studies showing how youthful patterns of consumption are orchestrated through adult, and mostly commercial, interests (Herring, 2008). This might seem to be just another turn in the argument that youth are manipulated by marketing and are victims, once again, of strategies they are too naïve to recognize and contest. But Griffin's (2008) research does more than this, placing some emphasis on what young people themselves have to say about their own experience (see also Bragg and Buckingham, 2003).

Perhaps one of the virtues of the often modest 'research' that is reported in some of the following chapters is that it often arose in dialogue with young people in classroom contexts, both in schools and in higher education. From a standpoint in teaching, 'research' is likely to be more participatory, more negotiated in day-to-day encounters with young people. This is a significant strength, though often, of course, such research finds it hard to shed the single inverted commas that imply that it isn't quite as credible as the research done more from a distance, from outside, by *professional* researchers.

Conclusion

This chapter has identified the kinds of research that seem significant, for education, in youth cultural studies as the first decade of the twenty-first century comes to an end. To represent research that is really new, in the sense of *very* recent, is difficult to do in a book. The process of writing and subsequent production is relatively slow. To find out what is going on in current youth research entails looking at websites (such as ESRC, 2010), at journals and e-journals. But, as I have suggested, research can also begin with your own experience of youth and education, or that of people you know or, if you are working in a school, with the students you teach or support. Research should not be seen as something that is done by remote specialists but as a mode of recording and reflecting on particular aspects of the social and educational life around you (see Buckingham, 1990; Schon, 1991; Etherington, 2004; Lassiter, 2005).

Points for reflection

What aspects of young people's lives outside school do they make visible in the classroom?

Do the schools that you know enforce a boundary between popular media and the classroom?

What do you think would be a worthwhile topic for new research?

Part 2
Culture, Media and the Curriculum

The second part of this book moves from the field of academic research and publication, dominant in Part 1, to more particular accounts of work with young people in schools and in Education Studies at undergraduate level. In keeping with the preceding chapters, these accounts are not confined to the 'present'. I have delved back into my own work as a teacher, to those occasions when, in the spaces afforded by secondary school English and Media Studies, I drew most directly on work in Cultural Studies. Each chapter also corresponds to a 'module' in the Education Studies degree that I taught in the late 1990s and the first decade of this century. Together, these modules formed a strand representing the cultural study of youth and popular media. The final chapter, like Chapter 3, considers current and future concerns. But, in each chapter, even where the discussion returns to past examples, those examples are considered as precedents for future work with young people.

Media Education

Chapter Outline

Introduction

This chapter explores the aspirations of media education in schools through an examination of particular examples of media teaching in practice. These examples are situated and discussed in the context of *continuing* debates about the meaning and value of both students' media-related production and the 'cultures' of young people.

Cultural Studies as a subject title has not had a visible presence in schools. As a field of study, it has been pursued and expanded, both in Britain and internationally, almost exclusively in higher education. Laced with an eclectic and often intimidating array of theory, Cultural Studies has sometimes seemed to be a problem for undergraduates, without also attempting to introduce it to those still less than 18 years old. And yet, Cultural Studies has informed what teachers do, especially in the development of forms of media education in schools from the 1970s onwards. In this chapter, I will outline a little of this history and also offer some examples of the kind of work done in media education, often under the title Media Studies. Though much of what I will discuss belongs to my own experience of media teaching, I intend these examples to serve as both historical documents and precedents for much more current concerns in the field of teaching about, for example, media representations of war, of young people and of sex. The priorities of media education in schools, in the second decade of the twenty-first century, are undoubtedly dominated by the new media (Gauntlett, 2000; Buckingham, 2007), but this does not justify an indifference to, and ignorance of, past attempts to develop media work with young people in schools.

There are several informative overviews of media education, giving varying degrees of attention to the history of its formation (Masterman, 1980, 1985; Buckingham, 2003). Among them, *Learning the Media* (Alvarado et al., 1987: 9–38) includes a significant attempt to locate the field historically. It is important to recognize that media education does not have a single source and that Cultural Studies has not always been its most obvious companion or resource in higher education. Film Studies, for example, had a significant part to play in the early formation of media education, and partly through its journals *Screen* (2010) and *Screen Education*, the Society for Education in Film and Television made some important contributions in the 1970s and early 1980s. Similarly, the British Film Institute has sustained support for teaching, mainly about film, though also other visual media, through several decades (BFI, 2010). David Buckingham, whose career and publications figure frequently in several chapters in this book, has made a determined and energetic attempt to engage with, but also to contest, the tendency of Film Studies both to circumscribe the concerns of media education and to produce a somewhat canonical approach to the field. Against a preoccupation with only those media that teachers themselves might revere, he has approached media education as a constantly shifting negotiation with emergent habits of media use among young people and, especially in the last decade, with the rapid proliferation of digital media (see Buckingham and Willett, 2006; Buckingham, 2007, 2008). In *Media Education: Literacy, Learning and Contemporary Culture* (2003), Buckingham takes a retrospective look at media education, but also outlines its future, offering a comprehensive sketch of the field at the point of its engagement with the new literacies of digital culture. Rather than reiterating Buckingham's thorough and informative account here, this chapter will address readers with interests in education but not necessarily with any experience of what media education looks like in the real world of the school classroom.

History

Teaching about the media used to take place in English lessons in secondary schools. Through the 1950s and 1960s, some teaching about print media, the press and advertising in particular, might well figure in even quite traditional schools (of course, books are print media too, but they were not often taught as such). Such teaching made these materials the object of critical scrutiny, borrowing methods of attentive analysis from the study of poetry or a passage from a novel. But whereas giving such attention to a literary text was mainly a matter of recognizing its value, the point of giving comparable time and thought to an advertisement was to refuse its power to influence or 'debase' both the English language and its users. The complex political history of this step towards the study of the media in schools can be traced through the work of key figures in twentieth-century literary criticism, notably F. R. Leavis and, through one influential joint publication, Denys Thompson (Leavis, 1930; Leavis and Thompson, 1933).

Francis Mulhern (1981) has provided a substantial and meticulously researched history of their influence and of the journal *Scrutiny*. Mulhern comments:

> At the most practical and pertinent level, it was evident that *Scrutiny* had opened up an educational space within which the cultural institutions of bourgeois-democratic capitalism could be subjected to critical analysis – a space which was to be utilized to remarkable effect, most notably by Raymond Williams and the Centre for Contemporary Cultural Studies founded by Richard Hoggart at Birmingham University. (Mulhern, 1981: 329)

Indeed, a recognizably Leavisite emphasis on critical and evaluative discrimination persists in Stuart Hall and Paddy Whannel's advocacy for teaching popular culture *The Popular Arts* (1964). Mulhern's critique of *Scrutiny* is, however, that it produced a literary critical discourse that has been politically disabling. In his final remarks, he suggests:

> . . . the basic and constant discursive organization of the journal, the matrix of its literary and cultural criticism and of its educational politics, of its radical and conservative manifestations alike, was one defined by a dialectic of 'culture' and 'civilisation' whose *main* and *logically necessary effect* was a depreciation, a *repression* and, at the limit, a *categorical dissolution* of *politics as such*. Nothing could be more disorienting for socialist cultural theory than the ingestion of

a discourse whose main effect is to undo the intelligibility of its ultimate concern: political mobilization against the existing structures of society and State. (Mulhern, 1981: 330–1)

As media education has had a close association with left politics in Britain and was also introduced and developed by teachers educated in English literary criticism, its struggle to achieve a coherent and credible practice has been protracted and difficult. Though now it is uncommon to find claims that media education is informed by the priorities of socialist politics, not least because such a politics has become so fragmented, the purpose of a critical and analytical approach to media texts remains a significant concern. Informed by social semiotics and multimodal analysis, it is an elaborate practice of reflective engagement with texts (Hodge and Kress, 1988; Kress and van Leeuwen, 1996, 2001; Burn and Parker, 2003; Kress, 2003). The production of meaning is traced across all the elements of the media text including, where relevant, design and layout, typography and colour, sound (including music), editing and so on.

Teaching: texts and politics

To recall and illustrate how Media Studies has negotiated the tensions of conducting classroom-based critical analysis of newspaper journalism in relation to immediate political events, I want to turn to an article I wrote in June 1982 for the magazine *Teaching London Kids*. This article, 'Topicality', was the first of two devoted to a critical engagement with the press in the first years of the Thatcher government. I will discuss the second, 'Media-Race-Riots', in the next chapter. Perhaps, at the time, Media Studies suffered from an excessive attachment to critical textual analysis. It was difficult to teach. It was not obviously enjoyable. It could also entail positioning students as disciples to a double cause – both that of critical reading and that of left political critique. But such priorities were central to, for example, Len Masterman's (1980, 1985) two influential books about media teaching. Here are some long extracts from my 'Topicality' article (Richards, 1982) written at the time of the Falklands (South Atlantic) war:

One of the issues which English teaching, and also Media Studies, faces is that of 'topicality'. English has a less fixed 'content' than many other subjects and it is often apparently easy to turn to 'current events' as material for classroom work. Sometimes what is on the 'agenda' of English lessons seems set inexorably by what the media dominantly present. There are good reasons for attending to the 'events', the 'themes', promoted in the press and on TV. To intervene in the field of preoccupations continually sustained and shifted by the range of news media, and to examine the processes through which that field is constituted, is one way of extending the already full debate around news issues which continues anyway amongst those one teaches. To encourage them to think more carefully about why, and with what consequences, 'topics' become 'topical' is, or should be, part of a larger process of challenging them to identify and to question the determinations of their own consciousness. But there are problems (Richards, 1982: 20.)

Some of the claims made in the preceding paragraph may seem contentious – and certainly articulate a version of media theory ('the determinations of their own consciousness') that I would now want to qualify quite radically. The article turns to a consideration of *The Sun* newspaper, at that time aligned with the Thatcherite form of popular authoritarianism. As a paper read and enjoyed by at least some of the students I taught, it was often difficult to persuade them to make it an object of analysis or indeed to persuade them that analysis was in any way a satisfying activity. I commented:

The Sun, The Daily Mail and *The Daily Express* (and others too) are profoundly anti-working class, sexist and substantially racist and yet sell themselves to an audience of millions whose real interests lie in opposing what these papers promote. The work of teaching in relation to this material is that of identifying contradictions, articulating them in classroom talk, challenging evasions of those contradictions ('everyone's entitled to their own opinion', 'people are just different', 'because my friends/parents do' etc) and, always avoiding the closures expected of teachers (Richards, 1982: 21).

These simplistic characterizations of both the press and its readers could not be sustained now and certainly contributed to the difficulty of teaching this material at the time. The adversarial stance was, predictably enough, the object of some mockery or, less obvious, silent refusal. The article struggles to understand, and to find a way of engaging with, the immediate and apparent political consequences of the Falklands War:

In the current Falklands crisis many anti-Tory working-class kids have manifested admiration for Thatcher: in this case the familiar contradiction between attacking her policies but doing so in viciously sexist terms has been reworked, but not resolved, into something like 'the bitch at war' – seen as a 'good thing' perhaps because the authoritarian and militaristic elements are now at least directed against foreigners. Such an appalling misconstruction of the situation should perhaps underline the need to contest the process of smoothing over contradictions in the name of unity . . . 'we, the British people . . . the nation united against the enemy' (Richards, 1982: 21).

These observations arose directly from what I observed among a class that I knew well and liked. In particular, one white working-class girl, Karol, had on one occasion turned on a Nigerian girl in the same class, telling her that if she didn't agree with Thatcher's stand on the British right to the Falklands, she should go back to her own country. As she was previously consistently hostile to Margaret Thatcher and the Tory Government, this was surprising and quite shocking. My discussion of her 'shift' was infused with the vocabulary of the various books I had read in the previous three or four years: Hall et al. (1978), Morley (1980), Foucault (1978), Laclau (1977), Dworkin (1981) and various novels by Kurt Vonnegut (1972; 1973/1975), satirizing war. The weight of political theory to be carried into thinking about teaching Media Studies was considerable. And its primary concerns, in those years, were more often than not with news and current affairs media (Masterman, 1985). So, this is what I had to say about, or in response to, Karol:

For as long as it lasts there seems to be a displacement of class positionalities and of the antagonisms between them in favour of a popular, racist unification. An anti-sexist deconstruction of militarism would have been a valuable way of pre-empting the popularization of military force which has been carried through on the basis of a discursive alliance with readers and an unchallenged ideology of sexism. To examine *both* the ideology of femininity inscribed on Page Three and the sexist labeling of Thatcher could well have made the comic book machismo seen in *The Sun* appear absurd and unacceptable. Thatcher's positive appropriation of the misconceived 'Iron Maiden' and 'Iron Lady' labels, long before the Falkland crisis provided fresh space for elaborating its most potent connotations, was evidence enough of how badly wrong criticisms drawing upon a traditional sexist repertoire can turn out. Against her small triumph on that there is a need for a fully developed refusal of the existing constitution of the sexual field as one of power and oppression: to be an 'Iron Maiden' depends upon notions of male identity grounded in sex-as-force, as the power to subordinate. The virginal connotations of 'maiden' suggest one who does not *submit* to sexual experience, because it can only be an experience of subordination, or lack of power. Thus, as one who does not submit, the 'maiden' is established in the position of 'man', aggressive, subordinating others by force. 'Iron' also carries connotations of chastity: hard, unresponsive, encased in/shielded by iron. It has a long history recalling the woman at war, leaving her (submissive) sexual identity behind, concealing the body in an armour which denies both the force of the military and the sexual attack. In times of war, so it goes, men must crush the enemy because that is the natural mode of masculinity and, sometimes, there are women who will overcome the natural mode of femininity, encase soft bodies in iron, and thereby defy the enemy. This may sound irrational but so is military action to 'reclaim' islands of no importance to people here, and whose people could have been extricated from their predicament through any number of non-military means. Being tough with the Argies, and for Thatcher, living up to the 'Iron Maiden' image, have become important means of winning popular support for the war; our task should be to unravel the net of militaristic and patriarchal concepts on which the construction of that popular support depends and in which much of left-wing thinking has itself become enmeshed. The heritage of imperialism must, in substantial ways, draw upon a patriarchal ideology in which male violence is privileged over other forms of negotiation or contest. Without such an ideology, it would be more difficult to secure the remarkable fiction that 'our boys' represent 'us'. The deaths and the wounds are made into the moral brace which holds 'the British people' together in unity: it is not for the Conservative Government but for 'our way of life' that people are dying. To refuse the construction of an 'us' for whom 'our boys' are getting killed has become a callous disavowal within the terms that are set in the majority of newspapers. And thus to challenge the commitment to killing/being killed is transformed into profound moral irresponsibility (Richards, 1982: 21–2).

Also in the early 1980s, Judith Williamson asked, in the title of a much debated article, 'How does girl number twenty understand ideology? (Williamson, 1981/1982). In a sense, I was asking the same question in reflecting on my own teaching about the media. Trying to understand Karol, and others, was not easy. And the concept of ideology itself contributed to positioning students as in need of enlightenment by a supposedly, but impossibly, 'ideology-free' teacher. Williamson acknowledges this in the conclusion to her article. In my discussion, in one long final paragraph I struggled, speculatively, with possible tactics, drawing on various strands in radical aesthetics, a mixture of Mukarovsky (1977), Brecht (Willett, 1978) and William Burroughs (1959/1969; Richards, 1974). Though perhaps eccentric as sources for thinking about classroom practice, at least *pleasure* emerged as a central concern. In short, students had to enjoy what they did:

Unless one can develop a pedagogy in which active enjoyment characterizes its most fundamental elements (and is not something marginal to the real process of learning) then I don't see much hope of engaging those one teaches in anything other than a wearying game of evasions and resistances (Richards, 1982: 22).

So, in the daily face-to-face teaching of Media Studies, it was becoming difficult to sustain a practice imagined as an intervention by teachers to liberate students from their subjection to the myths of the dominant ideology disseminated by the media. Perhaps the most significant challenge to such a practice was published in *Screen*, with the provocative title 'Against demystification' (Buckingham, 1986). Though primarily a review article devoted to Len Masterman's (1985) *Teaching the Media*, it opened up and gave momentum to the project of investigating both what students themselves enjoy and make of the media and how they negotiate being taught about it in school. Assumptions about the ideological effects of the media were, if not set aside, made matters for empirical enquiry.

Production and creativity

Probably the most enjoyable aspect of media education for students is production (Buckingham et al., 1995). This is not new. Arguably, it predates the development of the critical Media Studies described above. But where schools have encouraged and supported practical media production, before the turn to such activities in Media Studies, it was probably outside the taught curriculum, in school-based film-making and photography clubs. To assess to what extent such precedents might have also included the wider concerns of media education is a project for extended historical recovery and is thus beyond the scope of this chapter. Here, I want to comment on some of the forms of practical production within Media Studies.

At the Club and *Roots and Culture Pirate TV* are two studio-based examples from when I taught Media Studies in schools as long ago as the early 1980s. I want to recall these here, in some detail, rather than offering a generalized account of what 'practical' or 'production' work in Media Studies has aspired to achieve. These are very particular instances, of course, and come from one 'inner-city' London school at a time of some strain in its history as it merged with a larger school nearby. Of course, the broader social and political context of the first Thatcher government was also marked by stress and uncertainty, with very high levels of unemployment, confrontations between young people and the police in a number of cities (Centre for Contemporary Cultural Studies, 1982), and the miners' strike. Some description of the 'lived experience' of attempting to teach a two-year Media Studies course to students aged

14–16 years and, in many cases, in their final years of schooling, might illustrate how teaching is always a negotiation with people living through the particular circumstances of their lives. The students referred to here, teenagers then, are living through their mid-forties as this book is published.

At the Club (1982) was produced in a simple television studio operated by the Inner London Education Authority in Highbury, North London. It was made by an ethnically mixed group of students aged 15 or 16, girls and boys, and well known to each other through several years of shared schooling. In the context of a school in which the most elementary routines of time-tabled lessons and attendance often seemed precarious, they were regarded as relatively successful and were quite popular with teachers. But this should not be construed as the basis for a harmonious and unproblematic encounter either between the students or between the students and myself. I wrote in my teaching journal at the time, 12 February 1982:

Attendance problems are interfering with the progress of these groups – Samantha and Errol absent today, Thomas and Naomi (both absent now for several weeks) also relations within one group seem to be extremely difficult. I've made it clear that group work is central and important, that they must be committed to producing a result, whatever the social difficulties involved. The groups must commence work next Friday.

At this stage, around the mid-point of the first year of the course, they were doing work on film narrative (viewing *The Killers*, directed by Don Siegel, and *Halloween*, directed by John Carpenter). They were also asked to examine a short 'independent' video called *Us Girls* (produced by the Albany Video Project. Deptford, in south-east London). *Us Girls* was one example of low-budget alternative video production, offered in teaching as both a challenge to 'mainstream' television and a possible basis for planning production work of their own. I reviewed the video for the magazine *Teaching London Kids* (1981).

In the review, I gave the following account:

The narrative is constructed through the statements and conversations of five white working-class girls, situated at the point of entry into work, monogamous heterosexuality and pregnancy. There are no male actors and the presence of men is indicated through the presentation of the female half of the dialogues (which are almost exclusively also confrontations – with the police, with a father). The visual absence and the silence of the male addressee invites a recognition of the obviousness and predictability of the missing words: in classroom use, it would probably be worth asking groups to supply these words, and to concentrate attention upon how *set* these interactions are.

The video moves through discussions of the oppressive dreariness of their lives: babysitting, domestic work, factory and shop work, the controls and constraints imposed by police, parents and boyfriends. Against all this, they pose their assertive style and the possibility of going away together for a weekend, without parents or boyfriends. But, of course, even this is compromised by the rivalry between the girls for sexual rights to boyfriends and, retrospectively, their competing assertions of physical sexual development. By breaking their already precarious unity in the brief final scene, the tape refuses the possibility of 'a weekend away' being construed as adequate relief or an achieved solution. The lack of closure in the narrative structure, the absence of resolution, makes the tape a valuable means of posing questions; in what ways they will be answered, or refused, will obviously vary. Perhaps the worst that might be expected came from a group of about 20 fourth-year boys who, predominantly, dismissed the challenges to masculine dominance by defining the girls as 'slags' – and thus is reproduced precisely what much of the programme attacks. It is necessary to have ways of intervening in those situations in which a part of the programme provokes a refusal of the whole: there are, for example, one or two derogatory allusions to Asians, and as the programme presents only white girls, it may be that some groups of black girls would come close to the position taken by the boys I showed it to.

The programme presents the five girls as if they are the sole source of the text: look closely, therefore, at the credits (at the end of the programme), where at least some of the people active in its production are identified. It was scripted by a man. But this could be a useful way into a discussion of how the apparent identity between the speakers and the lines spoken is achieved and should not detract from the real sense of commitment displayed in the programme (Richards, 1981).

When the more mixed group (not that referred to in the review) watched *Us Girls* it did inform, eventually, some of what they produced as *At the Club*. Indeed, I noted that in preparing to visit the studio where video production would take place, they should not try to copy the TV programmes they were familiar with but should rather use the studio situation to develop group discussion and presentation of what concerned them. The group responsible for *At the Club* included five girls and four boys: Alice, Samantha, Pamela, Felicity and Sharon; Barry, Errol, Matthew and Neil. What they produced together was confrontational, contained within the frame of a brief realist drama set in a youth club, but constantly poised between pre-scripted artifice and scary, emotionally raw, improvisation.

The drama is framed within a single space – that of the studio organized to suggest a recreational area within a youth club. At the centre, towards the back, there is a table with drinks and a box for cash. Behind it stands Samantha, acting, with her own name, as a youth worker. To the right, there is an improvised table-tennis table and space for one or two people to sit low down with their backs to the wall. To the left, there is also space for two to sit together and talk. The video recording of the drama is in black and white; actually mostly a grainy, low-resolution, grey. Though focus is generally well maintained and cuts from one shot to another are mostly well timed, framing is often too loose. Some shots show the microphones rigged over each of the three divisions of space, others include actors not active within the shot and somewhat unaware that they are visible within the frame. It looks like a rough take, far from a finished 'product' to be subjected to evaluation in relation to standards of technical and professional 'quality'. But such an outcome would have been judged within the terms of the Media Studies coursework assessment as an aspect of the students' learning. I will return to this issue later. Here, I want to focus on the scripted, and partly improvised, encounters between the students.

The drama explores several themes, most centrally teenage pregnancy. But the regulation of the youth club also entails challenges to, for example, Alice for openly smoking marijuana and to Sharon, due for a court appearance and, later, suspected of stealing from the youth club itself. The dialogue I want to quote most extensively involves the pregnancy. All the students act with their own names. Errol is black, Afro-Caribbean. Pamela is perhaps of Indian-Caribbean origin. Felicity is black, West African. Sharon and Samantha, and Neill, are white.

Errol and Pamela are playing table tennis, to the right. Felicity arrives. Sharon sits with her, to the left of the table:

Sharon: So did you go the doctor then?
Felicity: Yeah.
Sharon: What did they say?
Felicity: It's positive.
Sharon: So what you going to do about it?
Felicity: Not much.
Sharon: You could tell Errol.
Felicity: He didn't really want to know in the first place.

Sharon: So what, you're just gonna leave it and not tell Errol.

Felicity: I don't really know.

Sharon: Oh Felicity, you know you've got to tell him, you can't just keep putting it off all the time.

Felicity: I will tell him but not right now . . . he's more interested in that little slag over there, y'know what I mean.

Sharon: What about having an abortion?

Felicity: Dunno, you have to get your mum's consent, don't you? You can see my mum giving me consent . . .

Sharon: You don't have to, you can go to that new place, Brook Street, whatever, go there . . . tell Errol.

Sharon moves back to the table and is involved in a conversation about her impending court case, with Samantha. In this encounter, it is Sharon who is now the recipient of insistent advice laced with disapproval. From telling Sharon what she must do, Samantha turns to Alice (a tall and slightly hippie-ish girl of East Asian origin) to forbid her lighting up a joint. Alice leaves, sullen, taking her companion Neill with her. The locus of the drama now shifts to an extended and tense triangular confrontation between Felicity, Errol and Pamela:

Pamela: So why are you giving me dirty looks?

Felicity: I can give you dirty looks if I wanna . . .

Pamela: No you fucking . . . [in a low voice]

Felicity: Whisper so I can't hear you . . .

Errol: Anyway what do you want?

Felicity
(to Pamela):   Just piss off . . .

Pamela: No, you don't own him . . .

Felicity: No I don't.

Pamela: Yer acting like it.

Felicity: No I ain't.

Pamela: Yes you are . . . so why are you telling me to get lost?

Felicity: 'cause I want to speak to him alone.

Pamela: I ain't got him on a lead . . .

Felicity: Errol I want to speak to you alone.

Pamela: Have I got a lead 'round his neck?

Felicity: It seems as if you have.

Pamela: You're the one who wants him back to give him his collar.

Felicity: Did I say I wanted him back?

Pamela: How come you're shitting 'round him?

Felicity:	I'm not shitting 'round him . . . really, on my life . . . Errol, I want to speak to you alone.
Errol:	What about anyway?
Felicity:	Look, could you just tell that slag to piss off?
Pamela:	I ain't the one that's flipping pregnant am I?
Errol:	Who's pregnant?
Pamela:	She is – haven't you heard about her?
Errol:	No, when?
Felicity:	When what?
Errol:	When was it confirmed you were pregnant?
Felicity:	This morning . . . so what're you gonna do? Stand there looking like a fish?
Errol:	There's nothing I can do about it.
Felicity:	What do you mean there's nothing you can do about it?
Errol:	I don't really want it anyway. Are you gonna have it then?
Pamela:	Don't you think the bitch has had it enough?
Felicity:	Just shut yer fucking face 'cause you're really getting on my fucking arse . . .
Pamela:	Good. Anyway I wouldn't wanna get up there, the amount of bloody pricks that've been up it . . .

[Samantha, probably unaware that she is within the frame of the shot as she sits at the back of the studio, smiles and her mouth drops open in amused amazement]

Felicity (to Errol):	Are you just going to stand there?
Errol:	I don't want it.
Pamela:	If you don't want it, what you standing here for, come on, let's go . . .

An intertitle shifts the time to 'three weeks later'. All the key participants return to engage in a series of closing dialogues. Errol and Felicity speak to each other alone, Felicity revealing that she has had an abortion and Errol that he has changed his mind and now wants the pregnancy to continue. Samantha and Alice chat briefly, and more amicably, about smoking. Sharon arrives and asks Samantha if she can borrow £20. Samantha refuses. When Samantha moves away from the table, Sharon takes the money anyway. The final dialogue between Samantha and Alice turns around how much money was raised at the disco, discovery that most of it has been stolen and Samantha calling the police to report a theft.

It is tempting to see this short drama as recording the authentic language and concerns of the participants. In this sense, it might be read as a document of the particular teenage working-class culture of north London in the early 1980s. Such an approach is not entirely invalid. For example, the use of a particular repertoire of sexualized insults and the somewhat misogynistic perspective they imply might be taken as evidence further supporting the analysis offered by Lees (1983, 1986). Indeed, it could be argued that this example illustrates how girls themselves turn a discourse associated with an abusive male view of women against each other (Mills, 1993; Hey, 1997; Holland et al., 1998; Muscio, 2002). But the use of such a repertoire in this short drama cannot be construed so straightforwardly as 'evidence' of how girls engage and enact misogyny in teenage culture. These students were attempting to stage a conflict within a form of realist drama informed perhaps by the specific, *Us Girls*, but also by many other, generic, precedents in television drama at that time (though note that this predates the long-running BBC 'soap opera' *EastEnders* by about three years). Felicity acts with considerable commitment and gravity throughout and presents emotional states extremely effectively. Because the actors used their own names and because the most aggressive confrontation (with Pamela) appeared to be improvised, it seemed as if the conflict might be real and might well extend beyond or disrupt its dramatic framing. However, this did not happen, and at the conclusion of these most tense dialogues, the students turn away from the camera shaking with laughter. In part, the transgression is of the school's constraints on behaviour and language. In the presence of teachers, they transform the space into one where they can be not who they are but what the school forbids them to be.

A further consideration, noted above, is that of what kinds of learning might have been achieved in this production. Viewing and reviewing the recording tend to suggest that the main focus for these students was in per-formance and that, therefore, what they learnt – the skills of acting out a script, but also of improvisation within the predetermined structure – could be located as much in Drama as in Media Studies. However, the form is that of studio-based television drama, and their acting had to be developed in relation to that form. The 'staging' of each encounter is specific to a studio setting and, though awkward and inadequately rehearsed, resembles scenes in TV soaps closest to British social realism. Recalling Williamson's (1981/1982) question, it is doubtful that any clear understanding of 'ideology' could be discerned in what these students did. But by translating their interests into a text form, they thus make available an object for enquiry – by themselves and others. The question is less that of ideology and more one of how these students represent themselves in the forms available to them. Potentially, of course, the question of how such representations might work, ideologically, could be explored. To some extent, discussions with the students involved were nudged in that direction. But evidence of understanding, of the kind advocated by Williamson, was difficult to identify.

Roots and Culture Pirate TV can be discussed with the same question in mind. Again, the production of the programme was mapped out in terms that invited the students to represent themselves or issues of concern to them in the forms associated with studio-based television. The studio used in this case, with the relocation of the Inner London Education Authority's facilities from Highbury to Battersea (1983–1984), was equipped with colour cameras. The boys, in particular, made much of this, showing up with a range of striking and tasteful jackets, shirts and jumpers. Two boys were central to this production. Both are referred to in my notes from the period as 'difficult' and 'disruptive':

Behaviour of various people in the group continues to be extremely disruptive and persistently obstructive of others . . . Their constant 'singing, dancing' activity, and their attention to the girls in the group, makes any consistent progress through the lesson difficult. Perhaps grouping them with an out of the classroom task might solve the problems temporarily. Meanwhile, they'll all have to be reported to form teachers and heads of year.

Eian and Desmond, both very articulate black 15-year-old boys, were clearly bored by much of the routine class work of Media Studies (and quite probably other subjects too). But, in the Battersea studio, they took control and assembled a witty studio talk show (cf. Richards, 1998a). They, and the others involved in this production, were clearly enjoying themselves.

Eian anchors the programme speaking in a strong black London voice long familiar in black music radio in London:

R-C-P-T – This is a test transmission for RCPT Roots and Culture Pirate Television.

[Speaking direct to camera; wearing a bright red 'anorak']

You may not have seen this face before but I guarantee you are going to see it again. This is the first and only TV station for the youth. So what if we're against the law, everything good is. Anyway, we're gonna guarantee you that everything we show tonight is just gonna be outstanding, outstanding, better than all that crap you see on all the other stations. Anyway enough of this chat and let's get on with it . . .

First of all, I know all of you youths out there are getting plenty of harassment from the police. So over in the next studio my friends out there are going to give you a little bit of advice, right?

The themes of racially targeted harassment of young black men by the police and of the daily stress of being young are consistent with those outlined earlier in this chapter (see also Chapter 5). In this school, they were given a specific local inflection through both particular students' and the school's experience of police activities (Richards, 1992). Relations between black youth and the police were an insistent concern. In the 'next studio' (a fictional shift in space), Eian reappears, dressed in more subdued colours, as the chair of a discussion between a black youth worker and a white police superintendent (Stephen). Though the conduct of the discussion replicates features of mainstream 'news-magazine' talk, there is also sustained reference to the 'pirate' status of the show. Indeed, the transmission ends, after several further items, with the inspector returning to close down the station shouting 'Pull the plugs' as the image and sound are abruptly terminated. Conflict, culminating in mock violence, figures repeatedly in the programme:

Eian:	On my right here I have a youth worker from Caxton House, Delbert Wilkinson [Desmond], and on my left here I have Superintendent B. from Highbury Grove, Holloway Road station and they've come to talk about the current situation, about the harassment between the black youth and the police . . . [turns to Delbert] Have you got any questions for him?
Delbert:	Superintendent, I'd like to know why black children, black youths, are so harassed by the police?
Superintendent:	Cause they are the main people to do it . . . they are the more likely to do it than any other child . . . muggings, wreck cars, smash windows, vandalism mainly.
Delbert:	How can you say that, have you ever caught one in the act?
Superintendent:	We have caught loads of 'em . . . I have caught loads of 'em . . . Police have caught loads of 'em.
Delbert:	Have you caught any white kids stealing and that sort of thing?

Superintendent:	I have caught some, some, but not very many, not as many as black people.
Delbert:	Do you find that blacks influence white boys or other children or youths to do this sort of thing?
Superintendent:	I reckon if a load of white boys hang around with black boys, they get influenced to become violent and cause all the things that black people are doing today.
Eian:	How can you say that?
Superintendent:	I say that, I say what's true . . .
Eian:	You're talking a load of shit . . .
Superintendent:	I'm not, it's absolutely true.
Delbert:	I find this appalling, how can you say this on the TV?
Superintendent:	It's true, I've got to tell everybody, I'd like to broadcast it to everybody in London.
Eian:	I'm an honest church-going citizen, I don't go around mugging people and breaking into cars.
Superintendent:	That's you, I mean I'm not saying that all the black people do it, just a lot of 'em. I mean I know a lot of black people who're very, very nice . . .
Eian:	All the ones with black hair . . .
Superintendent:	No, no, no . . . I mean black people, some of them are very nice but most of 'em are just like vandals . . . like you.
Delbert:	Like me? What do you mean like me?
Superintendent:	I mean so far you've already started swearing and everything.
Delbert:	I never said a word, you're just a mug, you know what I mean.
Superintendent:	I'm not a mug . . . I'll take you down . . .
Delbert:	You stupid copper.
Superintendent:	Listen son, any more of this and I'm gonna arrest you.
Delbert:	Well I'm 'ere, come on, take me.
Eian:	No violence, no violence.

[Brief mock fight and arrest]

Eian:	Well what can I say, that's the current state of things between black youth and the police, it goes on and on and on.

Some writers on media education in the 1970s and 1980s were witheringly dismissive of this kind of thing. Masterman (1980), though by no means entirely negative, remarked that, in his experience, school students produced 'an endless wilderness of dreary third-rate imitative "pop"-shows, embarrassing video dramas, and derivative documentaries courageously condemning war or poverty . . .' (Masterman, 1980: 140). But Masterman might not have applied these critical comments to either *At the Club* or *Roots and Culture Pirate TV*. Though both appear to be anticipated by his comments – and the next item in *RCPTV* is a mimed performance to a Chaka Khan track – he set out, albeit briefly, a more encouraging view of how such production work might develop:

> The precondition of video work which is centred in the concrete reality of the pupils' world, which reflects their real concerns and problems, and which is derived from their language, activities and preoccupations is talk – dialogue if you like – about themselves, their culture, their background and their community, and it is this material which must form the field of the teacher's own research and further study. Only when pupils value their own language, background and personalities and are not demeaned by them, will they recover their eagerness for expression. (Masterman, 1980: 141)

The implied mission of facilitating the expression of an authentic culture distinct from the world of 'pop-shows' is problematic. In this view, culture is in the 'folk' not in the pop song. Nevertheless, the approach to teaching that he advocates suggests how students can use such opportunities to do something more than learn technical skills and work through predetermined exercises and simulations. Indeed, Masterman (1980), from which these comments are quoted, was central among the sources that informed how I taught Media Studies in the 1980s and can be seen as contributing to the practice from which these studio products emerged. Further exchanges from *RCPTV* might illustrate this more fully:

Desmond:	Good evening ladies and gentlemen, home boys and fly girls, this is my programme, everybody, my programme. Today we are here to discuss a very interesting subject – about a man they call Nyabinghi. He originated in the land of Ethiopia, in Africa, and was executed in . . . god knows when. On my right, we have a man they call Professor Laird, who is studying the man, Nyabinghi.
Desmond:	Mr Laird, could you tell us a bit about Nyabinghi?
Prof Laird (Eian):	What you want fe know? [Speaking with a strong Jamaican accent, eyes closed]
Desmond:	Quite a bit really.
Prof Laird:	Be specific, me cyan tell you what you want to know. [silence]
	He has showed me the way to righteousness.

Desmond:	And can't you get that sort of thing from an ordinary god or a prophet such as Moses?
Prof Laird:	Moses? [Teeth kissing] Nyabinghi was Moses.
Desmond:	Nyabinghi was Moses now?
Prof Laird:	Is a fool?
Desmond:	Ladies and gentlemen, the man has called me a fool and he's on my programme . . . let me ask the right honourable gentleman, Professor Laird, how did Nyabinghi die, what did he do before he did die, what sort of things did he do?
Prof Laird:	Nyabinghi showed many people the way to righteousness and a good living and him never die, him still alive, in air, him never dead, Nyabinghi could never dead . . .
Desmond:	Alright so he's about with us now at this present moment in time, is that what you're telling me?
Prof Laird:	We . . . [what] you using all dem big foo foo words for?

This item continues and yes, predictably, culminates in some brief mock violence as the 'interview' becomes more confrontational. But this is play with both elements of the television form they have been asked to replicate and with the strongly religious components of their own black London culture. They are exploring, and imagining, how a black youth TV show might take shape. They are also identifying and rendering excessive (by fighting) the forms of power and authority typically enacted in the existing examples of such television shows. In many respects, this emphasis on student production, especially on forms of playful reworking of mainstream media forms, has taken a central place in the development of media education in England through the 1990s and since (Buckingham and Sefton-Green, 1994; Buckingham et al., 1995).

Media education is sometimes seen as driven by, and recomposed in response to, technological innovation. Of course, such innovations are of crucial significance, but to explain the concerns of media education only in these terms cedes too much to technological determinism, an approach that always gives precedence to this aspect of the media industries. Somewhat similarly, the primary rationale for media education can also appear to be that of keeping up to date with the new apparatuses of media *reception*, variously shifting its ground to both accommodate and challenge their place in young people's lives. Often the central assumption informing media education is that it is, above all, a line of resistance to such innovations, the place where education stands up to and refuses the power of the media to infiltrate and shape people's thoughts and lives. In the United States, this understanding of the role taken by media education is widespread and prevails in the active development of materials and advice for the extension of media education with young people. The cultural complexity of media texts, and of young people's engagements with them, tends to be displaced in favour of accounts of the media as monolithic and corporate industries (Steinberg and Kincheloe, 2004).

Demystification, again

The Media Education Foundation (2010), located in Northampton, Massachusetts, is an interesting and highly productive example. Founded by Sut Jhally with his video critique of MTV, *Dreamworlds* (1989), the Media Education Foundation claims to make its audience (mainly college and high-school students) aware of the medium (the combined media) in which they live. Proceeding from a metaphor equating people in contemporary media worlds with the immersion of fish in water, Jhally argues that the educational videos produced by his foundation enable students to reflect on determinants of their subjectivity of which they might otherwise be unaware. This is a view of the media as insidiously and overwhelmingly powerful and places its audiences in a relationship to the media imagined as an unconscious, subintellectual process, in Jhally's words, like breathing the air. As this makes a sweeping and negative assumption about the kind of involvement most people have with the media, it is an awkward starting point for teaching about popular media products, especially where a majority of students have a different history of media experience from that of their teachers. Inevitably, it positions academics and teachers as an enlightened elite stepping in to facilitate critical thought where, otherwise, it is implied, there is none.

Dreamworlds 3 (Jhally, 2009) and *The Price of Pleasure* (Sun and Picker, 2008) are among the educational videos produced by the Media Education Foundation in 2008–2009. Both are characterized by their intensely repetitive condensation of images of sexual display, exploitation and objectification, thus generating a visual text more powerful, and more memorable, than the words of the academic contributors. This paradox is further compounded by the way that though, again in both videos, there is no explicit claim that pornographic imagery causes sexual violence against women, each ends with visual displays of such violence. In Sun and Picker (2008), the images are taken from scenarios of rape and torture in pornography, in Jhally (2009) from documentary footage of mob assaults on women and the onscreen listing of statistics of rape and sexual assault (see Dworkin, 1981). Though both videos lament the dominance of one kind of (aggressive and masculine) 'story' about sex, they reproduce only those scenarios they condemn and offer no instances of, or even hints of what might be, alternative and *not* exploitative sexual representations. For media education, this is a lamentably narrow approach, doing little to support young people (or anyone else) in any effort they might make to imagine, or produce, images and stories of other kinds (see Kipnis, 1999, 2006; Williams, 2008; Attwood, 2009; Attwood and Hunter, 2009; Albury, 2009; McNair, 2009; Smith, 2009).

Conclusion

This chapter has offered specific accounts of media teaching drawn from my own experience in London. In doing so, it has addressed the need for descriptions of what constitutes Media Studies teaching in practice. By selecting examples from many years ago, it has also indicated how some of the concerns of British Cultural Studies were pursued in working with young people but, always, with considerable doubt about the outcome of such efforts. Such doubts have not gone away. Questions about war and its representation are prominent in 2009–2010, in relation to both Iraq and Afghanistan. Past precedents should inform media teaching in its engagement with debates both about the reporting of, and the construction of support for, these wars. Equally, the representation of 'youth' in the media is a recurring concern with a continuing emphasis on violence, crime and disorder. It is important to be aware of the longer history of these concerns and the persistence of rhetorical constructions of the 'feral youth'. Some media education initiatives (some contributions to Hall and Bishop, 2007; Jhally, 2009) appear to add to this pessimistic and anxious view of young people, others do not (Buckingham, 2003, 2008; Bragg and Buckingham, 2009). But, from a variety of vantage points, there is now a much wider background of research and debate supporting media education and enabling informed discussion and practice (Gauntlett, 1997, 2000, 2007; Buckingham, 2003, 2007; Buckingham and Willett, 2006).

Points for reflection

In what ways can you compare current debates about the representation of youth to the past examples explored in this chapter?

What do you think is the value of young people's media production work?

How can you evaluate conflicting views of the power of the media to shape and influence young people?

'Race' and Representation

Chapter Outline

Introduction

This chapter examines the idea of 'representation' through a case study of 'othering' in the reporting of 'rioting' in the early 1980s. The construction of 'race' as difference is also explored through a discussion of Paul Gilroy's work on 'raciology'.

For the sociology of education, and for Education Studies, 'race' has figured in a range of productive studies of the social relations of schooling; it has also entered into debates around the curriculum, educational policies and questions of educational attainment (Gillborn, 1995, 2008; Sewell, 1997; Mac An Ghaill, 1999). The focus of this chapter, by contrast, is on how debates in Cultural Studies have contributed to teaching about 'race' in media education. In this context, a central concept is that of representation.

Representation has been explored in some depth in the fields of Cultural and Media Studies (Berger, 1972; Hodge and Kress, 1988; hooks, 1992, 1994a;

Dyer, 1993, 1997; Hall, 1997). Here, it is necessary to give at least a brief outline of its meaning in this context of use. Simply, the argument is that we cannot communicate about the world in a way that is transparent and unmediated. The real world is not representable in a way that is ever complete, accurate and entirely truthful. When we communicate about any aspect of our world, by whatever means (including talk), we are also representing it in particular ways, from a particular standpoint, for a particular purpose, to some kind of audience and within the limits and capabilities ('affordances') of the specific medium of communication (Hodge and Kress, 1988). Even a snapshot on a mobile phone does not capture the real object photographed in any full and fully real way. Despite its immediacy and simplicity, the image is produced in terms of specific conventions (or 'codes') of representation: distance, angle, framing and definition. Furthermore, the characteristics of this digital technology contribute substantially to both the circumstances in which the image is produced and its material quality (pixels). There are layers and layers of 'constructedness' or 'fabrication' in the production of such an apparently uncomplicated image of a real moment in a real place with, most often, real people. Broadly, this emphasis on the 'fabricated' character of all representations informs the argument of this chapter as a whole.

On another level, this chapter also entails some careful reflection on what is meant by 'race', a term always used here only in those single inverted commas. The importance of the inverted commas is that they show, or intend to show, that the term is always problematic and that its reference, a category of people, is contentious. The term has a long history and is still in wide and everyday use in the English-speaking world. But its history has to be explored and challenged. The belief that human beings can be divided into distinct 'races' can no doubt be traced through many hundreds of years, but it had an especially influential phase, in the nineteenth century, when such a belief was underpinned by the authority of science (Hall, 1997: 243). Science, in the aftermath of the eighteenth century Enlightenment, has achieved the status of a master discourse, extending the principles of rational explanation to all of the known world and, in principle, to everything beyond it too. But scientific thought has a history and is, or should be, always open to critical debate, reflection and reconsideration (Kuhn, 1970). Scientific explanations of human difference in terms of 'race' have been challenged, within biology and genetics, for many decades, and though there are those who have clung to the idea of 'race' quite tenaciously (see Rose et al., 1984), it has been discredited to such an extent that current genetic theory no longer supports the concept at all (Rose et al., 1984; Appiah, 1992). However, in the domain of everyday discourse, changes in the scientific status of the concept have not been taken up widely or with any consistency. Sedimented layers of meaning, the accumulated past uses of 'race', persist in many contexts across the media and popular culture and between people in day-to-day life.

In everyday usage, 'race' and 'racial' are used with apparently simple reference to entities that exist out there in the real world, categories of people, for example, who seem unequivocally to belong to the same race, no inverted commas required. The 'Chinese' perhaps are widely understood, at least by those who are not Chinese, to constitute a race. Such Chineseness is not confined to those who are citizens of China or to those who live in China or Taiwan or Chinese communities around the world. Chineseness is assumed to inhere in the body, and any one individual, of whatever citizenship, and belonging to whatever community, might thus be defined as Chinese. This is 'race' as essence, enduring and unchanging. But such a construction of the Chinese depends on a dynamic of othering (Dyer, 1997; Hall, 1997). 'Chinese' looks like a secure and bounded category for those who see all those thus designated as different from themselves in ways that cohere as Chinese – hair colour, skin tone, shape of nose, eyes and so forth. Together, these various elements seem to confirm the reality of the category they represent and its difference from other clusters of elements constituting further distinct races. Among the Chinese, and despite the, not widely respected, idea of separate evolution, other differences may be far more salient and might be read as differentiating those from, for example, particular regions. 'Chinese' might then be a category of citizenship, but not a more broadly inclusive racial group. Or, indeed, differences between individuals may be salient and some wider notion of belonging to, or definition by, Chineseness be unperceived and, routinely, irrelevant.

Dyer (1997) highlights the shifting boundaries of 'racial' categories. He points, for example, to some periods in which the Irish were considered not white (by the English) and the very many circumstances in which Jews have been considered 'other' to those who are 'properly' white (Dyer, 1997: 52–7). Difference and belonging are defined along the lines of social and political interest and through acts of power and control.

Case study: 'race' and 'riots'

Following the discussion of media education in Chapter 4, I want to further illustrate its practice by retrieving an article I wrote, as a secondary school-teacher, in the early 1980s. This may seem a long time ago. But the article serves to depict what kind of work was done in media education in response to both Cultural Studies and current political events. It also examines 'race' in the context of media representations of particular relevance to this chapter and to *continuing* debates in Britain, 30 years later. The process of 'othering' through which categories of people are constructed as alien is a central theme then and now. I began my article with an extract from an editorial in the *Daily Telegraph*, then and even now, a staunchly Conservative newspaper. The editorial, 'Gospel of St Marx?' (published shortly after the Bristol riots in 1981), criticized those involved in the 'riots' and those who offered social explanations of them. The failure of both, it claims, lies in a lack of moral responsibility:

> . . . even the most case-hardened among us will be saddened by the utter deficiency of elementary Christian understanding in those reactions to the Bristol riots which blame material conditions . . .
>
> The unfortunate West Indian migrants emerged in the aftermath of slavery without any stable family framework within which to integrate to a wider society. Lacking parental care many ran wild. Incited by race-relations witch-finders and left-wing teachers and social workers to blame British society for their own shortcomings, lacking the work ethic and perseverance, lost in a society itself demoralized by socialism, they all too easily sink into a criminal subculture. (*Daily Telegraph*, 1981)

With the intention of challenging this 'othering' of black people of Caribbean descent, I wrote an account of the press coverage of 'rioting', strongly influenced by Hall et al. (1978). I wanted not only to situate my argument in a specific debate about the nature of recent urban confrontations ('riots') but also to report on my attempts to teach about these representations in Media Studies lessons with fourth- and fifth-year classes (Years 10 and 11). I began by noting that Conservative politicians were complacent about the social consequences of dramatically worsening unemployment. In particular, I questioned comments from William Whitelaw, Home Secretary in Margaret Thatcher's first government, when he was interviewed about inner city 'riots' on BBC radio 4. However, it is worth emphasizing that even the Thatcher government was not monolithic – the differences between Whitelaw and Michael Heseltine, the Secretary of State for the Environment, became apparent in the aftermath of the Toxteth 'riots'. The following account is an edited version of the article:

How the press represented the 'riots' of 1981 continues to be a crucial political issue: now, in February 1983, on *The World This Weekend*, William Whitelaw casually dismisses a suggestion, by an interviewer, that there is a connection between 'rioting' and unemployment. So again it's worth wondering what meanings those 'riots' have for people, and how the meanings which are dominant come to appear fixed in place. If it is so easy to deny a connection between unemployment and 'rioting' or, as the *Telegraph* argues, to exclude 'material conditions' completely, then the basis of that ease must at present be substantial and secure. One way into this, and one which can be pursued with those we teach, is to look in some detail at the repertoire of images, which became established as the definitive truth of those events.

At the time of the 'riots', I collected most of the daily newspapers and, later that July, with Andrew Bethell, sorted through them to find images that had been used particularly often, either within one newspaper or across several. We found that a small group of images had been used by almost every paper. I made slides of these, though photocopies could be as useful in most teaching situations. Of course, a selection of exclusively visual material arose out of both a prior concern with how images are read and a pedagogic preference for a mainly non-verbal text. The apparent ambiguity of images is a pedagogic advantage: there is less of that risk of closure threatened by the idea that there is a right answer and, unlike the verbal text, there may be a feeling that images are more neutral ground on which discussion can take place. The mass of verbal text is also important, as are the representations produced in other areas of the media, and no systematic or adequate account of the media representation of the riots can be expected to emerge from image analysis alone. But news photographs do have a metonymic power, itself underpinned by their 'actuality' status, which gives them wide currency as a 'shorthand' for major and complex historical moments. And in July 1981, just a few images did seem to stand for everything that was called the 'riots'.

If a photograph of a black person throwing bricks or petrol bombs is placed with an account of rioting in Toxteth, it is likely that the image will support and secure the text: to look, to have seen, is equated with to know, and in the news media, images serve to reassure the audience that there is an easy and immediate knowledge of events available. The apparent transparency of the image allows the equation between looking (itself equated with knowing) and the having-looked constituted by the image. Furthermore, the origin of images in supposedly non-human technological processes seems to offer an additional guarantee of unmediated reality. To resist the image as a definitive truth about Toxteth [a district of Liverpool] is not easy, particularly for the very large majority of a national newspaper's audience with no other source of knowledge but the media. An important emphasis in teaching around these images must therefore be placed on the means of deconstructing photographic images; it is essential that their quality of naturalness be undermined.

The history of representations of 'rioting' is of considerable importance, providing precedents for their continuing representation. The 'riots' are placed within such a history by the newspapers themselves: they are related to other apparently similar events and are represented in terms that recall those other events. It is here that *race* becomes a crucial term. 'Race' enters into the construction of the 'riots' not just because some of the 'rioters' were black or because some of the 'riots' occurred in areas with relatively substantial black populations. There is a selection made from a repertoire of precedents, and it is, to some extent, in terms of a 'popular knowledge' of those precedents that the new, the unexpected, is defined. One important set of precedents here is that drawn from the representation of 'rioting' in America in the 1960s. It was only when a high level of 'unusual' violence developed in areas of American cities that the particular places became newsworthy and thus a part of 'popular knowledge': an area such as Watts [Los Angeles, CA] became known because of an unusual level of violence and not because of the complex processes that produced the conditions for rioting there. Similarly, Toxteth became a place on the map for national newspapers when an unexpected level of violence occurred. An unexpected level and type of violence defines the basis of the similarity between Toxteth and Watts [in Los Angeles], but the historical particularity of each is displaced by the assumption that in other crucial respects these unexpected events are also equivalent. The use of local area names – St Paul's [Bristol], Toxteth, Moss Side [Manchester] and Brixton [London] – recalls the American precedent and thus invokes the connotations of the 'black ghetto'. Without even an explicit comparison, the *racial* basis of the American 'riots' is constructed as an already familiar framework of explanation; at a rhetorical level – summer, the city, the ghetto, blacks – the framework is brought into place. The *Daily Mail*'s headline on Toxteth was 'BLACK WAR ON

POLICE' and yet the racial composition of those 'riots' clearly did not justify an explanation centred principally on race.

The consequences of this rhetoric are enduring. One effect is to attribute blame to 'blacks' and another is to stress their separation from 'us'; the closer this rhetoric moves to denying the structural belonging of black people to this society, the more easy it is to construct a consensus view that is more right wing than even most recent official Tory policy. The equation of black people with ghettoes and therefore with foreign bodies lodged in the host society is a fundamental step in achieving a racist nationalism (Barker, 1981). The ideological expulsion of a social category from the 'consensus' is a solution to structural conflicts so fundamental that the 'unity' of the 'nation' has to be reconstructed in order still to 'make sense': 'we' can be united against 'them' (blacks, criminals, strikers, Russians and Argies [Argentinians as labelled by sections of the British press]). This solution is not openly or consistently articulated by all the newspapers, but it is the implicit conclusion to the forms of social explanation promoted by many. Looking back to the *Telegraph*'s editorial, one can see the means by which black people are placed elsewhere: 'migrants', 'lost in a society' and running 'wild'. The editorial doesn't mention compulsory repatriation because it doesn't need to. The success of this explanation of 'rioting' is what matters for not only does it draw on and reinforce the pre-existing racist rhetoric but also excludes those forms of explanation that do place the sources of conflict within British society.

The theme of 'outsiders' is central to the press coverage. Looking through the photographs in the papers, it is striking that, partly because of the processes of reproducing low-resolution black-and-white, rather than colour, photographs, it is very difficult to determine the racial identity of the 'rioters'. In such cases, ambiguity in the image can be anchored by verbal captions and headlines. Of course, putting a headline like 'BLACK WAR ON POLICE' above a picture fairly effectively fixes the reading that most people will make. But another important strategy here seems to be directed towards making the ambiguity of the images a major theme. There is a dramatization of the ambiguity in terms of a mystery and a panic about the identity of the 'rioters'. The appearance of masked and hooded figures in some of the photographs furthers this work on ambiguity and allows papers to construct a narrative hermeneutic across several days, each issue appearing to offer a partial disclosure of the mystery. [Think of the masked and hooded figures that appear regularly in the media 30 years later!] In the newspapers of the early 1980s, this theme is most obviously pursued through the use of a masked figure as a logo, marking as a key issue the identity of the 'rioters'. The *Mail*'s reference to 'masked coloured youths wielding pickaxe handles' (6 July 1981) is maintained by the logo, but in addition, it facilitates a further implication that the violence comes from another kind of *outsider*, the 'Marxist left'. Yet another link in the chain is added by a knowledge of prior representations of the Irish Republican Army (an organization fighting for the reunification of Ireland) and again the implication might be that all these categories are essentially reducible to one: the violent threat from outside, the subversion of the British social order by elements that *do not belong*. The masked figure logo condenses a plurality of connotations; it is a figure in which left-wing politics, terrorism, violent crime and black power are united.

Images of the police are somewhat different. In the *Daily Mirror* for Monday, 6 July 1981, a photograph of a policeman with a blood-spattered transparent visor is positioned on the front page as a key, emblematic image. Inside, in the centre pages, a policeman, possibly the same one, is represented being supported by a fireman and another policeman. There is also a photograph of a policeman in a hospital bed, with his wife: 'CASUALTY: Wounded PC Paul Noden 26, is comforted by his wife Pat'. Above, a much larger photograph, captioned 'The Front Line: Youths hurl missiles as the massed ranks of police advance behind their riot shields', compresses three ranks of police beyond which about ten people stand, some throwing . . . it's not clear what. The general point I want to make is that policemen, injured, tend to be named and their faces shown: the clear visor, like the black hood, has its place in the rhetoric of identity. Here, the police are individuals, ordinary people like 'us', doing a job and getting hurt on our behalf. This is a very different construction of the 'police' from that which is at work when 'elite' groups within the police, or military groups such as the Special Air Service (SAS), are represented in the press. This police force is made of ordinary coppers, and it is 'bloodied copper Chris Gregory . . .' (*Daily Star*, 6 July 1981) whose image comes to define their position and its relation to 'us', the audience addressed by these papers. The 'rioters' are not people with individual identities (the exception may be when an 'extreme leftist' is *exposed*), and given the racial closure around these images, the implication is that 'we', the white audience, look across the police lines at the mob *out there*; the position of having been in the riots is not offered by this photo-textual discourse. It is as 'individuals' that 'we' belong; the loss of individuality is itself synonymous with the collapse of the British social order, the menace of communism, or the flood of immigrants, blacks . . . 'you can't tell one from another'.

The comments I have made so far come out of discussions with other teachers and, in the context of those discussions, a reading of Hall et al. (1978). What I have said very little about is the reading of these images by the audiences to which we have some access. Clearly, the point is not to deliver the reading I have suggested but to pose questions that draw attention to the construction and reproduction of these images and the effects of the verbal context in which they are placed. Within the groups of teachers where these images were discussed, there is an exceptional homogeneity in terms of social and discursive positions: all belonging to a very specific sector of one occupational group, often all white, probably all with some degree of com- mitment to some form of left-wing politics, mainly in an age range stretching from mid-twenties to early forties, middle class; it may only be in terms of sexual identity that any strongly marked differences are apparent. The groups that we teach are markedly different from ourselves and are likely to be more heterogeneous, except, of course, on a criterion of age. The readings of these images produced in classrooms may not converge with our own or with each other. What I think may be a very useful strategy relies on the teachers' willingness to situate their own readings as those of a particular kind of group within the audience addressed by the press. Wherever possible, we should record the comments that are made when discussion of images takes place: this might be done by actually taping discussions or by moving from discussion to writing before there is too complete a resolution of ambiguities and instabilities of meaning. In itself, this could seem no more than the usual basis for an assessment of individuals, a scrutiny of how much and of how well each individual has spoken and thought. But this is not the point. The aim should be to document the differential readings produced with the group and to re-present those readings to those that produced them. By doing so, we should be able to group similar readings together and draw attention to differences, to the competition between these groups of similar readings. To take this further should entail discussing the reasons for these differences, reasons that must be situated within some understanding of the *social* formation of 'individuals'. This could well be a long-term process even with a particular group: why not preserve what was said at the beginning of the fourth year [Year 10] to be examined by the speakers themselves late in their fifth year [Year 11]? In using my own slides, and materials such as

Images and Blacks [a piloted but unpublished teaching resource] from the British Film Institute, I make much more effort now to have some record of discussion even if it has to be individually written. Most people respond well to having what they say preserved and thought about carefully.

What I am suggesting is that classes which remain reasonably stable for a year or two can be involved in producing an ethnography of their own reading of images (Green and Bloome, 1995; Pink, 2001/2007). On such a basis, one can work towards challenging the view that readings are the result of a rather random, free play on the object of attention and that differences are mostly a matter of individual idiosyncrasies. The aim should be to investigate the constant shifting of meanings through struggle: struggle between readings and against, or for, the reading 'preferred' by the photo-text. To develop an awareness among those we teach that *they* are involved in contests over meaning and not simply in a media-guessing game is essential.

It is possible, in order to maximize the range of different readings produced around an image, to so detach it from its context, and to separate the image itself into lesser fragments, that meanings are not just multiple but apparently infinite. To show just how high a level of ambiguity is particular to visual images, this is a legitimate strategy; but it is also important to show that this ambiguity is not ever available to the reader in the way that it becomes so when a formal deconstruction of this kind is enacted. In the actual journalistic practices through which the images here are produced and contextualized, there is a process of 'preferring' or 'directing' the reader to particular sets of meanings. This is not a consciously manipulative process on the whole, but more a matter of routine practices of image selection, cropping, positioning, captioning. To pretend that images are read somewhat like the ink blots in Rorschach tests seems to deny not only the particular context in which the image is inserted but its very specific connotations which, within the set of cultural relations in which the image is produced and consumed, are relatively stable and predictable. Of course an image transposed to an alien context, or 'consumed' in unusual circumstances, becomes the locus of widely varying meanings but a newspaper image is always already placed in specific ways that its audience recognizes.

An important type of newspaper image as yet unmentioned is the political cartoon. It is useful here because cartoons, like jokes, rely on quite particular assumptions about their audiences. They seem to be constructed within an idiom which reflects back to the target audience its own sense of humour; it is this idiom which is also constitutive of 'the social personality of the newspaper'.

One example here may illustrate the point. I showed a slide of a cartoon from the *Daily Telegraph*'s (1981) 'London Day by Day' to a small group of fifth-year [Year 11] boys. I had not said that the images we were to look at had any connection with the 'riots' and, though the cartoon was surrounded by text, there were no legible verbal indications of its topical reference. The cartoon shows a figure, a brick in either hand, looking at a street plan. To me it is apparent that the figure is supposed to resemble a skinhead. Among the comments made by two white boys were these: 'He's looking at the streets to find somewhere to live most probably. He's a builder. He's looking for a street . . .' and, 'He's a working-class . . . he's not a tramp.' Like the usual target audience of the *Telegraph*, the boys resolve the ambiguities of the cartoon into, at least, something like 'a working-class man is looking for somewhere connected with the bricks in his hands'. *Telegraph* readers, knowing the contexts of the cartoon much more fully than the boys looking at the slide and also being knowing consumers of a right-wing paper, might presumably further resolve the ambiguity of the image into the notion of 'rioter' (wantonly destructive, using a publicly available guide to further violent ends in a place to which he is a stranger). At least the humour of the cartoon, and thus its coherence as a 'joke', seems to depend on such a reading. However, the boys give a reading which contradicts that rough and tentative summary of what the 'preferred' reading might be: they establish a relation between the elements of the cartoon in a way which makes the bricks signify an ordinary working-class occupation – he may therefore be a builder looking for a site of work. Is this a negotiated reading of an image that is constructed in ways that privilege anti–working-class connotations or is it, particularly because the boys are deprived of its fuller context, just one among an infinity of readings? Of course, it is possible to say both that their reading is one among an infinite possibility and that it is structured by their social and discursive positions, but there are reasons for arguing that they *resist* the 'preferred' reading of the image. They seem to identify a probable negative meaning ('tramp') but subordinate it to one that carries no hostile implication for them. I suspect that factors such as the surrounding type (its density), the absence of a caption or one liner and maybe even the style of the drawing allow to place it as coming from a 'posh' paper. And against 'the posh people, having a go at the working-class again' they make sense of the image within the terms of everyday working-class life.

I've raised this problem of distinguishing between play and struggle because images are often regarded as *neutral*, bits of the real embedded in partisan verbal texts and, unfortunately, the argument that ambiguity is endless seems to lead back to a placing of images *outside* the discursive processes in which political ideologies are secured. To say that images are neutral and to say that images are *infinitely* ambiguous may well amount to saying the same thing: that they're not *very particular constructions* of social and political 'reality'. The detail of establishing that there is a preferring of meaning within the construction of the image itself is set out at some length in Hall (1972). To take the argument further must also entail empirical work on how particular images are read by particular groups of people (for subsequent developments, see Buckingham, 1990; Buckingham and Sefton-Green, 1994; Cohen, 1997).

All that I have said has been about challenging the very considerable power that photographic images acquire in the field of news production. There is much more that needs to be said and done; it is essential to locate press photographs within the whole field of media representations of the riots and to draw attention to the ways in which fictions share significant themes with news and documentary. One cannot isolate a particular form and deal with that alone. It is a *pedagogic* strategy to defer study of other forms and should not be allowed to generate quite false hierarchies of significance. After all, newspapers compete for their place among the products of other media institutions; they are not more important, or more powerful, than those other products. The achievement of William Whitelaw's sense of ideological security is hardly a matter of images alone but of how social explanations are produced and maintained across the whole range of the media. It would be a serious mistake to think that any one media discourse fulfils a supreme ideological role, as if, through images or the BBC voice, the whole ideological configuration of a particular moment was stitched together. It is necessary to take apart media products and to understand and challenge the achievement of their effects, but it is quite wrong to pursue a pedagogy that might therefore marginalize ways of thinking about the whole social formation and the institutional practices in which its ideologies are embedded. Doing concrete practical things with words and images and talking carefully about them are essential but not adequate: essential to fracture the already known, the familiar, the repeated *recognition* through which ideological elements are accepted as natural, but not adequate, because a knowledge of those effects must be coupled with a knowledge that is not just concerned with the discursive. Questions about material conditions should be answered, however immaterial the *Telegraph* editorial writer may wish them to be (Richards, 1983: 2–7).

Continuities

The themes explored in this case study remain salient to current debates. Perhaps, most obviously, the media preoccupation with both the veil and the 'hoody' suggests that a particular rhetoric of 'othering' persists, though taking new objects in the display of fearful abjection. The rhetoric of othering, in the construction of the masked rioter, the veiled terrorist, the street violent hoody, addresses and constitutes 'us', inviting the audience to position itself in the familiar dynamic of exclusion and boundary drawing (Said, 1981). What is more prominent in this more recent rhetoric, though by no means new, is the prioritizing and reifying of religion. Above all, Islam tends to be fixed, essential and immutable. Consistent with Hall's (1997) account of stereotyping, Islam is drastically reduced and simplified. Moreover, Islam is repeatedly located in an allochronic order of time as backward, belonging to another era, outside and alien to the modern world (Fabian, 1983). In part, the dynamic of these processes of othering might often be seen as driven by instability in the position from which such power is exercised. Who 'we' are is shored up by insisting on the boundary between 'us' and 'them', by an intolerance of any blurring, complication or ambiguity in the line of difference. Whiteness, for example, appears especially fragile (Dyer, 1997; Ellsworth, 1997b; Fine et al., 1997; Frankenberg, 1997; Hewitt, 2005; Preston, 2007), and its anxieties and uncertainties are addressed by right-wing political discourses, often with some enhanced success in periods of economic crisis and disarray. The election of members of the British National Party to the European Parliament in 2009 is a small-scale but arguably significant example of the response to racialization in the field of representations. Membership of the BNP was, until late in 2009, only open to 'whites'. Whatever changes were required for it to continue functioning as a legal political party, it could hardly renounce its racist constitution-in-practice.

Often, knowing how these discourses and representations are actively engaged in specific contexts remains just as elusive as I suggested in the 'riots' case study. Some attempts to show how such discourses might figure in the lives of Asian girls at school have been made by, among others, Farzana Shain (2003). In particular, she explores representations constructing Muslims as caught within a cultural pathology (see also Shain, 2010). Working from a very different repertoire of representations, Tony Sewell (1997) attempted to show how black boys engaged with the world of dancehall and hip-hop. However, to move from an analysis of representations to the lived experience of people themselves is invariably a difficult task. Research often aspires to explore these relations between representation and lived relations among young people, but at least in educational contexts, this has proved a challenging task (Dimitriadis, 2001; Dolby, 2001).

It needs to be emphasized that the concern with 'race' and representation should not remain fixated only on events given a highly political status in news media. There is scope to consider many other forms of representation, some located in educational settings of various kinds (museums, for example) and others encountered more in the domain of popular entertainment. Clearly, rather different issues can be raised about the modes of address found in such differing domains. Attention to the specificity of forms, contexts and intended audiences is essential.

Exhibitions, as forms of public education and 'official knowledge', deserve some careful scrutiny. Among those visited and discussed by my own students in London, the permanent Holocaust exhibition at the Imperial War Museum has been a particularly prominent and complex focus. Encountered not in the context of a study in Jewish history, but in relation to an exploration of fascist representations from the 1920s, 1930s and since, the exhibition not only illustrates but also undermines fascism's preferred imagery. In moving from the aesthetic heights of Riefenstahl's film *Triumph of the Will* (1934/1935/2008), shown in class, to the exhibit of shoes abandoned in the execution of the 'final solution', students are invited to ask in what way these images and objects 'stand for' and explain the destructive force of fascism in the 1930s. The exhibition, like the film, has its rhetoric of 'truth' and is thus subject to critical interrogation. For example, it might be questioned in terms of its preferred forms of evidence – black and white images, artefacts and models – and their adequacy as modes of explanation. It might be suggested, for example, that through its rhetoric of presentation, the exhibition places fascism and its consequences too firmly in the past, limiting engagement with more recent events both in Europe and elsewhere (Cambodia, the Balkans, Rwanda, Gaza and so on). Indeed, the work of tracing fascism in contemporary culture is perhaps not well served by historically distanced exhibitions alone (see Ellsworth, 2004). Paul Gilroy's (2004b) impressive, but difficult, exploration of such themes, *Between Camps: Nations, Cultures and the Allure of Race,* provides a critical guide – though one in need of some detailed illustration to achieve wider currency in teaching about 'race' and representation.

Gilroy's work is wide-ranging, challenging readers to follow arguments traced across, for many, unfamiliar ground. In teaching Gilroy's exploration of 'race' and representation, I have adopted the strategy of focusing on the career of a single figure, the film maker and photographer Leni Riefenstahl (1902–2003). Riefenstahl had a lengthy career, and in dwelling on its most significant phases in some detail, it is possible to provide a life-historical thread through the maze of complex and abstract debates (see Muller, 1993/2003). Riefenstahl's work, from her appearance in the *Bergfilm* ('mountain' films) of the 1920s (for example, *The Holy Mountain,* Fanck, 1926; Dyer, 1997: 21), her direction of both *Triumph of the Will* and the film of the 1936 Berlin Olympic Games, *Olympia* (1938/2006), to her 'anthropological' photography in the Sudan, provides a vivid and powerful source of debate.

Gilroy (2004b: 156) comments that 'vision's relation to other senses and dimensions of communication, in particular its apparent triumph over written language, is an extremely significant component in the history of raciology', adding that this is 'central to Riefenstahl's own story'. In the 1930s, her film *Triumph of the Will* was both admired, aesthetically, and condemned as unequivocal propaganda for the Nazi party led by Adolf Hitler. Of course, it may seem perversely backward looking to return to the events of the 1930s when 'race', both in education and in wider politics, has a continuing and immediate significance in the present. But the scope of Gilroy's argument suggests that such a focus can inform discussion of more recent developments:

> . . . whether Riefenstahl was fully aware of it or not, the success of the revolution in visualizing technologies and visual cultures which she pioneered changed forever the apprehension of solidarity and the synchronized collective life of national, ethnic, or racialized communities in just the way that her associates Hitler, Speer, and Goebbels had hoped that it would. (Gilroy, 2000: 157)

Gilroy comments further that this 'transformation in the power of images relative to words' has 'shaped forms of solidarity, identification, and belonging more generally' (Gilroy, 2000: 158). Indeed, he goes on to note the influence of fascist aesthetics in pop videos and political advertising and, as he argues at some length, in black popular culture too. The point is that the enhanced power of visual media has contributed to, without any means being the exclusive basis for, a process in which 'racial' difference is rendered visible, making division an unarguable fact of life. In Gilroy's words, spectators are delivered to 'a special place beyond the duplicity of words where fundamental historical and racial divisions could be immediately perceived'. (Gilroy, 2000: 164). The appearance of Riefenstahl's (Riefenstahl, 1976a, b) rich colour photographs of the Nuba in the 1970s invited both admiration and controversy (Sontag, 1983; see also Sontag, 2003; Peucker, 2004). Their value as documents of performance and of body art could not, and still cannot, be separated out from their status as representations of people positioned as 'other' and 'exotic' both to Riefenstahl herself and to the consumers of Sunday newspaper colour supplements, where these images were often most widely publicized. One strand in the debate focused on these images as evidence that Riefenstahl either never was, or was no longer, a 'racist'. How could a racist produce such elegant and often beautiful images of black people? For continuity in Riefenstahl's stance, it was often recalled that even in 1936, she very obviously celebrated the achievement of the black American athlete Jesse Owens (see, for example, Riefenstahl, 1994). But, in critique of Riefenstahl, it can be argued that she has sustained, and furthered, a very familiar rhetoric of 'racial' difference by celebrating the black body, both its strength and eroticism, rather than the mind. Gilroy argues that

> . . . associating blackness with intelligence, reason, and the activities of the mind challenges the basic assumptions of raciology – in common sense and scientific versions – whereas giving 'The Negro' the gift of the devalued body does not, even if that body is to be admired. The black body can be appreciated as beautiful, powerful, and graceful in the way that a racehorse or a tiger appear beautiful, powerful, and graceful. Beauty and strength are, after all, understood by Riefenstahl as exclusively natural attributes rather than cultural achievements . . . The underlying, implicit tragedy is the Aryan loss of physical power, not the African retention of it. (Gilroy, 2000: 174)

Though Gilroy's case is made very effectively and, in its account of the prevailing logic of 'raciology', is substantially correct, it is worth keeping the debate around Riefenstahl's work open. This observation arises in part from the evident enthusiasm for her photographs shown by some of my students, including those of African origin – but this offers no secure ground for their defence. However, it is possible to argue that at least some of Riefenstahl's images do actually draw attention to and celebrate the elaborate and stylistically sophisticated masks and motifs painted on the faces and bodies of her subjects. In this respect, it could be argued that her images record and acknowledge an intellectual and cultural skill by no means reducible to the body and to nature (see Riefenstahl, 1976b). It might also be suggested that such embellishments of the body are no longer so obviously markers of 'difference' and 'primitivism' because such practices – tattooing, piercing and hair stylization – have become relatively common-place among young people in the 'West'. How these images are read is thus not fixed and final, but a matter for continuing discussion and reconsideration.

Conclusion

This chapter has introduced some aspects of the inevitably complex debates around 'race' and representation. The history of the concept of 'race' deserves more detailed discussion than it has been possible to provide here. Among those sources that might be pursued in further reading, Appiah's (1992: 28–46) essay on 'Illusions of race' is particularly rewarding. Though always polemical, hooks (1992; 1994a) is essential reading, stirring debate around 'race' from a black feminist perspective. Gilroy's work, *Between Camps* (2000), from which I have quoted, and also *There Ain't No Black in the Union Jack* (1987), *The Black Atlantic* (1993) and *After Empire* (2004) constitute the most theoretically eclectic, but also coherent, challenge to 'race' in recent decades. Each of these texts explores and undermines 'racial' thought in both contemporary and more historically distanced settings.

The concept of 'representation' has been explored by many authors, but those cited here and worth reading further include Stuart Hall (1983, 1997) and Richard Dyer (1993, 1997). Hall (1997) is a key reference for work in this field, mapping out the conceptual intricacies of representation but is also much more engaged with psychoanalysis than other sources considered here. As was noted earlier, in Chapter 2, the exclusion of psychoanalysis from Education Studies often places students in some diffi-culty when they encounter its, mostly unfamiliar, vocabulary. Nevertheless, the way that Hall uses psychoanalytic concepts to explain the emotional force of 'racial' imagery should not be ignored. 'Race', despite the inverted commas, persists in daily life and is often a dangerously *emotional* matter (Shain, 2003, 2010).

Points for reflection

To what extent is the concept of 'race' still a part of common everyday talk?
What are the current 'imageries' of 'race' in the media?
What are the benefits of a historical approach to 'race' and representation?

Children and Television

Chapter Outline

Introduction

This chapter outlines the meanings commonly associated with the idea of 'childhood'. With an emphasis on the agency of children, the chapter also questions the belief that television is harmful to children and outlines other approaches to understanding how children engage with television in their talk and their play.

In this chapter, the concern with representation persists in the attention to visual media, especially television. But its focus is not primarily on how children are represented on television, though that is an important issue, but more on how they are 'addressed' by television. This formulation, 'modes of address', involves posing questions about the relationship between texts (television programmes in this case) and their viewers. What kind of viewers, what kind of 'audience', is implied by the construction and positioning of a particular TV show? More particularly, why and on what terms is it considered to be (by its makers and its viewers) 'for children'? In asking that last question, I imply another, one that will take some effort to answer. What do we mean by 'children' and 'childhood'?

Ideas about childhood have a long and complex history (Aries, 1960/1986; Steedman, 1982, 1995; Jordanova, 1989; Scarre, 1989; James and Prout, 1990; Lesko, 2001). Such ideas inform the way that we think and talk about children now and cannot simply be stripped away or ignored or, indeed, be displaced by the actual reality of living children. The strongest and most persistent strand in thinking about children, at least in the Anglo-American domain, is associated with the Romantic movement in the later eighteenth and early nineteenth centuries in Western Europe. Romanticism has contributed to the prevailing construction of childhood as a time of innocence, a special and distinctive period to be valued and protected. In some versions of this Romantic construction of childhood, growing up is inevitably to lose purity, poise and freedom; becoming an adult is thus a matter for regret, lived as a lament for a personal past that is irretrievable. Such feelings may thus inform an adult insistence that the childhood of children should be just as innocent and ideal as they imagine their own to have been. That this Romantic preoccupation with childhood was itself a part of a wider response to, and evasion of, industrial capitalism is perhaps too often forgotten (Sutton-Smith, 1997: 129–33). Whatever the real social benefits of according childhood respect and concern, the inheritance of 'childhood-as-innocence' is a misleading and inadequate frame for understanding the realities of children and childhood.

Brian Sutton-Smith comments on the construction of what he calls the 'paradigm of the imaginary child':

> What develops in the twentieth century is a complex of ideas in which the child's play and art are brought together with ideas about the imagination, about the child as a primitive, an innocent, an original, and, in effect, the true romantic, because he or she is untouched by the world and still capable of representing things in terms of an unfettered imagination. (Sutton-Smith, 1997: 133)

In debates over television and other media, the idea of childhood as innocence and of children as vulnerable to, and in need of protection from, the media has a central and enduring place. If childhood is taken to be a period of life innocent of sex, violence, conflict, death and work (for example), then what children watch can be seen as putting them, but also 'childhood', at risk. In this context, it is a common assumption that childhood has been eroded by television and other newer media (Kline, 1993; Postman, 1994). But it can be argued that this view of childhood, whatever its importance as the basis for the protection of children, is also one that firmly places adults in control of children, monitoring their lives and deciding on their behalf what they should know. Protection, if also entailing being kept in ignorance, might thus be productive of the vulnerability it claims to defend.

Among the most radical post-Romantic challenges to a belief in childhood as innocence, the work of Sigmund Freud (1856–1939), and of the wider psychoanalytic movement, deserves some further acknowledgement in this chapter. But before discussing psychoanalysis, it is helpful to introduce here, through some short quotations, the thoughts of the writer Reynolds Price on childhood. Price, in an afterword to Sally Mann's *Immediate Family* (1992), examines images of childhood and family, questioning the way that childhood is usually remembered and celebrated. Mann's, sometimes controversial, photographs show her own children at moments of distress, occasionally naked, often unsmiling. By invoking moments not photographed, except by photographers such as Mann, Price further unsettles the image of childhood innocence. Writing like a teacher, opening up the topic of childhood memory for a class of people beyond childhood, he invites reflection, investigation and speculation about how all of us recall and define our own childhoods:

> Think of your own shoe box of pictures, the dog-eared, fading and technically spotty record of your own childhood . . . Do the earliest pictures of you coincide with what you believe to be your earliest memories (and to what extent have the pictures 'created' those memories for you or merely served as reminders of them)? What important known events or persons from your childhood are omitted from the photographic record? Which of those events and persons do you wish you had pictorial evidence for? Do you have, as I do, seeming recollections of moments so happy that you want hard evidence the moments aren't simply dreams or longings?

> What if you were suddenly presented with a previously unknown box of old pictures – all of them made without your knowledge and focused clearly on the most embarrassing moments of your childhood, the most humiliating, the most enduringly damaging: how many of the negatives would you destroy? And how wise would even a single destruction be, given the mind's tendency to magnify bad news which it can no longer consult for accuracy of memory? What if

> I suddenly held toward you, in a plain sealed envelope, a picture you'd never suspected of that one instant in early childhood when the first great fracture of fear or loathing tore your mind and you knew that life would entail much pain – would you open the envelope and look?

This is a powerful and perhaps unwelcome sequence of questions, building a case for enquiry into some of what we may feel is too fundamentally personal to allow such probing. As a classroom project, such feelings might well constrain both teacher and students, limiting the scope and duration of the investigation. But, as a basis for more private reflection, his questions effectively pick away at what we might believe about our past selves. His own responses, giving considerably more weight to psychoanalysis than to a belief in childhood innocence, decline to accept the child his parents wished to construct in taking and collecting family photographs. It should be noted, however, that Price, like Freud, is still located within a Romantic paradigm as childhood is taken to shape so significantly the rest of an individual's life:

> . . . at the first glimpse of any emotion but joy or a premature amusing dignity, my parents' camera would refuse to click . . . like the great majority of middle-class children, I accepted from the cradle onward a near-perfect complicity in the fiction of our endless contentment with one another and with the world beyond us.
>
> So I can only reconstruct vaguely, in my mind, the seismic events and feelings of, say, the first sixteen years of my life – the years in which, most artists and psycho-analysts agree, a lifetime's dilemmas are laid in the cellars of the dark unconscious for curing or souring and for whatever strange conjunctions they choose to make before erupting in adult life with the useful work or the ruin that results.
>
> Like most veterans of family photographs then, my face and body – so far as they manage to outlast me – will survive as a highly edited version of the whole person I managed to be behind an ever-ready grin.

From Price, it is useful to take on, as a habit, the need to question and reconsider our own memories and assumptions about our own and others' childhoods. The importance of psychoanalysis here is that, though also insisting on the sustained 'influence' of childhood in any one individual's life, it provides accounts of childhoods that are far from contented. In psy-choanalysis, childhood is not innocent of sexuality and, emotionally, it may be a period of violence and turmoil. Such elements in childhood are often sharply denied. However, most people, with any day-to-day experience of young children, are likely to recognize that anger, rage even, is commonplace. They might also acknowledge, though this is now a very contentious matter indeed, that young children appear to feel, and to explore, feelings that are sexual (Bragg and Buckingham, 2009). Among the more famous of Freud's theories is that of the Oedipus complex, named after the Greek myth in which a boy grows up to murder his own father (in ignorance and in battle) and to subsequently marry (again in ignorance) his own mother. Freud used the myth to represent feelings of rivalry and jealousy felt by infant boys in their relationships with their fathers, powerful adult competitors for the attention of (their) mothers (Freud, 1977; Laplanche and Pontalis, 1985: 282–7). Freud made this emotional and sexual dynamic a commonplace element in infant life rather than only an aberration, dramatically enacted in *Oedipus The King* (Sophocles, 1962) and in *Hamlet* (Shakespeare, 1969). Attributing such desires to infants is clearly to undermine that peculiarly influential strand of Romanticism from which our own contemporary belief in childhood innocence is substantially derived. In this respect, psychoanalysis can appear to recall an older Christian view of children as somewhat monstrous, sinful beings in need of determined moral correction (Bazalgette and Buckingham, 1995: 1). But, as Adam Phillips notes, Freud was:

> a very late Romantic [finding] the passions and perplexities of the child exemplary; the child with her consuming interests, her inexhaustible questions, and her insisting body. The child who is learning to make mistakes, figuring out how to become a person, through the curious combinations of word and gesture, and the gaps between them. (Phillips, 1998: 1–2)

In psychoanalysis, rather than moral condemnation and correction, there is a central preoccupation with affectivity, the emotional dynamics constituting human beings, children included.

Too much . . . too young

There is a persistent and widespread belief that children watch too much television. 'Too much' is an expression worth bringing into focus. 'Too much' can be contrasted with, perhaps, 'not enough'. But it would be remarkable to hear that children do not watch enough television. Children may not eat enough, not sleep enough, not take enough exercise, or play enough. And, of course, they may well not read enough. But somehow television is not ever, *in everyday common sense discourse*, too little. Television appears therefore to be already understood as something to be reduced, restricted and regulated. It is a medium somehow thought to be intrinsically debilitating and possibly damaging, and especially for children (Postman, 1994; Mander, 1998; Winn, 2001; Schor, 2006). As either 'innocents' or 'monsters', children, it seems, are unlikely to benefit from watching television.

Such a brief hint at what everyday talk about children and television might be like is no more than an attempt to open up the question that, in various forms, has occupied many academic writers. A great deal of academic research has explored arguments about what 'effects' television has on children (Hodge and Tripp, 1986; Lowery and DeFleur, 1988; Buckingham, 1993b, 2000a). This has been, and to some extent persists as, the dominant theme in this field. Children, in this view, tend to be seen as *acted upon* by television, as passive recipients of a powerful and all pervasive medium over which they have no control. Meanings are imposed upon children by what they watch and the consequences of this are conceived as the effect of a cause, the response to a stimulus. This favours an understanding of television as having automatic and predetermined consequences for its child viewers (see Roof, 2007). In this scenario, more television is inevitably to increase the 'effect', and thus to intensify the harm. The particular forms of damage, depending on the concerns of the research and the wider frame of public debate, range from violence and its emulation (or the fear it instils) to the display of commodities and the resulting obsession with consumption. These are substantial and important concerns, and are often familiar to those who are involved with children on a day-to-day basis. But the attempt to think through these issues from within the 'effects' paradigm produces only very simplistic, meagre, accounts of what is going on. In accord with the emphasis on culture, throughout this book, the approach to these questions advocated here takes meaning to be a matter of negotiation and interpretation in the encounter between particular children and the TV shows that they watch. Sutton-Smith, in his extremely wide-ranging review of theories of play, comments:

> . . . even when children try their hardest to match their own play behavior to that modeled for them by television – in this case, to the actions of the *Power Rangers* television show – they are forced by their need for cooperation to make all kinds of compromises, such as bargaining for who takes the negative roles, deciding how they can adapt their unique 'power' feelings to the scenario, devising

costumes, weapons, gestures, and sequences. What they reproduce is a playful theatric adaptation. There is no tabula rasa. The point is, no matter what the cultural stimuli might be (toys or television shows), they have to be mediated by children's fantasy in order to be accepted, and adjusted to their play norms and social competence in order to be assimilated into the active theatric play forms of childhood. (Sutton-Smith, 1997: 154)

The most productive studies of children and television are those that seek to show how children engage with, and take further, the shows they watch, both those addressed to them ('children's television') and those they watch from the much broader repertoire of contemporary television and film (see Buckingham, 1987, 1993b, 1993c, 1996, 2000).

Decades of research

Though there is a great deal of published commentary, through several decades, in support of the belief that television is, on the whole, a bad thing, especially for children (for example, Postman, 1994; Winn, 2001; Schor, 2006) there is also a long history of enquiry into what children learn from television, going beyond, if not entirely abandoning, concerns about what forms of television are 'appropriate' for them (Hodge and Tripp, 1986; Buckingham, 1993b, 1993c, 1996, 2000; Buckingham et al., 1999; Kapur, 1999; Kenway and Bullen, 2001). Perhaps the earliest, qualified, defence of television can be found in the 1950s, in the work of Hilda Himmelweit et al. (1958), published in the same period as those precursors of Cultural Studies, Hoggart (1957) and Williams (1958). A comparable investigation in the United States was reported in *Television in the Lives of Our Children* (Schramm et al., 1961). In the 1950s, the implications of the relatively new medium of television, amidst wider shifts in the strengthening of a commercial popular culture, focused a growing research effort set to continue through the 1960s and 1970s. How people 'used' television became a core concern of audience research. Though not a study of child viewers, the contribution of Cultural Studies to qualitative audience research took shape most decisively in the mid-1970s with the publication of *The 'Nationwide' Audience* (Morley, 1980). This study, emerging from work supported by the Centre for Contemporary Cultural Studies, explored responses to an early evening BBC TV 'news magazine' (*Nationwide*) from groups, mostly of students in further and higher education. In giving detailed attention to what people had to say, the study opened up the nuanced complexity of actual viewers' relationship to what they watch (or in this study, often, what they did not watch!). Morley's concluding comments on the theoretical requirements of an adequate study of audiences proved to be influential for Media Studies throughout the last three decades. For example, he insisted that:

> We need to construct a model in which the social subject is always seen as inter-pellated by a number of discourses, some of which are in parallel and reinforce each other, some of which are contradictory and block or inflect the successful interpellation of the subject by other discourses. Positively or negatively, other discourses are always involved in the relation of text and subject, although their action is simply more visible when it is a negative and contradictory rather than a positive and reinforcing effect. . . . Crucially, we are led to pose the relation of text and subject as an empirical question to be investigated, rather than as an a priori question to be deduced from a theory of the ideal spectator 'inscribed' in the text. (Morley, 1980: 162)

The concept of 'interpellation', absorbed from the work of Louis Althusser (1971), is intended to define the process of being addressed by a particular discourse (imagine watching a TV presenter opening with the line 'Hey kids!), and accepting, or not, the position we are invited or expected to accept (do you take up the position – 'kid'?). Morley is trying to get at the complexity of how actual people engage with TV programmes (texts) by drawing attention to the combination of social positions and discourse positions through which any individual is located. In relation to studies of child viewers (never a significant part of Morley's own research, 1986, 1992, 2000), this would mean that the simple homogeneity of 'children' would need to be dismantled in terms of social divisions such as class and gender, but also discourses such as those of consumerism, education and age-phase, for example. A TV show might seek to address 'children' in some general, apparently all-inclusive way, but this might be seen as just a claim on the possible audience – not one that many may take up on the terms that it is made. 'Children' may well not be comfortable with being addressed as children in some discourses. The further lesson drawn from Morley's (1980, 1986, 1992) research is that how texts are engaged by their viewers cannot be predicted on the basis of an analysis of the text alone. Though many adults have presumed to judge what texts will mean to children, this is a fundamental problem and a focus for debate in many of those studies that, following Morley's cultural study of audiences, subsequently defined the field.

Bob Hodge and David Tripp's (1986) *Children and Television: A Semiotic Approach* was a seminal study, exemplifying the need to explore children's engagement with television empirically. Coming out of a three-year research project examining how children interpreted a single cartoon show, it was published in the same year as Morley (1986), a book that, despite its title *Family Television*, relinquished any claim to document children's viewing. Though carefully acknowledging the 'effects' paradigm, Hodge and Tripp go beyond its causal constraints with an eclectic array of theory thoughtfully applied to discussion both of the cartoon, *Fangface*, and of children's responses to it. They comment:

> Not to ask questions about the effects of television on children would be irresponsible. So parents and legislators look to experts for some answers; and that is where the dilemma turns into a miasmic and oppressive cloud of uncertainty – for although the experts have turned out study upon study for decades, the result has seldom been a progressive clarification, an increasing certainty and confidence about what is or is not so. . . . The problem . . . is that these 'experts' have been trying to answer the wrong questions in the wrong order, with theories and methods that have been overly partial and inadequate. (Hodge and Tripp, 1986: 2)

Their approach is to offer a very detailed and thorough adult analysis of the chosen cartoon but then to acknowledge that the meanings they attribute to it are not necessarily, and are indeed unlikely to be, those that various groups of children offer in response to it. Like Morley, they take the position that the text does not impose or predetermine the meanings readers, or viewers, derive from it.

Hodge and Tripp (1986) go on to make a more particular case for television's value to children and, despite some careful reservations, at various points they suggest that there are some good reasons for children to watch more, rather than less, television. The route they take to this apparently unprecedented proposal is interesting and well worth following, though some may find the relatively specialized semiotic vocabulary troublesome. In particular, the concept of modality, if unfamiliar, is essential to an understanding of their conclusions.

Modality, in Hodge and Tripp's usage, refers to the 'reality-status' of a text or, to be both more precise and more elusive, the degree of reality attributed to a text by its audience. For example, a cartoon such as *The Simpsons* represents human characters with flat, highly stylized drawings coloured, mostly, yellow.

By contrast with a situation comedy with human actors, like *Friends* (1994–2004), its modality is weak. It is further from what we take to be real. Further, a situation comedy, as formulaic television fiction, is weaker in its modality than, say, a documentary film about the lives of a family that actually exists outside of television. One reason for children to watch more television is for them to encounter such contrasts, and thus learn to recognize and understand the implications of differing degrees of modality. Watching too little television might result in a relative naivety about what is shown. But there are also good reasons for children to watch a lot of examples of the same genre of television.

For example, *The Simpsons* is unusual in its complexity of reference (for example, to American politics), in its use of sound (arguably relatively realistic) and in the strongly individualized voices of characters, again in aural terms, relatively realistic. Though sharing the weak modality of cartoons, these other elements heighten *The Simpsons'* modality in other ways (Wells, 2002; Gray, 2005). For children to appreciate this, they need to see many other cartoons and also computer animations, those produced by Disney, of course, but many others too. An extended range of viewing, even within one genre, can therefore facilitate competence in making more nuanced modality judgements. Such a competence can be acquired informally in day-to-day viewing but is also potentially a matter for further exploration in media education. This educational implication is also among Hodge and Tripp's (1986) conclusions, as they acknowledge that such learning can be extended in formal education. Among their ten concluding theses they list these:

> It has long been known that the reality factor – television's perceived relation to the real world – is variable, depending on age, experience and social conditions. Indeed, it is a decisive factor determining the nature of media responses and media effects. But the ability to make subtle and adequate reality judgements about television is a major developmental outcome that can only be acquired from a child's experience of television. (Hodge and Tripp, 1986: 215–16)

> All children need some fantasy programmes, such as cartoons for younger children. All children, particularly older ones, also need some programmes which touch more closely their reality. (Hodge and Tripp, 1986: 216)

> The school is a site where television should be thoroughly understood, and drawn into the curriculum in a variety of positive ways. (Hodge and Tripp, 1986: 218)

That they offer such condensed formulations is indicative of the often animated context of debate around children's responses to television. Clearly, they intend to do more than add to the uncertainty they identify in their introduction. Their research is thus far from merely academic, even in its elaboration of the medium's 'language' and 'grammar'. They aim to inform a wider public, including parents, rather than only a more circumscribed academic readership interested in the technicalities of semiotics.

Like Hodge and Tripp, Buckingham, in *Public Secrets:* EastEnders *and Its Audience* (1987) pursued the argument that children were active readers of television and more capable of sophisticated judgements about what they watch than adults might think. Buckingham has published many studies since this initial, and possibly somewhat overstated, claim that children are a sophisticated and 'knowing' audience. Each one has added empirical detail and more considered analysis of just how children and young people view, talk about, and appropriate television, and other media, in their lives (Buckingham, 1993b, 1993c, 1996, 2001). Again, in common with Hodge and Tripp (1986), some of these studies offer specific summary conclusions for a wider non-academic constituency. For example, Buckingham (1996) ends with a list of 16 conclusions and 6 implications for film and TV classification policy. Declining simply to reiterate the complexity of his findings, Buckingham presents the research as responsible to the real lives of children, young people and their parents. At the level of policy, he advises:

1. There should be more objective information for parents (and indeed for all viewers) about the content of programmes and videotapes, particularly where this relates to areas of general concern.
2. While some form of centralized censorship is inevitable, a great deal could be done to make the system more accountable.
3. The age classifications on video distribution – and particularly the '18' certificate – should be reconsidered in the light of changing cultural assumptions about childhood.
4. The debate about 'violence' needs to take much greater account of responses to factual material.
5. Our responsibilities towards children as an audience need to be defined, not merely in terms of prevention and control but also in terms of the positive provision that is made for them.
6. Media education, both for parents and for children, should be regarded as a major priority. (Buckingham, 1996: 314–17)

Though not following the populism of Maire Messenger-Davies's (1989) *Television is Good for Your Kids* – a title suggesting a manual for parents rather than an academic study – Buckingham attempts to avoid the insulation of one regime of value from another where, at best, participants in one agree to disagree with those in another (see Chapter 1 in this volume and Frow, 1995). Though the previous decades of research into children and television are somewhat lamented by Hodge and Tripp (1986), their own study and other research informed by the cultural study of audiences has been more productive both of appropriately complex accounts *and* of informed action, at least in education (Nixon, 2002; Wells, 2002; Buckingham, 2002, 2003).

The culture of children

The idea of 'children's culture' is highly ambiguous and problematic. But it is important to consider what it might mean. Recalling the discussion of 'culture', and particularly the idea of a culture 'of the people', in Chapter 1, it may now be appropriate to make a similar argument about children. Frow argues that 'the people' is 'not a given entity which precedes cultural forms, but is rather entirely the product of cultural forms . . . a fact of representation rather than an external cause of representation' (Frow, 1995: 84). To some extent, this is also true of 'children', if we take this to be a category constituted in the media and to which actual young people are 'recruited' or by which they are 'interpellated'. But, as I argued in relation to 'youth', such an age-phase is not only a media construction, and 'children' live their lives as such not only and not entirely in terms of representations. So, in part, the idea of a children's culture is constructed through its elaborately sustained presence in the media but it has other, additional, modes of existence.

There are those who have argued that children's culture is constituted by an enduring, if also variable, repertoire of games, jokes, rhymes, riddles and songs. The work of Iona and Peter Opie (Opie and Opie, 1959/2001, 1969; Opie, 1993) has been especially influential in documenting, and thus appearing to substantiate, the view that there is a separate and distinctive children's culture. One of their best-known early publications emerged in the late 1950s, thus, once again, at the same time as other seminal pre-Cultural Studies texts (Hoggart, 1957; Williams, 1958). *The Lore and Language of Schoolchildren* (1959)[1] reported on research accumulated through the 1950s and made a striking claim:

> . . . the folklorist and anthropologist can, without travelling a mile from his [sic] door, examine a thriving unselfconscious culture (the word 'culture' is used here deliberately) which is as unnoticed by the sophisticated world, and quite as little affected by it, as is the culture of some dwindling aboriginal tribe living out its helpless existence in the hinterland of a native reserve. . . . No matter how uncouth schoolchildren may outwardly appear, they remain tradition's warmest friends. Like the savage, they are respecters, even venerators, of custom; and in their self-contained community their basic lore and language seems scarcely to alter from generation to generation. (Opie and Opie, 1959/2001: 1–2)

The concept of 'culture' deployed here is marked by its usage in late nineteenth and early twentieth century anthropology and carries some of the more idealizing characteristics of Romanticism. Culture is regarded as somewhat outside history, as an enclave in a changing world, where the past persists largely unchanged. The 'savage' (often elevated in Romantic myth as 'noble') stands as the 'other' to the corruption and commerce of the modern world and is firmly located in another time before the present (Fabian, 1983; Stallybrass and White, 1986). Often, in this paradigm, childhood is equated with this other, uncivilized, and separate world. This is a problematic use of the concept of 'culture' and, whatever the weight of the empirical archive, needs to be carefully qualified. It seems especially dubious here in contributing to a construction of childhood as distinct and separate from the society in which it is lived (Evaldsson, 2009). However, Opie and Opie's (1959) emphasis on communication between children, without the involvement of adults, is an important corrective to approaches that reduce the scope of children's agency to a reactive subservience to the adult world. As Sutton-Smith (1997: 154) suggests in the passage quoted earlier, how children take on adult-produced media, for example, is subject to reworking in the context of children's own social relations, typically in play. But this is no basis for claiming an *autonomous* 'culture of childhood' (Steedman, 1982; Corsaro, 2009).

Allison James, among others, has made a case for considering childhood both in terms of agency and wider social relations (James, 2009). She identifies her position in a rejection of 'the passivity of functionalist roles/models' and emphasizes that young people are 'active in the construction and determination of their own social lives, the lives of those around them and of the societies in which they live' (James, 1995: 45; see also, James and Prout, 1990; James, 1993, 2009). Though endorsing many aspects of the Opies' research, she qualifies her concept of a 'culture of childhood' by drawing attention to the 'contexts within which they are *forced* to socialize' (my emphasis, James, 1995: 45) and the social marginality of children and young people. This implies some necessary distancing from the more celebratory accounts of children's play (see Marsh, 2008; Bishop and Curtis, 2001). In fact, beyond the rather loose rhetorical invocation of a 'culture of childhood' most authors (for example, those in Bishop and Curtis, 2001) when their accounts go into detail, acknowledge that both directly (through teachers and parents) and less immediately (through the media) the 'culture of children' draws continually on sources other than children themselves and is enacted in circumstances often, and perhaps increasingly, defined by adults (see also Herring, 2008).

Taste and distaste

When adults encounter, and sometimes write about, the 'culture of children', questions of taste appear with some force, though when the writers are academics, their feelings are often somewhat disguised with the rhetoric of critical analysis. In relation to children's television, two perspectives, those of Stephen Kline (1993) and Ellen Seiter (1993) can be usefully outlined here. They have been compared before (see, for example, the discussions in Buckingham, 2000: 159–63 and Kenway and Bullen, 2001: 36–7). Usually, Kline is taken to represent the Marxist tradition, giving priority to political economy. Seiter is taken to represent a form of feminism, attentive to the interests of young girls.

Kline (1993) is inclined to perpetuate the belief in a traditional children's culture now infiltrated and significantly weakened by the apparatus of the market, including television. The book's title, *Out of the Garden*, announces a central theme: a lament for lost innocence. He argues that the commercialization of children's culture has fundamentally destroyed the traditional activities and experiences of childhood. The book is a thoroughly researched and substantial study, but it is almost entirely focused on the interconnected industries involved in marketing the material components of a modern, and in his view debased form of, children's culture. What children actually do, and how they might make meaningful engagements with the products they encounter is not explored in any significant way. His nostalgic vision of childhood is invoked early in the argument: 'The rise of the electronic media seems to have undermined the traditional healthy preoccupations of street play, peer conversations and just wandering in the garden long associated with a happy childhood' (Kline, 1993: 12). From this standpoint, almost everything that children might do with the contemporary media, on screen and in play, is inauthentic. That the media might be a resource for street play and peer conversation is not given much consideration. And 'wandering in the garden' sounds more like what a weary academic might like to do after a long day at the computer! The 'culture' of this childhood is again to be found in the past.

Both *Out of the Garden* and *Sold Separately* were published in 1993. As they were writing mainly about developments in the 1980s, it may be helpful to illustrate the dispute through some detail of one example. I want to discuss *The Care Bears* (see Loubert et al., VVD284, 1986b; Loubert et al., VVD408, 1986a; *Care Bears Complete* DVD, 2010) – a show also examined by Kline – with reference to two episodes. My own reading, recorded in an unpublished document, was aided and informed by that offered by one of my daughters, six years old at the time (1989):

It is possible to read *The Care Bears* as little more than a form of fantasy preparation for adult femininity, confirming, extending and developing gendered modes of relating to others. While appearing to maintain the exclusion of children from adulthood, the cartoons seem to be offering girls entry into subordination within adult life, endlessly 'interpellating' them as 'nurturers'. Boys are addressed as in control, leading and initiating action. However, it may be that the narrative dynamic of these cartoons, often developed around Mr Beastly and the means by which he will fail or, temporarily and inadvertently, succeed in carrying out No Heart's plans, engages far more interest than the 'caring missions' of the Care Bears themselves. As an incompetent villain, he seems to be the focus of most uncertainty and humour. Is an interest in Mr Beastly evidence of a relative lack of interest in the 'lessons in caring'? Or are the 'proper' modes of femininity so well established by the age of 6 that their representation is relatively redundant?

The Care Bears family, though conceived around a set of traditionally female values, is actually led by male figures and is often addressed in a distinctively masculine language of command, perhaps with both military and frontier connotations: 'Care Bear Family – Move Out!' Such commands do sometimes seem to be a matter of exaggerated and humorous characterization (for example, Brave Heart Lion). The 'Care Bear Countdown! 5–4–3–2-1 STARE!' is, however, more serious: streams of hearts and stars, the collective power of caring feelings, are directed against the evil No Heart. In fact, the programmes are constructed in terms of a battle, a repeated conflict and test of good power, caring, against evil power, uncaring. Male leadership, female deference and emotionality are clearly marked; there is strong gender differentiation right across the Care Bears family and this seems closely related to traditional colour codings of gender. Browns, strong yellows, strong blues and orange are male (Tender Heart, Brave Heart Lion, Grumpy and Secret Bear); pinks and most pale pastel colours are female (Cosy Heart, Wish Bear, Love-a-Lot and True Heart).

A particularly marked example of traditional gender differentiation appears in *Care-a-Lot's Birthday*. The episode presents baby Hugs (pink female) and baby Tugs (blue male), both in nappies, but highly differentiated through voice and their modes of interaction. 'Hugs' and 'Tugs' define the priorities for each. Baby Hugs speaks in a kind of 'baby girl' idiom and is limited to a repertoire of emotional responses (concern, excitement, admiration and fear) to events in which her actions are framed by baby Tugs' initiatives: 'Ah Brave heart fell down-go boom' (Hugs hugs); 'Oh goody goody gosh! Oh we can dance, watch!' (Hugs dances, Tugs drums); 'Oh goody goody gosh! Oh you're so smart Tugs! And strong too!'. (Admiring/flirtatious touch/hug); 'I'm scared Tugs!'. Meanwhile Tugs' characteristic utterances are: 'Ah, don't worry Hugs. I'm not going to take this hanging up! I'll think of a way to get us out of here'. It is also of some importance to note that these 'baby bears in nappies' are a typical instance of that blurring of distinctions between human babies, animal 'babies' and toy 'baby' animals: the equation of one with another seems to imply a naturalization of being a baby or young child and, in this case, that naturalization could be construed as underpinning the gender difference. Their gender is represented as being as natural as their dependent playfulness.

The power of the Care Bears is an essential interior quality, which is always present, whereas No Heart's power is precarious and dependent upon external agencies: the gemstone, complex spells, shadows and demons. All fail him. In *The Cloud of Uncaring*, the spell-induced cloud is intended to wash away all feelings ('Sadness will rain down from my cloud') and briefly deprives Wish Bear of her capacity for emotion. She is restored by Dale, a 'neglected' child of separated parents, whose unexpected hug, expression of caring and tears revive her pastel green colour. Dale's discovery of a capacity to care is joined with that of the Care Bears in their collective resistance to the cloud and enables them to neutralize the rain, which would otherwise destroy all caring in the world. Dale, suitably educated in the importance and power of caring, is returned to Earth and to his mother, who expresses her regret at breaking her promise to take him swimming. The agency of the Care Bears thus overcomes the threat of uncaring in the domestic interior and in the global battle with No Heart. It may be that there is a distinction here between the power used against No Heart, similar to that used by many other superheroes, and the more interpersonal emotional power, which secures relationships and heals 'bad' feelings (see Rose, 1989/1999). Both are essential powers but the former seems to be directed and coordinated by male Care Bears and the latter is expressed, evoked and invoked by the female figures. The programmes referred to here date from 1986 (re-released in *Care Bears Complete*, 2010) and do include the Care Bear cousins. It may be that this dualism in Care Bear power is evidence of efforts to address both boys and girls, and thus to expand the audience for these cartoons. This is consistent with the argument put forward by Tom Engelhardt (1986) emphasizing market priorities in cartoon development. But it also raises some interesting questions for research into young children's engagement with texts which do attempt to address both boys and girls at the same time or indeed with those that illustrate the *continuing* gender differentiation of media addressing young children (for subsequent developments see, for example, Thorne, 1993; Griffiths, 2002; Mitchell and Reid-Walsh, 2002; Mitchell and Reid-Walsh, 2005; Bishop, 2007; Walkerdine, 2007).

Kline, like Engelhardt, has a well-assembled argument about the television industry and its profit-led strategies. But when it comes to engaging with the texts themselves, it is clear that his distaste for them takes over. He doesn't like *The Care Bears*. Whatever my own viewing preferences may have been at that time, probably *Hill Street Blues* (1981–1987) and films such as *Blue Velvet* (1986) directed by David Lynch, I did live with *The Care Bears* (and *My Little Pony*, DVD 2009) as a constant backdrop to domestic life. Even if I didn't always watch, I heard several episodes collected on video, many, many times. So, out of such familiarity and with some awareness of how and why my daughters enjoyed these cartoons, I can engage with *The Care Bears* both as an object of critical analysis and a text offering some, socially mediated, pleasure. The enjoyment my daughters found in *The Care Bears* was, more often than not, located in their humour, especially evident in the actions of the incompetent 'villain' Mr Beastly, rather than in their didactic 'pro-social messages' (see Richards, 1993, 1995).

Some of Kline's comments are not so different from my own. Others suggest growing irritation:

> The fantasy world of Care-a-lot is the same cuddly, friendly world of simple emotions and simple actions associated with character plush toys. The commercials contain no parable of play, no reference to human experience – just emotional icons drifting across the screen in a neat episodic package. (Kline, 1993: 261)

Curiously Kline invokes A. A. Milne (1928) as a standard against which to condemn the 1980s cartoon characters. Kline's regime of value is nostalgic and literary: 'the wit, individuality, and subtle humour of Milne's eternal characters' is offered as, it seems, a timeless guide to quality (Kline, 1993: 261). The wider argument in which these somewhat unsustainable judgements are made is more credible:

> Programmes such as *He-Man* and *Care Bears* are not scripted as moral parables or even innocent amusements. Character fiction must serve the marketing functions of introducing a new range of personalities into children's culture, orientating children to this product line, creating a sense of excitement about these characters, and ultimately leading children to want to use those characters in play. Most of the new children's television animations have been created explicitly for selling a new line of licensed goods. (Kline, 1993: 280)

Though it can be argued that the use of children's fictions for the marketing of toys is not, in itself, grounds for criticism of the fictions themselves, Kline is correct in his description of the market dynamic. But, again, when he writes about *The Care Bears*, his case disintegrates into a series of inappropriate, contradictory and inaccurate 'exasperations':

> There is . . . no whole personality among them . . .
>
> . . . the scripts focus on the loneliness, fear, clumsiness, foolishness, egotism, frustration and social misunderstanding typical of childhood.
>
> The situations are so contrived and abstracted from the child's experience that it remains difficult to know how children can connect them to real experiences in their own lives . . . Themes of abandonment, separation, incompetence and helplessness are all there, but there is little of the social context of real life, and there is no room in the tales for issues such as divorce, child brutality, poverty or negligence. (Kline, 1993: 292)

Presumably, at least some of these criticisms could also be made of A. A. Milne's (1928/1980) *The House at Pooh-Corner*. But what Kline leaves, as he moves on from *The Care Bears*, is a sense of bewilderment about what he would like a contemporary cartoon for children to do and how he would expect it to engage children.

Ellen Seiter construes both Engelhardt and Kline's distaste as not merely that of adults viewing programmes for children, but as that of middle-class men scornful of cartoons constructed to address young girls:

> In the 1980s, with the rise of home video,recorders and rental tapes, animated series were specifically designed for girls for the first time. The shows *Strawberry Shortcake*, *The Care Bears*, *Rainbow Brite* (1983–1987), and *My Little Pony* (1984–1986) were denigrated as the trashiest, most saccharine, most despicable products of the children's television industry. Yet these series were the first animated shows that did not require girls to cross over and identify with males. (Seiter, 1993: 145)

Seiter discusses *My Little Pony* in some detail and not uncritically. But she also draws on the work of Pierre Bourdieu (1984) to inform her analysis of adult reactions to children's tastes, tracing the horror of middle-class parents faced with the 'low' cultural choices made by their children. Moving between detailed discussion of particular cartoons and the toy stores where parents and children act out the tensions between conflicting tastes, she provides an elegant model for further enquiry. Indeed, many of my Education Studies students, following her lead, have carried out investigations in a variety of toy stores, reporting in detail on the class and gender politics of shopping with and for children. In this respect, the embedding of texts in social practices, and the complex negotiations of their meanings, are a key focus for the attention of those wishing to understand how such cultural commodities enter the 'lived experience' both of adults and children.

Conclusion

This chapter has introduced, and reviewed, some of the central arguments about children's relationship to television. The volume of published work in this field is immense. Further reading on 'Teen TV', beyond the scope of this chapter, includes Davis and Dickinson (2004), Osgerby (2004), Jowett (2005),

Williamson (2005) and Richards (2008). In addition, with the rapid expansion of new media (computer games and the Internet especially), a new wave of publication has taken shape (Livingstone, 2002; Snyder, 2002; Kress, 2003; Buckingham and Willett, 2006; Carr et al., 2006; Willett et al., 2008). To some extent, the debates around children and television are replicated in those around children and new media. The main emphasis of this chapter, that 'childhood' is never simple and cannot be approached without an awareness of its historically accumulated meanings, is particularly relevant to enquiries focusing on young people's engagement with new media. Long familiar ideas about childhood are sustained and circulated in debates, both academic and popular, around the threat, the power and the promise of new media forms (Buckingham, 2007; Livingstone, 2009; Livingstone and Haddon, 2009).

However, in my own research into media-related play in primary school playgrounds, current at the time of writing (2009–2010), there is no straight-forward evidence of immersion in new media, to the exclusion of other older media forms.[2] On the contrary, there are many different sorts of media accumulated and combined in the experience of children between the ages of five and eleven. Younger girls (Year 2) sing Abba songs (mostly from *Mamma Mia*) and adopt routines from *Hannah Montana*, *Camp Rock* and *High School Musical*. Many children watch CBeebies and CBBC (for example, *The Story of Tracy Beaker*; *Spirit Warriors*; *Relic: Guardians of the Museum*; and *Deadly 60*). Across the years, lunchboxes carry the imagery of *Dr Who*, *The Simpsons*, *Ben 10*, *Bratz*, *High School Musical*, *Hannah Montana*, *Star Wars* and sometimes *The Little Mermaid* or *WWF*. Some boys still collect and trade *Pokemon* cards. One boy in Year 5 claims his favourite film is the *Seven Samurai* (Kurosawa, 1954) and is enthusiastic about *The Incredibles*, *Kung Fu Panda*, *Spy Kids* and *X3*. Another Year 5 boy names *The Wizard of Oz* as his favourite film. Some boys read *His Dark Materials* (Pullman, 2007), *The Lord of the Rings* (Tolkien, 1968) and the *Harry Potter* novels (though the films are perhaps engaged with more widely). There are other series of novels that are popular with boys, for example, *Percy Jackson* (see Riordan, 2008) and the *Diamond Brothers* (see Horowitz, 2004). The same children *are* devoted players of computer and video games, among them *New Super Mario Brothers* (Nintendo Wii, 2009) and *Wizard 101* and *Teenage Mutant Ninja Turtles* (Play Station 2, 2007). This is an outline of a complex and dense pattern of media use. The important point to end with here is that new texts do not entirely displace older titles and nor do new media forms squeeze out a continuing engagement with 'old media' such as books and films (Jenkins, 2006; Richards, 2008). It is important to be wary of caricatures (for example, 'cyber kids') that construe whole generations as singularly devoted to just one, whether celebrated or reviled, newly emergent media form (Buckingham, 2000: 41–57; Buckingham and Willett, 2006; Buckingham, 2007).

Points for reflection

In your own experience as a child, how important was television in the daily life of your home?

As a child, do you think that you were vulnerable to television?

How should children be taught about television and new media?

Young Adult Fictions

Introduction

This chapter considers the meaning of the category 'young adult' and, through examples from two authors, Melvin Burgess and Francesca Lia Block, explores debates about the reading and teaching of novels 'for' young people.

This may seem an improbable chapter in a book of this kind, largely preoccupied with youth culture. The common assumption is that new media replace the old, and the latter fade away and become marginal to most people's lives. Progressively, film, television and new media such as video and computer games have, it is believed, eroded the reading of novels and other print media. Moreover, given the still persistently male connotation of 'youth' and the even more entrenched assumption that boys do not read, to introduce literature, or even fiction, here is bound to appear incongruous. Exactly this perception has been addressed by Ulf Boethius (in Fornas and Bolin, 1995). Boethius writes that:

> Although we know that young people do also read – and write – more than other people, literary texts have largely been neglected. Why? One important reason is,

of course, that music, pictures and the body incontestably . . . play a greater role in the lives of young people than does the printed word. For researchers, more interested in modern youth culture than in older cultures, it has been natural to concentrate on what is presently most widespread. (Boethius, in Fornas and Bolin, 1995: 145)

Boethius discusses Swedish youth in the early 1990s. To what extent his argument was accurate and credible in the Swedish context is not my concern. However, his *general* case that it is a mistake to separate off and ignore this aspect of youth consumption is pursued in the rest of this chapter. In Britain, Charles Sarland investigated young people's enthusiasm for fiction in *Young People Reading: Culture and Response* (1991) and, in Canada, Meredith Cherland produced an ethnography of reading in the lives of 11- to 12-year-old girls, *Private Practices: Girls Reading Fiction and Constructing Identity* (1994). A little more recently, Holly Virginia Blackford, in the United States, investigated young pre-teenage and teenage girls in *Out of This World: Why Literature Matters to Girls* (2004). These suggest that the degree of neglect identified by Boethius may be exaggerated. But, with just a few boundary-crossing exceptions, he is right to suggest that 'literary studies' and 'youth culture studies' are quite distinct academic domains. The old, and high, culture location of the 'literary' has certainly made it appear irrelevant to youth researchers. And there are more studies of girls' engagement with literature than there are of boys. The tensions between these areas of enquiry have certainly been evident in teaching a course on 'Young Adult Fictions' and these will be addressed in this chapter.

I wrote this course, first of all, for a three-week summer school at the upstate Cortland campus of the State University of New York, in 2003. But it was subsequently taught in Education Studies at London Metropolitan University. The course was intended to explore issues relating to the broadly defined field of young adult fictions. It aimed to encourage critical investigation of, on the one hand, the way that 'young adult' as an audience or category of readers has been defined through the activities of publishers, bookshops and libraries and other media and educational institutions. On the other, it focused on the reading and analysis of a selection of novels and other texts, from various genres, marketed as 'for young adults'. Taken together, these two aspirations can be explored as a coherent project provided the interrelationship between the institutional apparatuses of publishing and book selling and distribution and both the positioning and construction of particular texts is kept in play.

For example, *Doing It* by Melvin Burgess (2003) serves well as a focus for such study. It is a novel deliberately addressing a readership of supposedly teenage boys, written by an author with a history of writing for children but, since the publication of *Junk* (Burgess, 1996) very publicly renegotiating his relationship to schools as key gatekeepers of young people's reading. In this respect, Burgess's novel also provides a highly controversial example in relation to the third aim of the course: to explore debates around what should, or should not, be included in the secondary school curriculum and, though somewhat more marginally, to consider approaches to the classroom study of selected texts. Texts, even where their 'literariness' is not challenged, are often judged 'controversial'. Sexual content, drug use and the use of 'street' language, and sometimes violence, are routinely regarded as inappropriate in texts to be taught in school classrooms or otherwise educationally legitimated – by their availability in school libraries, for example. Given the wider context of popular media culture and young people's affective engagement with many aspects of it, attempts to maintain strong boundaries between educational and popular knowledge often become a little desperate. I will return to this, and to Burgess, later in the chapter.

The course, at the State University of New York and at London Metropolitan University, like this chapter, carried the title 'Young Adult Fictions'. Giving it this name implied a number of questions that, in a sense, persistently troubled the easy assumption that there is a body of work, a list of novels, that can be offered as the 'appropriate' content of the course (see McCallum, 1999, for very detailed textual studies that do draw on a corpus taken to be well defined and stable). But the intention was to look at young adult literature, fiction and writing in social and institutional terms and thus to examine the meaning and currency of the terms themselves. For example, each of these categories – 'literature', 'fiction' and 'writing' – suggests a different, if overlapping, definition of the field of concern. Not all writing is fiction, not all fiction is judged to be literature, and so on. Young adult 'literature' is typically seen as including writing *for* young adults and writing *about* young adults – mostly, in effect, writing by adults, not young people themselves. Often, and this has been central to English teaching, the category includes only what adult 'experts' (teachers, librarians and critics) believe that young adults should read. The 'literariness' of the texts deemed appropriate to this category, often taken for granted within particular regimes of value, needs to be a matter for explicit debate rather than assumed to be a legitimate criterion of inclusion. In some versions of 'young adult literature', the texts chosen are all by well established, 'canonical', literary figures and are selected because they include young protagonists – Mark Twain's (1884/1966) *The Adventures of Huckleberry Finn*, for example.

'Fictions' suggested a more widely defined field of texts than that implied by 'literature', or even 'writing', alone. Print texts unlikely to be regarded as 'literary' (graphic novels and contemporary popular fiction) and other texts addressed to young adults in the interrelated media of music, television and film are all implicit in the addition of an 's' to the singular 'fiction'. But it also acknowledges, because 'Young Adult' fiction(s) is not just one kind of thing, that it could include writing *by* young people themselves (see Hinton, 1970; Carlip, 1995; Block and Carlip, 1998). The agency of young people, as actual (or potential) producers of fiction, is often disregarded in the marketing, distribution and promotion of young adult fiction by adult authors (see Richards, 2008). An enduring debate about what is meant by 'children's literature' foreshadows this concern and is perhaps most sharply stated first in Jacqueline Rose's (1984) *The Case of Peter Pan or The Impossibility of Children's Fiction* and, many years later, by Jack Zipes (2001) in an essay mysteriously entitled 'Why children's literature does not exist'. Both Rose (1984) and Zipes (2001) point out that 'children's literature' is an adult institution driven by adult activities to which children (and young people) themselves are outsiders.

The more 'youth cultural' concern with how young people actually live their lives and, in that context, how reading might figure in their experience is difficult to sustain in this field. As I have noted above, there is sociological and ethnographic research into young people's reading practices (Sarland, 1991; Cherland, 1994; Blackford, 2004). Certainly, how young people become readers and how they engage (or not) with writing presented as 'young adult literature' is an important focus but to make any effective connection between, for example, a study of Burgess's (2003) novel *Doing It* and the question of what and how teenage boys (and girls) are actually reading (or not) demands research that, on the whole, is relatively scarce. Detailed empirical studies of young people as readers need to be conducted far more widely and consistently than in the past two decades, especially given the substantially new configurations of the media available to most young people (see Moss, 1989, 1993; Sefton-Green, 1993; Buckingham and Sefton-Green, 1994; Livingstone, 2002; Jenkins, 2006; Buckingham and Willett, 2006; Hoechsmann and Low, 2008).

The idea of the 'young adult' is odd, when you pause to think about it. It could seem something of a contradiction if not quite an oxymoron. It belongs to particular kinds of discourse familiar in education and in related sites (library services and publishing) but begins to sound a little stilted if spoken (but it almost never is) in a more commercial context where young people are directly addressed as consumers. It is possible to imagine a teacher addressing a class in secondary school, perhaps even in the final year of primary school, with the intention of instilling or eliciting more 'mature' behaviour – 'You are all young adults now . . .'. But this is not how those intending to attract and sell to young people would address their 'market'. In one way or another, some version of 'teen' or 'teenage' is likely to figure more prominently (see Richards, 2008). This 'interpellation' is one that, it is assumed, young people might more willingly accept. If 'adolescent' appears too pejorative (Lesko, 1996, 2001) and 'teen' too commercial, it is not difficult to see why, in education, 'young adult', or some close equivalent, seems to offer just the 'right' mix of respect and subordination. But outside institutional sites where positioning as a 'pupil', 'student' or even 'youngster' suggest the unequal power relation with adults in authority, to accept being addressed as a 'young adult' might imply that you are content to be put in your place.

In schools, the 'young adult' age-phase might be understood to refer to 11–16 or 13–18, though its upper and lower boundaries drift in actual usage. In more commercial uses, though not in direct address to young people themselves, it is likely to designate either material suitable for distribution to schools or, and these are not always mutually exclusive, texts of interest to 'younger' adults – potentially at least up to thirty-something though sometimes even up to 40 and 50 (Buckingham, 2000; Richards, 2007, 2008). Among the most interesting texts to examine in this field are those with complicated publishing histories, either because they have been repositioned in various ways or because they have been published simultaneously for different audiences or ambiguously float between them (Richards, 2008).

Reading Francesca Lia Block

Francesca Lia Block's career, from 1989 and continuing, is an interesting example of a publishing history marked by boundary confusion (Richards, 2007, 2008; Marshall, 2009). Better known in the United States than in Britain, her reputation mainly grew out of a series of five very short novels begun in her mid-twenties (Block, 1989, 1991, 1992, 1993, 1995, 1998a). Her father was Irving Alexander Block (1910–1986), an artist and Hollywood science fiction writer and special effects specialist (story writer for the 'cult' science fiction film *Forbidden Planet*, 1956). In her account, she began writing 'for herself', after her father's death. She has become well established, and very controversial, as a 'young adult' author without actually identifying herself as such. But this is a significant element in her success because she declines to address young people within the boundaries that schools may wish to preserve. Some of her work may have been taught in schools but much of it is unlikely ever to be accepted as 'classroom material' (Reid and Hutchinson, 1994; National Council of Teachers of English, 1994). I want to emphasize that, in teaching the 'Young Adult Fictions' course, it was always essential to include texts regarded as problematic, disconcerting and troublesome and thus to question how, in particular, English teaching might contribute to quite narrowly conceived ideas of 'appropriateness' in relation to young people (Blume, 1975). Both Block and Burgess offer risky and, to some people, outrageous examples (see Richards, 2008; McDonell, 2002; Haddon, 2003; Stoehr, 2003).

However, one key writer on young adult fiction would almost certainly disagree with, at least, the unsettling value I place on her writing. Roberta Trites (2000) has written a significant and influential critical study of 'young adult' fiction, arguing that it is, in her words, an 'ideological tool' through which adults exercise power over young people. She makes her case on the basis of critical readings of many well-known examples of 'young adult' fiction. Her title, *Disturbing the Universe: Power and Repression in Adolescent Literature*, hints at her approach and indeed her critique of 'adolescent literature' (of which she identifies the Young Adult novel as a subcategory). Wide-ranging and theoretically well informed, her study is essential reading. However, she pursues an argument that the Young Adult novel is a means to exercise power over young people, by adults, and is thus a repressive form of address to its readers. As I have noted above, the category 'Young Adult' certainly implies the 'putting in place' of younger, lesser, persons and I can therefore share her critical wariness of any text proffered in this way. But she also attributes the subordinating implications of the category to the texts that are deemed to belong to it:

> adolescent literature is as often an ideological tool used to curb teenagers' libido as it is some sort of depiction of what adolescents' sexuality actually is . . . Some YA novels seem more preoccupied with influencing how adolescent readers will behave when they are not reading than with describing human sexuality honestly. Such novels tend to be heavy-handed in their moralism and demonstrate relatively clearly the effect of adult authors asserting authority over adolescent readers . . . (Trites, 2000: 85)

She discusses a range of contrasting examples, many introducing sex as trouble, but also some contradicting her primary case that sex is virtually always portrayed as a problem and a source of distress. So, the following summation of this strand in her argument is somewhat monolithic:

> Whether a novelist writing for adolescents depicts sexuality as a matter of pleasure or displeasure . . . Characters who have explored their sexuality usually learn something from the experience, which is why sex is a rite of passage in so many adolescent novels. This tendency to link sexuality with maturation has a certain didactic impulse to it: as long as the adolescent learns something from the experience, then the literary representation of sexuality seems more acceptable within a genre dedicated to teaching adolescents how to become the Other – an adult. Ultimately, the connection between sexuality as a site of power, knowledge, and pleasure proves to be one more occasion for ideological indoctrination in the genre. (Trites, 2000: 102)

It seems that any novel judged to be 'for adolescents' is going to be skewered in this way. But there is a serious contradiction here. For in her concern to show that this 'genre', whatever the variation in particular examples, is a mechanism for 'ideological indoctrination', she constructs an argument that completely ignores how young people themselves might engage with the texts she discusses. Like some who lament the consequences of television for children (for example, Kline, 1993), but who neglect to find out what children themselves might think of what they watch, she builds her account only on textual analysis and on theories that attribute overwhelming power to texts. There is nothing wrong with offering critical analyses of texts, but they should be acknowledged as insufficient (Hodge and Tripp, 1986), one part of the process of understanding how texts are made, circulated and consumed in the 'circuits of cultural production' (Johnson, 1986/1987; Carspecken, 1996: 184–7). Trites (2000) presumes to tell her readers what these novels will do to young people. If she investigated how they may be read by young people themselves she might undo the awkward irony of her position.

Trites (2000) is one of the first critics to write extensively about Francesca Lia Block's novels. She provides some detailed and thoughtful discussions of several of the novels brought together as *Dangerous Angels* (Block, 1998a). However, her conclusions are predictable, attributing a strict legitimation of 'permanent' monogamy to the narrative arc of the series:

> Block cannot escape the trappings of our culture: writing within a post-AIDS culture, she only sanctions sex that occurs between committed, loving couples in

permanent relationships. Block's books carry no more approval for promiscuous sex than do [Judy] Blume's. Weetzie, in fact, gets beat up and date-raped when she does not carefully guard her sexuality in a blaming-the-victim scene early in the novel . . . (Trites, 2000: 93)

Ignoring the hints of impermanence and uncertainty in Block's endings, she expresses satisfaction that 'ideologically trained readers' (her students) will recognize that:

the text [*Weetzie Bat* – Block, 1989] affirms the status quo, for Block does not rest easy until everyone in her novels is paired off, two by two, even if gender and orientation are irrelevant to her dyads. Students trained to read for competing dialogues intuit that in Block's novels, ultimately, nothing all that radical really happens. (Trites, 2000: 149–50)

Given the historical circumstances of the later 1980s and 1990s, especially the continuing right-wing direction of American politics and the pathologization of gays in the immediate aftermath of AIDS, it is not clear which 'status quo' Trites has in mind here. The representation of a long-term gay relationship and of a household assembled as a 'family', but not governed by paternity, certainly do not belong to a status quo that many of Trites' fellow American citizens would acknowledge and endorse (see Hedges, 2007; Richards, 2008). Unfortunately, Trites' approach is 'theoreticist': it privileges theoretical arguments at the expense of attention to historical particularity and empirical research. It encourages 'correct' and singular readings (by 'ideologically trained readers') and is thus indifferent to the positions from which people might actually read and otherwise interpret the texts in question. Significantly, neither 'culture' nor 'Cultural Studies' are listed in the index to her book and no empirically grounded research into reading and readers is acknowledged (see Radway, 1984; Cherland, 1994).

Block has been both condemned and honoured, by Christian fundamentalists on the one hand and the American Library Association on the other (see Richards, 2008). She was given the Margaret A. Edwards lifetime achievement award in 2005. Her work continues to be controversial. In June 2009, it was reported in *The Guardian* (Flood, 2009) that:

In a scene which appears to have been lifted straight out of Ray Bradbury's *Fahrenheit 451*, a group of Christians in Wisconsin has launched a legal claim demanding the right to publicly burn a copy of a book for teenagers which they deem to be 'explicitly vulgar, racial [sic], and anti-Christian'.

The offending book is Francesca Lia Block's *Baby Be-Bop*, a young adult novel in which a boy, struggling with his homosexuality, is beaten up by a homophobic gang. The complaint, which according to the American Library Association also demands $120,000 (£72,000) in compensatory damages for being exposed to the book in a display at West Bend Community Memorial Library, was lodged by four men from the Christian Civil Liberties Union.

For at least some of the residents of West Bend, Wisconsin, their 'status quo' is not 'affirmed' by *Baby Be-Bop* (1995), the concluding novel in the *Dangerous Angels* collection (Block, 1998a). The activities of West Bend Citizens for Safe Libraries may not seem of much wider consequence. But they do illustrate the common strategy of adults seeking to condemn what they themselves do not like on the grounds that it will damage and corrupt those younger than themselves. Moreover, the approach to reading taken by such groups (see also Parents Against Bad Books in Schools, 2010), typically involves the extraction of single words or utterances as emblematic of a text's evil intent. Such clumsy reductionism is easy to challenge but, as Henry Jenkins (2006: 198) has pointed out, these anxieties about the flow of cultural commodities also represent very powerful feelings about a loss of control.

In schools, teachers are faced with many variants of this kind of conflict and need to know how to justify the choices that they may have made. Clearly, the meanings that may be attributed to particular choices across differing regimes of value (Frow, 1995) make this a complex and potentially awkward matter. Block's novels do legitimate gay relationships. Some of her stories, though not those positioned as 'young adult', include explicit and quite detailed descriptions of (hetero)sexual acts (Block, 2000a). It is quite probable that in attempting to defend the inclusion of her writing in the school curriculum, arguments would have to be made in the terms that Trites (2000) uses to criticize its apparent conservatism. The discourse prevailing in such an educational site is one that brings into play notions of learning, progress and the achievement of emotional stability. Block's novels can be read, in that context, in those terms: as showing how young people live through difficult experiences and attain a more settled and perhaps more 'mature' state (Block, 1994, 1996, 1998b, 1999, 2000b, 2001). But this is just one kind of reading, strongly privileged in the school context and likely to contribute to the 'public' rationale for many of the texts classified as 'young adult' (see National Council of Teachers of English, 1994). How young people might construe what they read is unlikely to be confined within the terms of such public discourse;

indeed, they will inevitably interpret what they read from within different regimes of value.

The differences, conflicts and struggles that may arise between different regimes of value may require some complex negotiation, sometimes between what may appear to be irreconcilable positions: if in one regime of value gay sex is a grossly unnatural and sinful activity, then the argument that might be made in favour of acknowledging different sexualities (perhaps by a teacher seeking to justify offering a Block novel to a class of 13- to 14-year-old students) is going to be difficult to pursue (see Carspecken, 1996: 143–4). John Frow's discussion of 'taste' is relevant here and though it offers no way out of relativism, it suggests the further social dimensions of claims to the value of one text rather than another:

> In arguing for a more complex correlation of social position with cultural practice I nevertheless retain Bourdieu's key thesis: that the primary business of culture is distinction, the stratification of tastes in such a way as to construct and reinforce differentiations of social status which correspond, *in historically variable and often highly mediated ways*, to achieved or aspired-to class position. Cultural discrimination involves a constant negotiation of position with the aim of naturalizing one's own set of values, distinguishing them from the values of others, and attempting more or less forcefully to impose one's values on others. It is thus not just a matter of self-definition but also of struggle for social legitimation. (Frow, 1995: 85)

Teachers might be considered as enacting particular social interests, not in any unified or entirely predictable way, but from within the horizon of interests of a professional group and in relation to cultural repertoires (ways of speaking, habits of reading and viewing, for example) not exclusive to but associated with such groups. Within a school, though not experienced as enacting power in a very forceful way, choosing a book such as *Baby Be-Bop* (Block, 1995, 1998a) will seem entirely legitimate within that professional domain. But to an outsider, perhaps a parent who sees homosexuality as deeply offensive, this may appear to be an act of arrogance from a self-interested member of a professional middle class. My own view of this is that an argument has to be made for the interests of, and in consultation with, school students themselves. The classroom, in this argument, is a place where differing, and conflicting, tastes, values and texts can be considered and discussed (see Richards, 2008). But this attempt to secure such a liberal forum for exploration would be unlikely to meet objections from parents who regard their own children as having no right to engage with material and debates beyond the boundaries of their own beliefs. As Carspecken remarks:

> Whether actual agreements can ever be fully established between diverse cultural groups is an empirical question, with as-yet-unanswered implications for a theory of universal human interests. People disagree (almost violently) on this question. (Carspecken, 1996: 143)

Reading Melvin Burgess

If Block is a problem for some Americans, then Burgess is certainly somewhat troublesome even in the more liberal political context of Britain. Unlike Block, he has built a career with writing for quite specific audiences, of children and, later, teenagers. But this has not led him to be more cautious in his choice of material, despite a continuing acknowledgment that schools are an important support for the distribution of books to young people. *Junk* (1996) has been taught in schools and teaching guidance has been published by the London English and Media Centre (Grahame, 1999; see Rosen, 1997). As it deals with heroin addiction and prostitution, it was necessarily defended as intervening to inform young people about drugs. Michael Rosen commented that 'no matter how uncompromising we say that a piece of children's literature is, it always has to be seen to be negotiating with a notion of a "developing" personality on the way to something "more mature"' (Rosen, 1997: 6). Burgess has been involved in making, and responding to, these arguments (Burgess, 2010) in a way that Block, on the whole, has declined to do. He positions himself as addressing a young audience and, despite distancing himself from any explicitly pedagogic role, has mainly framed his writing in terms that secure its place within the discourse of liberal education. The publication of *Doing It* (2003) made this precarious self-positioning extremely difficult to sustain.

The National Association for the Teaching of English published quite a favourable review, but with serious warnings:

> Melvin Burgess' books are controversial and *Doing It* is no exception. Based on the premise that teenagers (some? most? all?) are sexually active, or even hyperactive, it is a full frontal attack on the reader's sensibilities. Some will be appalled by the frankness of the language and the explicitness of the sexual descriptions. Nor will objections be raised only amongst easily shocked conservatives.

> Forget about love, the excitement of new experiences or even the joy of sex, this is a book about teenage lust, a book about boys having sex; and in the process the female characters (with the exception of Deborah, a more fully realised girl) are reduced to servicing the needs of the rampant boys. Parents and teachers will look in vain for role models to set before their charges. This is a book to be handled with care. It is unlikely to be bought as a classroom set and a copy on the classroom library shelf could well be a time bomb. (Clarke, 2004)

Despite the claim I made above, that a classroom can be a kind of liberal forum for exploration, it is unlikely that many teachers would attempt to introduce this novel in such a context. It is important to think about why it would be so difficult, even assuming a classroom located in the upper secondary phase, in Year 10 or 11 (14–15 and 15–16). Reading, and perhaps especially reading novels, has a history strongly anchored in individual privacy (Watt, 1957/1979). The reception of a novel has not been primarily a social act, conducted in the presence of others. Reading a novel is mostly something done alone or, if in the presence of others, at least silently. Of course, radio serializations, film and television dramatizations, audio books, book clubs and authors' public readings transmute and transpose the silent printed text to speech for an audience of multiple others. These offer important additional forms of reception but each variously presumes, invokes or invites a mainly individual engagement with the novel at some point.

To draw in and encourage a class to read a novel, it is sometimes necessary to read it chapter-by-chapter. When I first taught English in a secondary school, I did this with *Black Boy* by Richard Wright (1970) and *The Wizard of Earthsea* by Ursula Le Guin (1993) but found the approach faltering when I tried to read aloud, to 'Sixth Form' students, some short stories from *Fireworks* by Angela Carter (1974). The sexual scenarios in Carter's stories felt disconcerting, read aloud to a group of 17-year-old students. Ian Watt suggests, given 'the novel's concentration on private experience and personal relationships', that 'the most powerful vicarious identification of readers with the feelings of fictional characters that literature had seen [is] produced by exploiting the qualities of print, the most impersonal, objective and public of the media of communication' (Watt, 1957/1979: 233–4). Teaching gets caught up in this paradox. Print, a public medium, is securely legitimated in education and the *public* sharing of what is in print can seem an equally safe and unexceptional practice. But novels are 'designed' to be alone with, to be engaged through often quite sustained, attentive and solitary reading. Some of what novels have been most effective at representing – personal, subjective feelings and thoughts and the subtleties of inter-subjective relations with others, including sexual experience – also seem most appropriate to modes of absorbed, introspective and individual reception. Reading a novel aloud can bring the private into the public, seeming to exhibit before everyone present what many may prefer to encounter alone. The tension between modes of reading (the novel) and modes of classroom reception and participation, there anyway in every attempt to teach novels, can be excruciating when the novel represents sex.

Transposed to a school classroom, the reading (aloud) of a novel is further entangled with the social relations of that site. Relations between students, but also between the student and the teacher, become the context of reception, a context absent when the novel is read alone and, most often, in silence. Where the material taught is explicitly sexual, challenges to the boundaries of self-presentation and self-disclosure most often unacknowledged and routinely maintained, in the negotiation of classroom relationships, between students and between teacher and taught, are inevitable.

Furthermore, to attempt to contain and control the consequences of engaging with sexually explicit texts by reading extracts can misrepresent and even undermine the narrative construction of a novel. As I have noted, some pro-censorship groups do this deliberately, to render the texts they wish to proscribe 'quantifiably' offensive. But, teaching can risk the same outcome. To read *Doing It* entails sustained attention and a commitment to go on reading to the very end. The NATE reviewer (Clarke, 2004) recognizes its value because he has read it. This may seem obvious, but it underlines the risks involved in ignoring the form of the text to be taught. Teaching a TV 'soap' cannot proceed on the basis of viewing a single episode, unless the class is composed entirely of loyal and long-term viewers. The form requires a particular level of commitment, an accumulation of knowledge over some months, even years, of familiarity with the text (Allen, 1983). Reading a novel, though more compact, demands a similar loyalty.

Take the following short quotations from *Doing It*:

> She took everything off, one after another, as if she was unwrapping him, until there he was, stark bollock naked in the middle of the room with an erection on the front of him like a concrete pillar. In some ways, it was uncomfortable standing there like that with your teacher stalking round you, but what came next was so indescribably delicious, he could put up with just about anything for it. She took his erection in one warm hand and gave a long, deep kiss. He could have harpooned a walrus with it. He pulled up her blouse and slid his

hands round to unhook her bra, and then she crouched down and took it in her mouth.

He was one lucky boy. (Burgess, 2003: 20)

Every evening, Ben went to visit. Ali sat in her chair with her head up staring at the wall as if she'd lost her sight. He felt so stitched up. He kept thinking, She's done this on purpose, but it made no difference. On purpose, by accident, under your heels, over your head, because God wanted it or for no reason at all, whatever. She had him just where she wanted him. There was no way out. Just thinking about leaving her made him break out in prickles of guilt. (Burgess, 2003: 287)

Ben and Ali, early and very late in the novel. The first quotation is just the kind of thing that those wishing to proscribe a novel such as this are likely to present as unambiguous evidence of the moral decadence they deplore. But reading the earlier quotation, after reading the second, from more than 260 pages later, suggests the tensions and plays of power in this 'relationship' in ways that, on first reading, are more muted hints. Given the claustrophobia and despair that Ben feels late in the novel, 'He was one lucky boy' becomes a pointed irony. Reading the novel as a whole involves a process of reflection and reappraisal, a turning back and reconsideration of events and their meanings. Anyone's reading will involve a lot more too, depending on the position and life history of the reader. All of this is by no means beyond attention in a classroom setting but is insubstantial without the basis of a full reading of the novel as a whole.

Doing It can be taught. It is possible to teach the debates that took shape around its publication, most strikingly in the furious challenge to it presented by Anne Fine (Fine, 2003) and Burgess's response (Burgess, 2004). Reading just the first chapter or dipping into some of the more graphic sexual descriptions might lend favour to Fine's argument. Reading to the end complicates an assessment of her case. It is worthwhile to look at the covers of various editions and to explore how it is positioned for various potential audiences through the choice of images and the selection of reviewers' comments. It is also important to consider its form more carefully and, especially, to identify its use of comedy, despite the very serious and unsettling themes it pursues. By complete contrast, Ian McEwan's *On Chesil Beach* (2007) is a novel in which premature ejaculation figures as a central event, but construed as bleak tragedy. Blackford cites Henry James in her thoughts on these contrasts between both the forms chosen and the authors making such choices:

'The spreading field, the human scene, is the "choice of subject": the pierced aperture, either broad or balconied or slit-like and low-browed, is the "literary form"; but they are, singly or together, as nothing without the posted presence of the watcher – without, in other words, the consciousness of the artist.' (Cited in Blackford, 2004: 34, from his preface to the New York edition of *The Portrait of a Lady*).

Once again, questions of representation, in this case in relation to the construction of 'authored' fiction are a necessary focus (see Culler, 2000). So why has Burgess chosen the form of a comic novel for this story of three boys and their struggles with sex and its emotional realities?

There are important things to do to situate *Doing It* and to rescue it from the kind of censorious condemnation to which, in common with other titles associated with the 'young adult' category, it has been subjected. But this cannot be a substitute for an individual reader's engagement with the text itself, on terms that he or she determines outside the classroom context. Moreover, it should also be recalled that many of the titles now associated with 'young adult' fiction are no longer written within the constraints of school-based reading and might, as *Doing It* does, appear to deliberately challenge mediation by teachers. In Burgess's case, this ambition does raise other problems, for it contributes to exaggerated claims both to authenticity in representation and to a direct engagement with young people, as if Burgess, at fifty-something is 'forever young' (Richards, 2008). Research into how 'teenage readers' engage, or not, with *Doing It* might question the correspondence between his representations and the cultural specificities of 'their' experience. I would argue that such research ought to be wide-ranging enough to allow discussion of how differently youth may be lived or, as is often necessarily the case, should be acknowledged as limited rather than representative of 'youth-in-general'.

Conclusion

This chapter has outlined some of the issues that now figure prominently in the remaking and proliferation of 'young adult' fiction, once a category of writing closely linked to school-based consumption of fictional texts (for example, Wilson, 1996, 1997, 1998, 1999; Fine, 1996) but increasingly oriented to a wider 'younger adult' market (for example, Meyer, 2005, 2006, 2007, 2008). Print fiction should be examined on the same ground as other media and thus without resorting to ideas of literary value lingering from English literary criticism. To explore 'young adult' fiction should not be a matter of drawing on a canon or of composing a new canon for future decades. However, choices are made by all readers and value placed on some texts rather than others. In this respect it is again necessary to consider the regimes of value from within which such judgements are made and thus to understand 'value' as embedded in social practices. By contrast with the approach taken by Trites (2000), there is a significant need for further ethnographies of young people's reading and thus to bring the study of texts more fully into the cultural study of youth.

Points for reflection

What assumptions about 'masculinity' are made in classifying some texts as 'for boys'?
How could you investigate young people's reading habits?
How can decisions about what to teach be justified and explained?

Popular Music, Youth and Education

Introduction

This chapter proposes an approach to music as embedded in everyday life. It shows how it can be documented and recalled through autobiographical forms of writing. Through case studies from Muslim students it explores, and complicates, some of the generalizations about youth and music that circulate in sociological writing.

By contrast with the last chapter, the focus on music in this one will not be a surprise. Popular music has been strongly associated with 'adolescence' and with being a 'teenager' at least since the 1950s when, arguably, the 'teenage' emerged as a distinct, if transitional, identity (Osgerby, 1998, 2004; Savage, 2007). Though it is probably unwise to assume that popular music is always privileged among the various media that engage teenagers' attention, it does continue to figure quite vividly in the way people live their youth. It can also be a way into recollections of youth for adults supposedly long past such identifications. In this chapter, my main concern is with popular music as it is encountered and adopted in the everyday lives of young people rather than with particular genres of popular music, the music industry or questions of performance.

This chapter, unlike others in this book, draws substantially on Education Studies students rather than, as in Chapters 4 and 5, school students. It offers examples of the kind of autobiographical work encouraged in Education Studies at London Metropolitan University. A background consideration, but an important one, is that of whether and how the school curriculum should make space for similarly autobiographical studies of popular music. In reading this chapter, the form of enquiry – individual case studies – should be considered as potentially transposable to the school context.

There are several, often interrelated, strands of recent research that contribute to this chapter's main concerns. A number of mostly school-based studies of young people's engagement with popular music have been published in the 1990s and since. Some were researched in England, but others come from the United States, Canada and South Africa (McCarthy et al., 1999; Yon, 2000; Dimitriadis, 2001; Dolby, 2001; Perry, 2002; Rampton, 2006). Each examines music in the context of young people's experience in institutional sites removed from both family and more informal leisure settings. There are also interesting case studies of youthful participation in music scenes, but at some distance from educational sites, again from the United States and England but also representing research in Sweden and Germany (Shank, 1994; Thornton, 1995; Fornas et al., 1995; Gaines, 1998; Bennett, 2000; Pini, 2001; Hodkinson, 2002). With their emphasis on youth 'at leisure', these studies mainly focus on young people at the upper end of school age and beyond. The exploration of music in everyday life, some of which includes research with young people, is also an important and growing field (Crafts et al., 1993; du Gay et al., 1997; DeNora, 2000; Bull, 2000; Williams, 2007). In relation to popular music and the school curriculum, a further body of research, mostly conducted in England, has been produced in media education (Buckingham and Sefton-Green, 1994; Buckingham et al., 1995; Richards, 1998b) and, often without much obvious interaction, in music education (Green, 1988, 1997, 2001).

There are some early precedents for the study of youth and popular music. Paul Willis, though best known in Education Studies for *Learning to Labour* (1977), wrote his PhD on two distinct youth cultures, motor-bike boys and hippies, focusing especially on the meanings given to their preferred music, rock 'n' roll on the one hand and psychedelic (hallucinatory) rock on the other. The thesis, *Pop Music and Youth Groups* (1972), became *Profane Culture* (Willis, 1978). Though an enduring example of ethnographic enquiry into youth cultures, this research did not document the lives of those still at school. But in 1972, Simon Frith pursued some research with '14- to 18-year-olds', school students, in Keighley, West Yorkshire. This research was reported, if not in great detail, in *The Sociology of Rock* (Frith, 1978) and in its re-edited successor *Sound Effects* (Frith, 1983). Frith's brief sketch of the school students' lives and of the place of music evokes youth as lived through music. Rejecting the fixity of subcultural approaches, he tends towards an emphasis on ephemeral and shifting engagements with popular music shaped largely by patterns of access to leisure, related somewhat to the town's 'social structure'. Despite retaining an emphasis on class differences, he takes issue with the case for a stronger correspondence between class and young people's choices of popular music reported in *Mass Media and the Secondary School*, a study by Graham Murdock and Guy Phelps (1973). In this respect, and in revising *The Sociology of Rock* for the American market, he was moving towards positions elaborated subsequently in Frith (1987) and Frith (1996).

Frith (1987) writes:

> It is a sociological truism that people's heaviest personal investment in popular music is when they are teenagers and young adults – music then ties into a particular kind of emotional turbulence, when issues of individual identity and social place, the control of public and private feelings, are at a premium. People do use music less, and less intently, as they grow up; the most significant pop songs for all generations (not just for rock generations) are those they heard as adolescents. What this suggests, though, is not just that young people need music, but that 'youth' itself is defined by music . . . This is to reiterate my general point about popular music: youth music is socially important not because it reflects youth experience (authentically or not), but because it defines for us what 'youthfulness' is. I remember concluding, in my original sociological research in the early 1970s, that those young people who, for whatever reasons, took no interest in pop music were not really 'young'. (Frith, 1987: 142–3)

This is a persuasive statement giving substance to the often rather empty abstraction of claims that youth is 'socially constructed'. It certainly reminds me that among those with whom I attended secondary school, the few with no apparent interest in popular music seemed 'older', more like their parents than other young people. But Frith's comment can also be read as a powerfully 'normative' construction of 'youth', disallowing 'youth' lived in ways not defined by 'pop music'. 'Pop music' is now an even more differentiated field than it was in the 1970s and 1980s, to such an extent that 'pop' can be used to designate just one, not necessarily dominant, subcategory. And there are people who would certainly regard themselves as having lived their 'youth' without much, or any, interest in pop music. For example, the opera director David McVicar (born in Glasgow in 1966), interviewed for BBC Radio 4's *Desert Island Discs* (5 October 2008), represented his youth virtually without reference to popular music (see also Richards, 1998b, Chapter 7). He lived his youth through opera. In the context of more distinctively different ethnic, sexual and religious identifications than those acknowledged in Keighley, West Yorkshire in 1972, Frith's claim requires more explicit acknowledgement that it refers to the construction of 'youth' within the range of 'youth culture' as defined by the commercial market in pop music.

In fact, going further with the argument that the social construction of identities always involves something more than what we are (young, black, white, male, female) or where we are socially, Frith has argued that musical scenes are a resource for narratives of identification unavailable within the limits of socially bounded categories such as class, ethnicity, gender and sexuality (see also Alexander, 1996; Hall, 1996b). Such narratives enable people to contradict the positioning force of discourses privileging cultural 'belonging'. Frith comments:

> . . . identity is always already an ideal, what we would like to be, not what we are. And in taking pleasure from black or gay or female music I don't thus identify as black or gay or female (I don't actually experience these sounds as 'black music' or 'gay music' or 'women's voices') but, rather, participate in imagined forms of democracy and desire . . . But if musical identity is, then, always fantastic, ideal-izing not just oneself but also the social world one inhabits, it is, secondly, always also real, enacted in musical activities. (Frith, 1996: 123)

The work of Tia DeNora, though not specifically with youth, complements Frith's in its concern with the production of emotional states in negotiating the routines of day-to-day living. Music is, for those she interviewed:

> . . . a resource for modulating and structuring the parameters of aesthetic agency – feeling, motivation, desire, comportment, action style, energy . . . its rhythms, gestures, harmonies, styles and so on – are used as referents or representations of where they wish to be or go, emotionally, physically, and so on. Respondents make, in other words, articulations between musical works, styles and materials on the one hand and modes of agency on the other, such that music is used, prospectively, to sketch aspired and partially imagined or felt states. (DeNora, 2000: 53)

Student case studies: music, Islam and youth[1]

At London Metropolitan University, some Education Studies students, mainly young women, self-identifying as Muslim, wrote vivid and often complex accounts of their past and current relationship to music. The students, mostly between the ages of 19 and 23, were directed to document their current everyday encounters with music as well as write a more autobiographical piece about their experience of music as teenagers. Framed by readings discussed early in the course from, among others, Frith and DeNora, Muslim students' autobiographical writing suggested some unexpected variations on the core themes they identify.

In particular, there seemed to be a tension between musical experience and devotion to Islam, as if these constituted competing claims on the 'affective self'. Such claims, it seemed, could not be reconciled easily and were rarely, if ever, mutually supportive. As the course was taught in the Autumn and I always began by asking students to keep a diary of their daily encounters with music, Ramadan sometimes presented some interesting challenges. The exclusion of music from the month of Ramadan, observed quite strictly by many students, did not, in fact, stall what I was asking the students to do, and in some respects, it focused discussion more effectively on the issue of the affective power of music. The question thus posed, among others, was that of how these students represent their various religious and musical identifications as coexisting in their experience as teenagers and young adults.

Many of the students entered university with some expectation that their degree would lead to training as a teacher, often for the primary sector. Such an aspiration might be characterized as 'lower middle-class', given that teaching, and especially teaching in primary schools, does not have the high professional status accorded careers in law or medicine, for example. The class position of the families from which these students came was, to simplify, working class and lower middle class. It was suggested to me, by Kareema, an Anglo-Moroccan student, that teaching appears to be a fairly 'safe' and 'respectable' occupation for young Muslim women, especially in primary schools, typically staffed largely by women.

Many Muslim students' families are from Bangladesh or Pakistan. The broader context of their experience includes, particularly in London in the months following the bombings on 7 July 2005, a heightened sense of 'othering', a positioning as 'different' to such a degree that they might be represented as 'incomprehensible' – though as young women, rather than young men, not 'dangerous' (Back, 2007: 144–9; Maira, 2009). Writing in 2003, Farzana Shain, in a study of Asian schoolgirls, draws attention to the prevailing discourses positioning, in particular, Muslims from Pakistani and Bangladeshi backgrounds:

> The cultural pathology discourse, despite much criticism, remains a powerful and central reference point in popular conceptions of Asian family life and femininity in the UK. This discourse positions Asian girls as the victims of oppressive cultures in which men dominate women. Asian girls are characterised as caught between the two worlds of home, where they are restricted, and school, where they experience freedom. Public discussions in the aftermath of inner-city disturbances of 2001 and the events of September 11, 2001 have further reinforced characteri- sations of the poorest Asian communities, the Pakistani and Bangladeshi Muslims, as isolationist and refusing to integrate. These communities have been accused of holding on to backward and barbarous practices that prevent girls from partaking in mainstream activities and encourage boys to take up dangerous and fanatical positions. (Shain, 2003: 125)

In fact, from 2002 onwards, there was a very marked increase in the numbers of young Muslim women participating in the Education Studies programme at London Metropolitan University. In this respect, they were by no means 'isolated', though it may be that the university was the main site for contact with non-Muslims. Whatever their circumstances, however, Islam often appears to be assigned an increasing importance as they move into their twenties.

One former student, Kareema, agreed to be interviewed. In the course of the interview, she explicitly positioned herself as not 'normal', contrasting her own experience and her conduct with both that of friends and that of the self-identified Muslim students she had encountered at the university. She commented:

> . . . you're not going to get them to come and do an interview . . . they're not going to come and see you by themselves . . . if they don't even listen to music Chris, then of course they're going to observe the rule that says you're not allowed to sit by yourself with a man unless accompanied by a chaperone and the chaperone has to be either your brother or your dad so I doubt they'd be able to get their brother or their dad to come down here . . . which is why they say email questions . . .

Though presenting herself as untypical, and emphasizing her difference from the other respondents discussed here, she is explicit about tensions that may well figure in my conduct of this enquiry as a whole. At one point, for example, when I asked about the position of women in Islam, she asked, if with amused tolerance: 'Why are you laughing? Are you trying to diss my religion?' Responding to questions which, perhaps, implicitly position her as a victim, she challenges the implication that Islamic belief is a kind of cultural pathology (Shain, 2003, 2010). She positions me as an atheist. This disjunction between Kareema and myself is significant:

> . . . all Muslims strive to become better Muslims . . . I don't think you would understand it because you're not Muslim. You can't comprehend it just like you can't comprehend belief in God because you don't believe in God . . . there are a lot of things you won't understand.

She positions me as an outsider to her beliefs and construes non-belief as disqualifying me from 'understanding'.

In his discussion of miracles in a Sufi order, the anthropologist Michael Gilsenan makes this comment:

> Those who are regarded as living their lives entirely in the realm of appearances (the zahir) will not, by definition, see the miracle even if it happens under their noses (the anthropologist originally failed to do so, but his Muslim friends understood his blindness and sought to cure it). Thus, those who challenge the miracle that a particular individual or group accepts . . . show by the very fact of their doubt that they are incapable of seeing the inner and 'true' world. Their attempt to discredit it is thus taken as triumphant demonstration of their own failure, and they are themselves discredited! [. . .] Every denial by the outsider is a proof to the insider that it is really he, helpless or impoverished or disprivileged, though he may be, who 'knows' and experiences the truth. (Gilsenan, 1982: 79–80)

So, in these exchanges, between myself, as her former teacher, and Kareema as, variously, a respondent, informant, collaborator, there is always a sense in which I am *both* ignorant and in a position of some authority – and able therefore to be ignorant without embarrassment. Of course, despite this, I have also tried to claim that I can represent their relationship, as Muslims, to music. But there is no doubt that the 'disjunction' persists, limits the responses made to my enquiries and constitutes a significant challenge to my claim to 'knowledge'.

In most of the students' written narratives, there was evidence of involvement with popular music, especially at school, but this was also represented as largely belonging to a past from which they significantly distanced themselves.

Their emphasis is on a gradual 'focusing' within Islamic precepts. Somewhat unusually, Helena (born 1985) presents an account that includes a more rapid process of strengthening religious identification. Though recalling being a teenager:

> . . . in my teenage years I would argue with my mum over small things. I would try to avoid the problem by listening to slow songs as loud as possible to escape from my tensions . . . it would calm me down slowly but on the other hand certain songs taught me to stand up against my mum showing it is my life and let me live it how I want to.

she relegates this to a past predating a kind of epiphany:

> . . . I now believe that music is the whispers of the Satan, calling me to his path and the path of wrongdoers . . . This is due to my spiritual journey to hajj in Saudi Arabia, which I undertook [for] two weeks without music. It was a miraculous feeling.

Her opening description of conflict with her mother, and the musical means to 'deal with' her feelings, is reminiscent of the accounts of emotional self-management presented by DeNora (2000). The emphatic shift to the 'miraculous' experience of the hajj, a journey without music, suggests that music is, in her early twenties, to be abandoned. But this is not entirely sustained. 'Nasheeds' are identified as a form of Islamic popular music, to which she can listen without compromising her religious self-identification:

> After understanding how music [is] defined in Islam, I begun to listen to nasheeds (Islamic song) that has become recognizable and popular in the Muslim community . . .

Another student, Mamoona, also born in 1985, offers a comparable account. She lived in Pakistan from the age of six and came back to Britain in her later teens. In Pakistan, she suggests that, especially for girls, music was subject to some disapproval from male adults in the family:

> My cousin would ask me to sing . . . once when we were sitting in the car, which was being driven by an uncle when I started singing, I could hear my uncle's eyes getting angry with me. This act confirmed that singing was a bad thing to do. Growing older I developed a secret singing mind where I sang but it was to stay in my head . . .

Knowing that music was not a good thing, but growing into my teenage years, I started to keep a careful ear out for music being played outside our house. At home I had never put a cassette on, thinking I might damage the cassette player and dad would know we have been listening to music . . .

At the age of 19 and since, she notes, like Helena, a significant shift:

These [Islamic] teachings have stopped me from listening to Indian Bollywood music and limiting myself to a cappella's in local mosques

. . . being aware of the latest music use[d] to make me feel confident to socialise and make friends, [now I experience] music as noisy, irritating, and . . . a cause of headaches.

There is a strengthening and narrowing of the frame within which music is experienced as acceptable. She goes on to note the existence of a variety of Muslim-orientated hip hop and, provided the music can be reconciled with her religious project, she expresses some enthusiasm for it (see Muslim Hip Hop, 2010). Her preference for such music is represented *not* as acquiescence in her male relatives' earlier proscriptions, but as a consequence of her progress in understanding Islam. Indeed, all the students represent these choices as their own, placing varying degrees of emphasis on their autonomy in relation to parents and other adult figures.

A third example comes from Naima, a Punjabi speaker, born in 1986. These are brief extracts from a lengthy account:

The majority of the music and songs I liked and listened to when I was 11 to 14 were those that the television programme *Top of the Pops (TOTP)* played and what the radio station *Kiss 100* played. In other words I listened to pop music as well as garage, R'n'B and Hip Hop. I liked boy and girl bands such as Boy Zone and the Spice Girls . . . All of the girls in my school also listened to these songs, so I did not feel ashamed or embarrassed to be listening to those songs, even though I am now.

I can remember when five girls in my class each named themselves after a spice girl. One became known as 'sport spice' another as 'baby spice' and so on. None of these girls actually resembled the spice girl they were naming themselves after. For example, 'Baby Spice' was a dark haired Asian girl, instead of having fair skin and blonde hair.

. . . at my cousin's house . . . I heard bhangra music for the first time on an Asian music channel. I would spend most of my time there listening to Bhangra and R'n'B songs. One day, when my cousin was dropping me home, she played a song that I liked as soon as I heard it and still like it to this day. The song was called '*Nari Nari*' ('It Burns, It Burns' – as in the heart burning with passion) and it was sung in Arabic with a bit of Hindi. It was from here that my love for Arabic (and bhangra) music began and it continued when I started college.

In February 2003, there was an Eid party in college, where only bhangra songs were played. Almost everyone was dancing to the music being played, and were dressed up in their best Asian outfits in order to show off their Asian identity. I did not particularly enjoy this party as I felt quite uncomfortable for some reason and did not join in with the dancing . . . Maybe it was here that I began to let go of part of my Asian identity – in terms of music choice at least.

. . . at college I was introduced to a new kind of music . . . one I knew nothing about before. I was introduced to what was called 'Islamic Hip Hop' by my friend. The artists were Native Deen and they sung for a project aimed at promoting Islamic awareness which was called MYNA [Muslim Youth of North America] Raps . . .

Reflecting further on the growing centrality of Islam in her life she comments:

Islamic songs can be contrasted against music played at clubs and raves because Islamic songs make Muslim youth realise who they are, whilst club music . . . can make you forget who you are.

. . . I mentioned an Eid party where everyone was dancing and I did not join in. This was because I felt I would not be true to myself as a Muslim if I did dance as dancing is not encouraged in mixed gender environments . . . people . . . were dancing rather suggestively at the party . . . it was as if they were 'letting go' of their Muslim identity . . . Islamic songs are about bringing people closer to who they are, raving is a way to let go and switch off.

Her 'life project' is defined both in terms of a degree of autonomous self-identification and, through Islam, a separation and distancing from many aspects of the cultural worlds in which she has grown up. Islam becomes the primary frame within which a sense of self-identity is constructed and activities lying outside that frame are seen as, increasingly, putting that self at risk. Though music as such is repeatedly identified as a somewhat dubious medium, where there is religious content, or instrumentation is largely eliminated, it can serve a liminal function, enabling progress in a direction consistent with sustaining an Islamic self.

The importance of nasheeds is that, though they are emotive, they are supposedly purely religious in their content. As devotional songs, they keep the self within the appropriate emotional frame. In terms of the students' narratives, their movement is from relative variety in musical experience 'inwards' to a more singular self-location within Muslim belief.

It might also be argued that such a commitment to religious duty is also an assertion of some autonomy from the requirements of the family. In her research in the 1990s, Claire Dwyer argues that, among the resources drawn into young Muslim women's negotiations of their parents' authority, Islam has been of particular importance. She points to the evidence of agency, rather than subordination, in identifications with Islam:

> . . . 'new' Muslim identities were characterised by a search for 'orthodox' Islam. This version of Islam was often counterposed to views of Islam transmitted by parents which were rejected as being more about 'Pakistani culture' than religion. Adherents to a 'new' Muslim identity sought authority through a close reading of the Koran, rejecting the oral teachings of parents or the authority of Pakistani clerics (maulvis). An important emphasis here was the rejection by the young women of parental prohibitions about 'appropriate' feminine behaviour or attire, which were regarded as being the result of cultural prejudices rather than having any rooting in orthodox religious teaching. (Dwyer, 1999: 146)

The distinction between Islam and particular Muslim cultures does figure in these students' accounts. If the authority of Islam can be elevated above that of their parents, this might also suggest why nasheeds, as 'Islamic' music seemingly somewhat apart from the music encountered in parental cultures, offer a position from which to continue to assert a degree of legitimate autonomy.

Kareema (born 1979), quoted earlier, offers a self-account echoing, but also complicating, some of Dwyer's observations. For her, everyday life is consistently defined by both Islam and an enthusiasm for music. Kareema's mother is white, middle class and English but converted to Islam early in the 1980s. Her father is Moroccan, a telecommunications engineer. Kareema lived in Saudi Arabia, briefly, in early childhood and, for approximately two years, in a mountainous region in the north of Morocco. From the age of six (1985), she attended schools in London and came to university in her mid-twenties. She strongly and consistently positions herself as Muslim:

> I've always been a Muslim. There's never been a doubt . . . and although I may have gone out clubbing . . . drinking and although there was a point in my life when I was taking drugs, there was always something I was holding on to, there was always 'I am a Muslim' and especially when I was younger and didn't have kids I would go to the mosque . . . I mean it's such a contradiction I know but I had

to hold on to that for some kind of sanity . . . you know there was never a doubt in my mind that I was a Muslim.

I know that I can be better at many things in my life, one of them being a better Muslim and I do strive. Some things, like for example I need to give up cigarettes, I know that it's forbidden for me to be smoking and I will do it and I know I need to wear a headscarf and start dressing more modestly. I know that's something in my religion I have to do and I will eventually one day do it but for now I don't want to do that . . . it's like listening to music, I can't see myself cutting that out of my life 'cause as soon as I wake up in the morning the stereo goes on and at two in the morning, that's the last thing that goes off, so as soon as I get in my car, again, it's the CD track that I want to listen to . . . so I know where I need to be and I know how to get there . . . and I will get there one day but for the time being, I like listening to music, I like smoking, I like having my hair [out].

The construction of time in her account is spatial: the present, now, is 'here', the future is 'there'. Through this metaphor, time is lived as a journey from one 'place' to another (Lakoff and Johnson, 1980). Life as a journey is also embedded within a larger, and familiar, topography: at the end of life, we 'go to' either heaven or hell. Like others, she orientates herself to a 'hereafter'. As Kareema comments:

Well it's about when you die, wanting to go to heaven, so you need to get rid of all the crap in your life and become a good person . . .

The structure of the belief evident in Kareema's account is comparable to that evident in the written autobiographies I have already discussed. However, unlike those students in their early twenties, still close to their teenage years and to school, Kareema is married, a mother of three children, and has no need to distance herself from 'youth' quite so sharply. So though phases of time are constructed topographically, there is more continuity, a greater persistence, in the engagement with popular music. Living, rather than transitions from one age phase to another, appears as a liminal phase, 'where she is', and death is the boundary at which, if not achieved before, music must be relinquished.

A little earlier in the interview, Kareema recalls listening to Grave Diggazs, Cypress Hill, The Pharcyde and, mainly through friends, some R&B such as Mary J. Blige and Jodeci when she was at secondary school in the 1990s. She follows these recollections with an apparently non-negotiable statement:

it's not good to listen to it [music] full stop . . . at any time . . . that's what I believe . . . it's not good to listen to music, it alters your state of mind, it changes your mood.

And later, commenting on Sami Yusuf (an enormously popular 'mainstream' singer) she adds:

> Well I don't really buy into Sami's music 100% anyway, well occasionally some of his music is good . . . but to me he doesn't represent Islam because I know that music is forbidden . . . don't try to bring me music on an Islamic level because for me that makes no sense . . .
>
> You just do in your life what you want to do and the end of it all you'll either get punished for it or rewarded . . . that's as simple and clear cut as it is. I know music in Islam is forbidden . . . that to me is the be all and end all. I can appreciate though that I would rather my kids listen to Sami Yusuf than to bloody 50 Cent without a doubt. Sami Yusuf is doing positive things and he is singing about God and he is trying to make people remember God . . . and trying to give young people a different type of music to listen to than the bitch pimp ho party type of music.

Kareema ran away from home at 16 and 17, largely because, in her account, by marked contrast with her brother, she was so persistently expected to carry out domestic work and observe restrictive rules. Elsewhere in the interview, she details, at some length, her own criticisms of the subordination of women, though she also attributes this primarily to particular forms of Moroccan working-class culture, not to Islam (Dwyer, 1999). Towards the end of her description of 'running away', she makes some quite extensive comment on her participation in raving:

> It was for about a year and half I was raving hardcore . . . and then I met my husband who was my husband to be but throughout those years although even my husband misunderstood me, he didn't get me, a lot of people didn't because yes I'd be sitting there in my short miniskirt drinking and smoking and stuff and flirting and kissing a lot of people . . . I was still a virgin until I met my husband . . . Yes contradictions I know . . . Well I think when you have kids that just gets put to the backburner anyway . . . I think I raved so much in those years that I think a logic takes over and you kind of think I'm paying £20 to go into a sweaty place where it stinks – to what? To go and dance, I can go and dance in my house and you know when I go to Amsterdam I'll be going out every now and again [So you're going raving in Amsterdam?] Hell yes!
>
> . . . but I don't cuss and I don't drink anymore, so it's different because if you don't drink and you don't take drugs and you go back you kind of sit there and think right what exactly am I doing here? Like I did actually go to Ministry of Sound, I think it was last July, with my husband, for my friend's birthday, yeah and it was all nice 'cause I was with him but if I wasn't with him I think it would've been shit

> because men are a bit more lecherous now because I think women are easier . . .
> I don't know what it is but I'm not into being touched [laughs] by random people
> in clubs, I don't like that you know, what I mean, some women get off on it, not
> me, don't touch me 'cause I'm going to have to fight . . .

Raving is both vehemently endorsed in this account and somewhat disowned as entailing subjection to male attention at odds with who she wishes to be and what she wants. The full pleasure of participation is compromised by the need for male protection (her husband), her abandonment of drink and drugs and the increased risk of violence she attributes to such public spaces. The pleasure remains in potential (Hell yes!), but it also belongs to another 'place', 'back in the day'.

To some extent, her distancing from past involvement in rave can be construed as achieved through the more determined assertion of Muslim rules of conduct, and in this respect, her religious beliefs are a resource for her refusal of 'random' male objectification as just another female body available for transient pleasure. But the negotiation of public space is also more dependent on male power – the presence of her husband saves a trip to Ministry of Sound from being 'shit'. And the domestic, familial, context is invoked as much more strongly framing her present life:

> I'm one person, I don't split myself up and categorize myself under different
> headings. I am me. For me I'm a woman, I'm a mother, I'm a Muslim, I'm a wife,
> I'm a daughter, I'm all these things. I'm into hip hop you know, I like smoking, I'm
> all these things under one umbrella, I'm me, I don't pretend to be this you know
> I can't do this whole pigeon-holing myself, I don't do that because I am a contra-
> diction you know I love listening to my hip hop and yet I won't let my kids listen
> to it you know and for my husband he finds it embarrassing . . . one time he bor-
> rowed my car, he was getting his car done, and he was in there with his friend and
> he turned the engine on and all he heard was 'motherfucker . . .' and it was
> Immortal Technique and he got so embarrassed 'cause his friend knew it was my
> car . . . yeah hardcore hip hop, you know the baby seat in the back . . . I don't
> listen to that when I'm in the car with the kids but when I'm by myself I blast it, I
> listen to it really loud and I like it. . . .

In this anecdote, she both identifies herself very clearly through her familial position and pursues her self-construction as not 'normal', as a contradiction. In this case, her taste in music sounds out unexpectedly in a place with which she is identified (her car) but in male company effectively making her (private) place known – with uncomfortable implications for the masculine status and authority of her husband. The more anonymous 'blast' of hardcore hip hop, driving around alone, is less problematic because it does not implicate the masculine identity of her husband. The juxtaposition of the 'baby seat' and the language of hip hop, 'motherfucker', suggests a continuing refusal to represent herself as fully or exclusively positioned by discourses privileging maternal responsibility and obedience to male authority (an issue evident in her earlier account of conflict with her father). In this respect, again, she is locating herself in an extended liminal state, acknowledging a point at which this involvement with music and its meanings will end but 'meanwhile' resolutely continuing with it in combination with being a wife, mother and committed Muslim. Moreover, her choice of hip hop (Immortal Technique, in particular), rather than pop or dance music, might also imply a distancing from positioning in the heterosexualized matrix she identifies with dance scenes where men feel entitled to touch women they do not know.

Soon after making these comments, she further defines herself by invoking the contrasting futures of some of her friends:

> . . . my friends who get married and settle down start wearing hijab immediately, stop listening to music, cut themselves off from nearly all of their friends who are Kafer [sinful] . . . and when I go 'round to their houses and their husbands see me with the piercings and I don't cover my hair and I'll wear funky clothes or bright colours and that sort of pisses me and I cuss them as well . . . [. . .] where does it say in the Quoran you must wear black all the time, it doesn't.

Here, once again, Kareema positions herself as much closer to the authentic core of Islam than those who concentrate so much on their outward appearance, following what she dismisses as a 'fashion trend' (see Sandikci and Ger, 2005). But in this, and in her sustained movement between seemingly contradictory positions, she is also refusing the authority of others to fix her in place or to devalue her as contradictory, inauthentic or improper.

If, in Islam, music is forbidden, how do these respondents reconcile their religious belief with their experience, as teenagers and young adults, of music? As I have suggested, one tentative answer is that music is put in its place. By this, I mean that these respondents construct their experience through distinctions between visible, physical places (mosque, family home, school, college, tube, street, and car) where, in accord with constructions of 'public' and 'private', secular and sacred, male and female, music belongs, is tolerated or is excluded. Between these places, at their thresholds, music is subject to (self) monitoring. More obviously, metaphorical places are also significant.

In particular, a metaphorical topography of time – the lived time of youth, of the present, of the future and the time of death – is apparent in the respondents' self-accounts. It is also between these 'places-in-time' that imaginary thresholds, liminal boundaries or phases, frame how, as Muslims, to move from one 'place' to another. Music is variously positioned as confined (for example, to a past place – adolescence/school), as a facilitator or catalyst (nasheeds) and as extending through life-as-liminal-phase (Kareema's 'investment' in hip hop). This complicates Frith's argument that 'the most significant pop songs for all generations (not just for rock generations) are those they heard as adolescents' (Frith, 1987). Whatever might be considered a 'pop song', there are, among these students (and those cited in Richards, 2008), those who appear to reject all that they heard as teenagers and those who very strongly identify with music heard somewhat later than 'adolescence'. As young women, the students' negotiations of music and of religion are also framed by their responses to positioning by heterosexualizing and consumerist discourses, defining them as they move through their teenage years and into early adulthood as sexual beings. Rather than equating intensified interest in Islam with subjection to the authority of a patriarchal religion, it may be that such interests are indicative of their unwillingness to be objectified. Islam, including 'Islamic music', appears in this analysis as offering positions from which young women can contest the authority of their parents and perhaps especially their fathers. It also allows them to contest, or somewhat refuse, positioning by me as respondents to a research inquiry. Indeed, it is worth ending this account with a reflection from Gleeson and Frith (2004) on their research encounters with young women:

> It did not occur to us that our participants might choose not to be understood and that ambiguity might be essential to their complex presentations of self and identity. We have positioned young women as knowable, but they may choose not to be known. (Gleeson and Frith, 2004: 111)

Conclusion

In the introduction to this chapter, I suggested a 'background' concern with the place of popular music in the school curriculum. Obviously, this has been left implicit throughout. But, in giving some detail of particular students' responses to the teaching of a course on popular music, I have intended to show how their experience of music is embedded in the cultural complexity of the social worlds in which they live. Together with the account of students' autobiographical reflections on music in Richards (2008), I intend this chapter to inform a particular kind of investigation of musical experience anchored in autobiographical writing and other forms of self-documentation. This approach to popular music is alert to change and complexity across the various sites of people's lives, including in particular the family, education and peer friendships. Similar enquiries might well be possible and worthwhile in schools too, especially in English, in Media Studies and in Music. Perhaps the most important difference, however, is that in secondary schools students are positioned in, rather than beyond, 'adolescence' and, unlike the students discussed in this chapter, may be less able, and less interested, in 'looking back'. Nevertheless, documenting the present, through diaries and blogs for example, is a viable and potentially rewarding approach.

Points for reflection

Try keeping a diary or comparable document of the place of music in your everyday life.

How and why is music important in your everyday life?

To what extent can you relate your own experience of music to debates about 'identity' and 'identification'?

Futures: Youth, Politics and Citizenship 9

Introduction

This chapter discusses the supposedly apolitical 'youth' of the early twenty-first century and suggests some of the main lines for further enquiry and debate in youth cultural studies.

As the previous chapter on music suggested, there is considerable complexity in the way that 'popular culture' is lived. Modest forms of enquiry, including the autobiographical, life-historical and tentatively ethnographic approaches drawn on in previous chapters, have an important place in Education Studies. They enable students to investigate their own experience of youth, popular culture and education. Such enquiries do produce important and sometimes surprising data; students are able to produce accounts of what, for lecturers, would otherwise remain largely unknown, glimpsed fleetingly and allowed little serious attention. But the work of thinking about 'lived experience' in ways informed by wider social and cultural theory is always difficult to pursue and, perhaps too often, there is a tendency to settle for the more personal, seemingly more 'concrete' document. But such documents do not, unfortunately, speak for themselves. If Education Studies is to provide an adequate framework for thinking about 'lived experience', it needs to challenge, politically and theoretically, the terms in which such experience is represented (Goodson and Sikes, 2001). However interesting, emotive, and particular, any 'experience' may be, questions need to be posed and pursued and analyses offered. The 'authenticity' of experience, perhaps implicit in some of the autobiographical material I have cited, should not be allowed to displace critique. This chapter's brevity entails a sharp focus on some of the questions that need to be asked and which should be a matter for further work and debate.

Youth and politics

Young people are often represented as uninterested in politics and in the responsibilities of being active citizens in a democracy. David Buckingham examined this issue in his study of news media addressing young people (Buckingham, 2000b). In an incisive concluding chapter, he comments that:

> . . . young people's alienation from the domain of politics should not be inter-preted merely as a form of apathy or ignorance. On the contrary, I would see it as a result of their positive exclusion from that domain – in effect, as a response to *disenfranchisement* . . . young people are not defined in our society as political subjects, let alone as political agents. Even in areas of social life that affect and concern them to a much greater extent than adults – most notably education – political debate is conducted almost entirely 'over their heads'. (Buckingham, 2000b: 218–19)

This opens up an important alternative to blaming young people for their own lack of power. Buckingham's argument is that both the media and education have a responsibility for informing and supporting young people in becoming active participants in a broadly defined democratic politics. What does youthful participation in politics look like? Cultural Studies in the 1970s answered this with accounts of resistance in school, on the streets and in deciding what to wear. Finding a politics in the everyday, or spectacular, cultures of the young was one insistent theme through that decade. Such efforts to read the 'cultural' as political do survive. And there are more conventionally visible forms of youth participation in politics – in anti-war demonstrations and in protests against environmental damage. But Buckingham argues, primarily, not that a politics is already there to be recognized but that it must be developed:

> The . . . challenge for teachers, as for news journalists, is to find ways of establishing the *relevance* of politics and of *connecting* the 'micro-politics' of personal experience with the 'macro-politics' of the public sphere. (Buckingham, 2000b: 221)

Looking back to the previous chapter, it might well be asked how the accounts of personal experience cited there could be the basis for furthering a political self-understanding. Music and religion and gender and age intersect in the way the students represent their experience of becoming adult. How they complicate notions of 'Muslim' identity is a political matter and might well be regarded as worthwhile even within the boundaries of a written assignment or an interview. But such statements could also be translated into other, more public, forms, thus encouraging 'young people's *critical participation* as cultural producers in their own right' (Buckingham, 2000b: 222). Of course, these students have every reason to be close to political concerns in their self-descriptions. As young Muslim women in London in the first decade of the twenty-first century, perhaps they could hardly be otherwise. Jonathan Freedland, writing in *The Guardian* (18th October 2006), commented:

> Right now, we're getting it badly wrong – bombarding Muslims with pressure and prejudice, laying one social problem after another at their door. I try to imagine how I would feel if this rainstorm of headlines substituted the word 'Jew' for 'Muslim': Jews creating apartheid. Jews whose strange customs and costume should be banned. I wouldn't just feel frightened. I would be looking for my passport. (Freedland, 2006; see also Back, 2007: 117–49)

What might other youth, less visibly political in the British media, make of the invitation to connect their personal experience with the politics of the public sphere? It is not within the scope of this book to answer that question (see Wells, 2009). But it is worth noting a further dimension to the disenfranchisement to which Buckingham refers. The notion of 'cool', and of what is 'uncool', is of some importance here. 'Cool' is in wide and frequent use. It has quite a long and complicated history (Danesi, 1994; Frank, 1997; Pountain and Robins, 2000; Kenway and Bullen, 2001; Skeggs, 2004; Richards, 2008). Pountain and Robins (see Robins and Cohen, 1978) observe that:

> Having conquered popular culture, the final step must be for Cool to invade politics. Following the collapse of the ideologies of the left – from Soviet communism and

Trotskyism, through new left Marxism to democratic socialism – a whole generation of young people in the UK finds great difficulty engaging in politics because current politics contains nothing to engage them. (Pountain and Robins, 2000: 170)

Writing from the earlier years of the 1997–2010 (New) Labour government, they are not at all convinced that young people will be 'recaptured' to political enthusiasm. The 'cool attitude', which Pountain and Robins both admire and regret, is a part of the problem:

There is . . . a . . . serious problem for politicians who attempt to harness the energy of UK youth culture under the banner of Cool. The main planks of the New Labour project are to restore our disintegrating sense of community (by shoring up the traditional family and eliminating drug abuse), to halt the rise of crime and to improve the performance of our education system. But Cool stands for almost exactly the opposite values: it is intrinsically anti-family, pro-drug, anti-authority and admires criminality (it is more than coincidence that criminals say 'he's cool' to indicate that someone is one of them). What's more, ironic detachment is a poor adhesive for any society as well as being extremely difficult to harness to any sort of collective endeavour. The plain fact is that the Cool attitude is an obstacle to several of the more important goals of New Labour's programme: the promotion of work, school and family, and the reduction of violent crime and drug abuse. (Pountain and Robins, 2000: 174)

There are weaknesses in their analysis of the concept of cool but, tentatively, and in conjunction with Buckingham's more rigorous and more empirically informed account, it is worth considering to what extent 'ironic detachment' figures in the way that many young people (dis)engage from the political domain (from the same period, see Ball et al., 2000). It is not only New Labour that has no doubt suffered from a lack of youth support. Other political groups may well have similarly small constituencies among the young. But it is also evident, and has been throughout the 1990s and since, that the political motivations of Cultural Studies, which was not supposed to be *just* another university department or *just* another wall of packed shelves in the university bookshop, have not been easy to sustain in practice. However, one central point of this book is that where Cultural Studies can connect with and inform more directly both Education Studies and practice in schools, its political rationale is more likely to revive and become more a part of the way that young people think about their lives. In this respect, the cultural study of youth and education should challenge the political marginalization of young people.

Youth and feminism

If politics in the relatively general sense discussed so far appear to exclude young people, a further distancing from political activity might be traced through the 'generational' decline of feminist politics among young people (see Modleski, 1991; Lumby, 1997; Whelehan, 2001; Harris, 2004a, 2004b). Some of the difficulties of sustaining and reconstructing feminist political initiatives dating from the 1960s and 1970s have been examined by Angela McRobbie who, as I noted in Chapter 1, has pursued a career in both feminism and youth cultural studies. This challenge to the depoliticization of gender and sexuality comes from *Interrogating Post-Feminism*:

> . . . the new female subject is, despite her freedom, called upon to be silent, to withhold critique in order to count as a modern, sophisticated girl. Indeed, this withholding of critique is a condition of her freedom. There is quietude and complicity in the manners of generationally specific options of cool and, more precisely, an uncritical relation to dominant, commercially produced, sexual representations that actively invoke hostility to assumed feminist positions from the past in order to endorse a new regime of sexual meanings based on female consent, equality, participation, and pleasure, free of politics. (McRobbie, 2007: 34)

McRobbie, like Pountain and Robins (2000), pinpoints politics, in this case for young women, as 'uncool'. What counts as 'cool' might, sometimes, seem surprising. In a BBC TV investigation of the making and distribution of pornography, *Hardcore Profits* (Samuels, 2009), 'Nikki Jayne', a young woman from Lancashire, pursuing a career as a porn star in Los Angeles, interviewed overlooking Muscle Beach (Santa Monica), tells the presenter Tim Samuels: 'I'm not totally dumb, I know that us porn girls are just guinea pigs . . .'. Later, facing two Christians seeking to challenge the porn industry, she responds to their questions about her future, positioning her within a traditional heterosexual life course: 'I'll just be the coolest mum on earth'. The logic of her position is that of the individual, not naïve but knowing, 'self-possessed' and though not in control, aspiring to be so, on the 'other side of the camera' (see Levy, 2005; Hall and Bishop, 2007; Attwood, 2009).

A wide-ranging discussion of 'new femininities' is developed further in McRobbie (2009). In relation to New Labour, she suggests that the extended educational participation of girls, especially in higher education, has provided the government with a basis for claiming the success of its policies. Feminism is seen as 'fading away on the basis of its work being done, substantial degrees of equality having been won, and enduring inequities . . . now attended to by mainstream governmental processes' (McRobbie, 2009: 74). In education, 'feminist pedagogy is seen to be a thing of the past, frozen in educational history as marking out a moment of outmoded radicalism' (McRobbie, 2009: 76). The figure of the educationally successful, 'working girl' becomes a kind of proof that young women can now 'wave goodbye' to feminism's values 'in favour of pursuing . . . personal desires' (McRobbie, 2009: 78; see also Rose, 1989/1999: 230). Turning to popular culture, McRobbie also discusses 'phallic girls', who like the porn star quoted above, appear to 'overturn the old double standard and emulate the assertive and hedonistic styles of sexuality associated with young men' (McRobbie, 2009: 84). She adds:

> The phallic girl is epitomized in the so-called glamour model, who earns most of her money posing naked for the soft-porn pages of the press and magazines and who, if successful, will also launch herself as a brand, lending her name and image to various products, usually ranges of underwear, make up, perfume or other fashion items. (McRobbie, 2009: 84)

Across both education and the popular domain, individualization is a key theme here and situates McRobbie's argument within a broader analysis of the decline in social and political consciousness (Frow, 1995: 80; Ball et al., 2000).

Education Studies has a responsibility to counter such asocial forms of self-understanding through informed reflection on educational experience both in students' schooling and in their more immediate circumstances as university students working for a degree and, perhaps, intending to become teachers. The prevalence of young women in Education Studies, and in training for primary school teaching, should itself be a matter for analysis and debate.

Youth and new media

The new media, the internet in particular, might be seen as offering new democratic platforms for a politicized youth. But as Buckingham (2007) points out, such expectations need to be considered somewhat carefully. There is a substantial and constantly expanding body of research focused on young people and new media (Gauntlett, 2000, 2007; Livingstone, 2002; Lievrouw and Livingstone, 2006; Buckingham, 2007, 2008). David Gauntlett's (2010) website, at the University of Westminster, is one significant source of information, guidance and debate in this field. He favours a view of the World Wide

Web as a 'network of creativity' and is keen to show how, among others, young people are increasingly participating in such a network as 'makers' and 'sharers'. The more participatory Web, Web 2.0 as it is known, facilitates a wide range of activity, some of it directed towards issues such as climate change, some more idiosyncratic and personal – but shared. Gauntlett has also been prominent in arguing that Media Studies needs to be fundamentally recomposed in the light of these developments as Media Studies 2.0. He presents a benign, optimistic and seemingly untroubled perspective that, if nothing else, is a striking contrast with the critical gravity of the media analysis offered by the Media Education Foundation (2010), discussed briefly in Chapter 4. Certainly he is alert to engagements with the media, including the Web, that figure in young people's lives outside school and, in this respect, he contributes to the case made from within media education for many years – that young people experience their lives through extensive everyday involvement with the media and that therefore schools should support and further educational initiatives to engage with that experience. Again, for Education Studies students, a recognition of these developments and an exploration of them, in part through autobiographical reflection, is essential to understanding how differently childhood and youth may be lived amidst these new media technologies (Herring, 2008). Identifying and exploring change and difference relies on some willingness both to document individual experience and to exchange it with others.

It is extremely difficult to know what the longer-term uses of these technologies might contribute to the political effectivity of young people (Loader, 2007). But there is no doubt that the 'new media' are, if in uneven and unpredictable ways, central to their lives. Buckingham (2008), cited in Chapter 3, is one among a short rush of publications offering detailed empirical accounts of what young people appear to be doing with the new media. But, as its authors might acknowledge, current investigations, however expert they may be in youth cultural studies, do struggle with the disproportion between modest, small-scale research projects and the rapid and somewhat overwhelming proliferation of new media.

As I implied in Chapter 3, to be conclusive is always difficult and, in the midst of significant political changes, is a fragile aspiration. So both this chapter and this book have ended with only tentative outlines of a future. However, the preceding chapters have been both a *record of*, and *advocacy for*, an approach to education open to and informed by both the wider field of popular culture and the complex, transdisciplinary projects known as Cultural Studies.

Points for reflection

Do you think that young people are 'apolitical'?

What does 'feminism' mean to you?

How important are the new media in young people's everyday lives?

Notes

Chapter 6

1. The cover photograph for the first edition of *The Lore and Language of Schoolchildren* was taken by Roger Mayne. His work was also used for many other publications in the late 1950s and 1960s, including Colin MacInnes' novel *Absolute Beginners* (1959) and a number of Pelican (Penguin) sociology and psychology titles such as *Children under Stress, Childhood and Adolescence, Attachment* and *Adolescent Boys of East London*. See Mayne, R. (2001).

2. My research is conducted as part of a project funded by the Arts and Humanities Research Council, entitled *Children's Playground Games and Songs in the New Media Age*. The research team includes staff from the Institute of Education, the University of Sheffield, the British Library and the University of East London.

Chapter 8

1. An earlier discussion of Muslim students' writing about music was presented at the American Educational Research Association Annual Meeting, New York (March 2008) and is included in Richards (2008). This chapter draws on papers presented at both the AERA Annual Meeting (April 2009) in San Diego and Twenty First Century Teenager: Media, Representation, Theory and Policy, Trinity and All Saints College, Leeds, July 2008.

Bibliography

Albury, K. (2009) 'Reading porn reparatively', *Sexualities*, Volume 12, Number 5, 647–653.

Alexander, C. (1996) *The Art of Being Black: The Creation of Black British Youth Identities*, Oxford: Oxford University Press.

Alexander, R. (ed.) (2009) *The Cambridge Primary Review Research Surveys*, London: Routledge.

Allen, J., Potter, J., Sharp, J. and Turvey, K. (2007) *Primary ICT: Knowledge, Understanding and Practice*, Exeter: Learning Matters.

Allen, R. (1983) 'On reading soaps: A semiotic primer', in Kaplan, E. (ed.) *Regarding Television*, Frederick, MD: University Publications of America and the American Film Institute, pp. 97–106.

Althusser, L. (1971) 'Ideology and ideological state apparatuses', in *Lenin and Philosophy and Other Essays*, London: New Left Books, pp. 29–68.

Alvarado, M., Gutch, R. and Wollen, T. (1987) *Learning the Media: An Introduction to Media Teaching*, London: Macmillan.

Anderson. B. (1991) *Imagined Communities: Reflections on the Origin and Spread of Nationalism*, London: Verso.

Appiah, K. A. (1992) *In My Father's House: Africa in the Philosophy of Culture*, Oxford: Oxford University Press.

Archer, L. (2005) 'Muslim adolescents in Europe', in Fulop, M. and Ross, A. (eds) *Growing Up in Europe Today: Developing Identities among Adolescents*, Stoke-on-Trent: Trentham Books, pp. 55–69.

Aries, P. (1960/1986) *Centuries of Childhood*, Harmondsworth: Penguin.

Arnold, M. (1869/2009) *Culture and Anarchy*, Oxford: Oxford University Press.

Asad, T. (ed.) (1973) *Anthropology and the Colonial Encounter*, London: Ithaca Press.

Attwood, F. (ed.) (2009) *Mainstreaming Sex: The Sexualization of Western Culture*, London: I. B. Tauris.

Attwood, F. and Hunter, I. Q. (2009) 'Not safe for work? Teaching and researching the sexually explicit', *Sexualities*, Volume 12, Number 5, 547–557.

Back, L. (1996) *New Ethnicities and Urban Culture: Racisms and Multiculture in Young Lives*, London: UCL Press.

Back, L. (2007) *The Art of Listening*, Oxford: Berg.

Bakhtin, M. (1994) *Speech Genres and Other Late Essays*, Austin, TX: University of Texas Press.

Ball, S. J., Maguire, M. and Macrae, S. (2000) *Choice, Pathways and Transitions Post-16: New Youth, New Economies in the Global City*, London: Routledge.

Banaji, S. (2006) *Reading 'Bollywood': The Young Audience and Hindi Films*, Basingstoke: Palgrave Macmillan.

Barker, C. (2007) *Cultural Studies: Theory and Practice* (third edition), London: Sage.

Barker, M. (1981) *The New Racism: Conservatives and the Ideology of the Tribe*, London: Junction Books.

Barker, M. and Petley, J. (2001) *Ill Effects—The Media/Violence Debate* (second edition), London: Routledge.

Bartlett, S. and Burton, D. (2007) *Introduction to Education Studies* (second edition), London: Sage.

Bennett, A. (2000) *Popular Music and Youth Culture: Music, Identity and Place*, Basingstoke: Palgrave.

Bennett, T. (1979) *Formalism and Marxism*, London: Methuen.

Bennett, T., Grossberg, L. and Morris, M. (eds) (2005) *New Keywords: A Revised Vocabulary of Culture and Society*, Oxford: Blackwell.

Berger, J. (1972) *Ways of Seeing*, Harmondsworth: Penguin.

Bernstein, B. (1996) *Pedagogy, Symbolic Control and Identity: Theory, Research, Critique*, London: Taylor and Francis.

BFI (British Film Institute) (2010) at http://filmstore.bfi.org.uk/. Last accessed 16 March 2010.

Bianchi, J. (2008) 'Cultural connections in learning', in Ward, S. (ed.) *A Student's Guide to Education Studies* (second edition), London: Routledge, pp. 172–181.

Bishop, J. and Curtis, M. (2001) *Play Today in the Primary School Playground: Life, Learning and Creativity*, Buckingham: Open University Press.

Bishop, M. (2007) 'The making of a pre-pubescent porn star: contemporary fashion for elementary school girls', in Hall, A. and Bishop, M. (eds) *Pop Porn: Pornography in American Culture*, Westport, CT: Praeger, pp. 45–56.

Blackford, H. V. (2004) *Out of This World: Why Literature Matters to Girls*, New York: Teachers College Press.

Block, F. L. (1989) *Weetzie Bat*, New York: A Charlotte Zolotow Book/Harper and Row Junior Books.

Block, F. L. (1991) *Witch Baby*, New York: A Charlotte Zolotow Book/Harper Collins.

Block, F. L. (1992) *Cherokee Bat and the Goat Guys*, New York: A Charlotte Zolotow Book/Harper Collins.

Block, F. L. (1993) *Missing Angel Juan*, New York: Harper Collins.

Block, F. L. (1994) *The Hanged Man*, New York: Harper Collins.

Block, F. L. (1995) *Baby Be-Bop*, New York: Joanna Cotler Books/Harper Collins.

Block, F. L. (1996) *Girl Goddess #9*, New York: Joanna Cotler Books/Harper Collins.

Block, F. L. (1998a) *Dangerous Angels: The Weetzie Bat Books*, New York: Harper Collins.

Block, F. L. (1998b) *I was a Teenage Fairy*, New York: Joanna Cotler Books/Harper Collins.

Block, F. L. (2000a) *Nymph*, Cambridge, MA: Circlet Press.

Block, F. L. (2000b) *The Rose and the Beast: Fairy Tales Retold*, New York: Joanna Cotler Books/Harper Collins.

Block, F. L. (2001) *Echo*, New York: Joanna Cotler Books/Harper Collins.

Block, F. L. and Carlip, H. (1998) *Zine Scene: The Do It Yourself Guide to Zines*, Girl Press.

de Block, L. and Buckingham, D. (2007) *Global Children, Global Media: Migration, Media and Childhood*, Basingstoke: Palgrave.

Blume, J. (1975) *Forever*, London: Gollancz.

Boethius, U. (1995) 'Controlled pleasures: youth and literary texts', in Fornas, J. and Bolin, G. (eds) *Youth Culture in Late Modernity*, London: Sage, pp. 145–168.

Bourdieu, P. (1984) *Distinction: A Social Critique of the Judgement of Taste*, London: Routledge.

Bourdieu, P. (1993) *Sociology in Question*, London: Sage.

Bourdieu, P. et al. (1999) *The Weight of the World: Social Suffering in Contemporary Society*, Cambridge: Polity.

Boyden, J. and Ennew, J. (eds) (1997) *Children in Focus—A Manual for Participatory Research with Children,* Stockholm: Radda Barnen.

Bragg, S. and Buckingham, D. (2003) *Young People, Sex and the Media: The Facts of Life?* Basingstoke: Palgrave Macmillan.

Bragg, S. and Buckingham, D. (2009) 'Too much, too young?: Young people, sexual media and learning', in Attwood, F. (ed.) *Mainstreaming Sex: The Sexualization of Western Culture*, London: I. B. Tauris, pp. 129–146.

Britzman, D. (1998) *Lost Subjects, Contested Objects: Toward a Psychoanalytic Inquiry of Learning*, Albany, NY: State University of New York Press.

Brunsdon, C. (1996) 'A thief in the night—stories of feminism in the 1970s at CCCS', in Morley, D. and Chen, H.-K. (eds) *Stuart Hall: Critical Dialogues in Cultural Studies*, London: Routledge, pp. 276–286.

Buchmann, M. (1989) *The Script of Life in Modern Society: Entry into Adulthood in a Changing World*, Chicago: University of Chicago Press.

Buckingham, D. (1986) 'Against demystification—*Teaching the Media*', *Screen*, Volume 27, Number 5, September-October, 80–95.

Buckingham, D. (1987) *Public Secrets: EastEnders and Its Audience*, London: British Film Institute.

Buckingham, D. (ed.) (1990) *Watching Media Learning: Making Sense of Media Education,* London: Falmer Press.

Buckingham, D. (1993a) *Changing Literacies: Media Education and Modern Culture*, London: Institute of Education/Tufnell Press.

Buckingham, D. (1993b) *Children Talking Television: The Making of Television Literacy*, London: Falmer Press.

Buckingham, D. (ed.) (1993c) *Reading Audiences: Young People and the Media*, Manchester: Manchester University Press.

Buckingham, D. (1996) *Moving Images: Understanding Children's Emotional Responses to Television*, Manchester: Manchester University Press.

Buckingham, D. (ed.) (1998) *Teaching Popular Culture: Beyond Radical Pedagogy*, London: UCL Press.

Buckingham, D. (2000a) *After the Death of Childhood: Growing Up in the Age of Electronic Media*, Cambridge: Polity.

Buckingham, D. (2000b) *The Making of Citizens: Young People, News and Politics*, London: Routledge.

Buckingham, D. (ed.) (2002) *Small Screens: Television for Children,* London: Leicester University Press.

Buckingham, D. (2003) *Media Education: Literacy, Learning and Contemporary Culture,* Cambridge: Polity Press.

Buckingham, D. (2007) *Beyond Technology: Children's Learning in the Age of Digital Culture,* Cambridge: Polity Press.

Buckingham, D. (ed.) (2008) *Youth, Identity, and Digital Media,* Boston, MA: MIT Press.

Buckingham, D. and Scanlon, M. (2003) *Education, Entertainment and Learning in the Home,* Buckingham: Open University Press.

Buckingham, D. and Sefton-Green, J. (1994) *Cultural Studies Goes to School,* London: Taylor and Francis.

Buckingham, D. and Willett, R. (eds) (2006) *Digital Generations: Children, Young People, and the New Media,* London: Routledge.

Buckingham, D. and Willett, R. (eds) (2009) *Video Cultures: Media Technology and Everyday Creativity,* Basingstoke: Palgrave Macmillan.

Buckingham, D., Grahame, J. and Sefton-Green, J. (1995) *Making Media: Practical Production in Media Education,* London: The English and Media Centre.

Buckingham, D., Davies, H., Jones, K. and Kelley, P. (1999) *Children's Television in Britain: History, Discourse and Policy,* London: British Film Institute.

Bull, M. (2000) *Sounding Out the City: Personal Stereos and the Management of Everyday Life,* Oxford: Berg.

Burgess, M. (1996) *Junk,* London: Andersen Press.

Burgess, M. (2000a) 'Ban sex and drugs? Not in my book', in *Times Educational Supplement* (see 'Rethinking Literacy' at http://www.melvinburgess.net. Last accessed 16 March 2010.

Burgess, M. (2000b) 'Teenage fiction comes of age', in *The Bookseller,* August 11, at http://www.melvinburgess.net. Last accessed 16 March 2010.

Burgess, M. (2001) *Lady: My Life as a Bitch,* London: Andersen Press.

Burgess, M. (2003) *Doing It,* London: Andersen Press.

Burgess, M. (2004) 'Sympathy for the Devil', in *Children's Literature in Education,* Volume 35, Number 4, December, 289–300.

Burgess, M. (2010) at http://www.melvinburgess.net. Last accessed 16 March 2010.

Burn, A. (2009) *Making New Media: Semiotics, Culture and Digital Literacies,* New York: Peter Lang.

Burn, A. and Durran, J. (2007) *Media Literacy in Schools: Practice, Production and Progression,* London: Paul Chapman.

Burn, A. and Durrant, C. (eds) (2008) *Media Teaching: Language, Audience and Production,* Kent Town, SA: Wakefield Press/Australian Association for the Teaching of English.

Burn, A. and Parker, D. (2003) *Analysing Media Texts,* London: Continuum.

Burr, V. (2003) *Social Constructionism* (second edition), London: Routledge.

Burroughs, W. (1959/1969) *The Naked Lunch,* London: Transworld.

Butler, J. (1990) *Gender Trouble: Feminism and the Subversion of Identity,* New York: Routledge.

Butler, J. (1993) *Bodies That Matter: On the Discursive Limits of 'Sex'*, New York: Routledge.

Care Bears Complete (2010) Lace DVD. Those Characters from Cleveland Inc. UK Publisher/ Distributor: Lace International, Walton-on-Thames, Surrey.

Carlip, H. (1995) *Girl Power: Young Women Speak Out! Personal Writings from Teenage Girls*, New York: Warner Books.

Carr, D., Buckingham, D., Burn, A. and Schott, G. (2006) *Computer Games: Text, Narrative and Play*, Cambridge: Polity.

Carrington, V. and Robinson, M. (2009) *Digital Literacies: Social Learning and Classroom Practices*, London: Sage.

Carspecken, P. F. (1996) *Critical Ethnography in Educational Research: A Theoretical and Practical Guide*, New York: Routledge.

Carter, A. (1974) *Fireworks: Nine Profane Pieces*, London: Quartet Books.

Centre for Contemporary Cultural Studies (Women's Studies Group) (1978) *Women Take Issue: Aspects of Women's Subordination*, London: Hutchinson.

Centre for Contemporary Cultural Studies (1981) *Unpopular Education: Schooling and Social Democracy in England Since 1944*, London: Hutchinson.

Centre for Contemporary Cultural Studies (1982) *The Empire Strikes Back: Race and Racism in 70s Britain*, London: Hutchinson.

Centre for Contemporary Cultural Studies (1991) *Education Limited: Schooling, Training and the New Right in England since 1979*, London: Hutchinson.

Chambers, I. (1975) 'A strategy for living: black music and white subcultures', in Jefferson, T. (ed.) *Working Papers in Cultural Studies Number 7/8: Resistance through Rituals*, Birmingham University: Centre for Contemporary Cultural Studies, pp. 157–166.

Chambers, I. (1985) *Urban Rhythms: Pop Music and Popular Culture*, Basingstoke: Macmillan.

Chambers, I. (1986) *Popular Culture: The Metropolitan Experience*, London: Methuen.

Cherland, M. R. (1994) *Private Practices: Girls Reading Fiction and Constructing Identity*, London: Taylor and Francis.

Clarke, G. (1981) 'Defending ski jumpers: a critique of theories of youth sub-cultures', in Gelder, K. (ed.) (1997/2005) *The Subcultures Reader* (second edition), New York: Routledge, pp. 169–174.

Clarke, J. (2004) Review of Doing It, National Association for the Teaching of English at http://www. nate.org.uk/index.php?page=3&rev=41. Last accessed 16 March 2010.

Clarke, J., Hall, S., Jefferson, T. and Roberts, B. (1975) 'Subcultures, cultures and class: a theoretical overview', in Jefferson, T. (ed.) *Resistance through Rituals, Working Papers in Cultural Studies 7/8*, England: Centre for Contemporary Cultural Studies, University of Birmingham, pp. 9–74.

Cockburn, A. and Blackburn, R. (1969) *Student Power: Problems, Diagnosis, Action*, Harmondsworth: Penguin.

Cohen, P. (1997) *Rethinking the Youth Question*, London: Macmillan.

Connell, R. W. (1987) *Gender and Power: Society, the Person and Sexual Politics*, Cambridge: Polity.

Connell, R. W. (1993) *Schools and Social Justice*, Philadelphia, PA: Temple University Press.

Connell, R. W. (1995) *Masculinities*, Cambridge: Polity Press.

Connell, R. W., Ashenden, D. J., Kessler, S. and Dowsett, G. W. (1982) *Making the Difference: Schools, Families and Social Division*, London: Allen and Unwin.

Corrigan, P. (1975) 'Doing Nothing', in Jefferson, T. (ed.) *Working Papers in Cultural Studies Number 7/8: Resistance through Rituals*, Birmingham University: Centre for Contemporary Cultural Studies, pp. 103–105.

Corrigan, P. (1979) *Schooling the Smash Street Kids*, Basingstoke: Palgrave Macmillan.

Corsaro, W. (2009) 'Peer culture', in Qvortrup, J., Corsaro, W. and Honig, M.-S. (eds) *The Palgrave Handbook of Childhood Studies*, London: Palgrave Macmillan, pp. 301–315.

Crafts, S. D., Cavicchi, D. and Keil, C. and the Music in Daily Life Project (1993) *My Music*, Hanover, NH: Wesleyan University Press, University of New England.

CRESC (Centre for Research on Socio-Cultural Change) (2010) at http://www.cresc.ac.uk. Last accessed 16 March 2010.

Culler, J. (2000) *Literary Theory: A Very Short Introduction*, Oxford: Oxford University Press.

Danesi, M. (1994) *Cool: The Signs and Meanings of Adolescence*, Toronto: University of Toronto Press.

Davis, G. and Dickinson, K. (2004) *Teen TV: Genre, Consumption and Identity*, London: British Film Institute.

de Certeau, M. (1988) *The Practice of Everyday Life*, Berkeley, CA: University of California Press.

DeNora, T. (2000) *Music in Everyday Life*, Cambridge: Cambridge University Press.

Dimitriadis, G. (2001) *Performing Identity/Performing Culture: Hip Hop as Text, Pedagogy, and Lived Practice*, New York: Peter Lang.

Dimitriadis, G. (2003) *Friendship, Cliques, and Gangs: Young Black Men Coming of Age in Urban America*, New York: Teachers' College Press.

Dimitriadis, G. and McCarthy, C. (2001) *Reading and Teaching the Postcolonial: From Baldwin to Basquiat and Beyond*, New York: Teachers College Press.

Dimitriadis, G. and Carlson, D. (2003) *Promises to Keep: Cultural Studies, Democratic Education, and Public Life*, New York: Routledge/Falmer.

Dolby, N. (2001) *Constructing 'Race': Youth, Identity, and Popular Culture in South Africa*, Albany, NY: State University of New York Press.

Donald, J. (ed.) (1991) *Psychoanalysis and Cultural Theory: Thresholds*, London: Macmillan.

Donald, J. (1992) *Sentimental Education: Schooling, Popular Culture and the Regulation of Liberty*, London: Verso.

Downes, G. and Haywood, S. (2008) 'ICT, computer games and learning', in Ward, S. (ed.) *A Student's Guide to Education Studies* (second edition), London: Routledge, pp. 162–171.

du Gay, P., Hall, S., Janes, L. Mackay, H. and Negus, K. (1997) *Doing Cultural Studies: The Story of the Sony Walkman*, London: Sage and the Open University.

Dworkin, A. (1981) *Pornography: Men Possessing Women*, London: The Women's Press.

Dwyer, C. (1998) 'Contested identities: challenging dominant representations of young British Muslim women', in Skelton, T. and Valentine, G. (eds) *Cool Places: Geographies of Youth Cultures*, London: Routledge, pp. 50–65.

Dwyer, C. (1999) 'Negotiations of femininity and identity for young British Muslim women', in Laurie, N., Dwyer, C., Holloway, S. and Smith, F. (eds) *Geographies of New Femininities*, Harlow: Longman, pp. 135–152.

Dyer, R. (1993) *The Matter of Images: Essays on Representations*, London: Routledge.

Dyer, R. (1997) *White*, London: Routledge.

Education Studies Definitive Course Document (July 1993) University of North London, Faculty of Humanities and Teacher Education. London: University of North London.

Ellsworth, E. (1997a) 'Double binds of whiteness', in Fine, M., Wong, M., Weis, L. and Powell, L. (1997) *Off White: Readings on Race, Power and Society*, New York: Routledge, pp. 259–269.

Ellsworth, E. (1997b) *Teaching Positions: Difference, Pedagogy, and the Power of Address*, New York: Teachers College Press.

Ellsworth, E. (2004) *Places of Learning: Media, Architecture. Pedagogy*, New York: Routledge.

Engelhardt, T. (1986) 'The shortcake strategy', in Gitlin, T. (ed.) *Watching Television*, New York: Pantheon, pp. 68–110.

English and Media Centre (2010) at http://www.englishandmedia.co.uk. Last accessed 16 March 2010.

Ennew, J. (1986) *The Sexual Exploitation of Children*, Cambridge: Polity Press.

Epstein, D. (1993) *Changing Classroom Cultures: Anti-racism, Politics and Schools*, Stoke-on-Trent: Trentham Books.

Epstein, D. (1997) 'The voice of authority: on lecturing in Cultural Studies', in Canaan, J. E. and Epstein, D. (eds) *A Question of Discipline: Pedagogy, Power, and the Teaching of Cultural Studies*, Boulder, CO: Westview Press, pp. 178–191.

Epstein, D. and Johnson, R. (1998) *Schooling Sexualities*, Buckingham: Open University Press.

Epstein, J. (ed.) (1998) *Youth Culture: Identity in a Postmodern World*, Malden, MA: Blackwell.

ESRC (Economic and Social Research Council) (2010) at http://www.esrcsocietytoday.ac.uk/ESRCInfoCentre/index.aspx. Last accessed 16 March 2010.

Etherington, K. (2004) *Becoming a Reflexive Researcher: Using Ourselves in Research*, London: Jessica Kingsley.

Evaldsson, A.-C. (2009) 'Play and games', in Qvortrup, J., Corsaro, W. and Honig, M.-S. (eds) *The Palgrave Handbook of Childhood Studies*, London: Palgrave Macmillan, pp. 316–331.

Evans-Pritchard, E. (1940) *The Nuer: A Description of the Modes of Livelihood and Political Institutions of a Nilotic People*, London: Oxford.

Fabian, J. (1983) *Time and the Other: How Anthropology Makes Is Object*, New York: Columbia University Press.

Fanck, A. (1926/2004) *The Holy Mountain*, London: Eureka Entertainment DVD.

Fine, A. (1996) *The Tulip Touch*, London: Hamish Hamilton.

Fine, A. (2003) 'Filth whichever way you look at it' (Review of *Doing It*), *The Guardian*, 29 March at http://www.guardian.co.uk/books/2003/mar/29/featuresreviews.guardianreview24. Last accessed 16 March 2010.

Fine, M. and Weiss, L. (1998) *The Unknown City: The Lives of Poor and Working-Class Young Adults*, Boston: Beacon Press.

Fine, M., Wong, M., Weis, L. and Powell, L. (eds) (1997) *Off White: Readings on Race, Power and Society*, New York: Routledge.

Firestone, S. (1972) *The Dialectic of Sex: The Case for Feminist Revolution*, London: Paladin.

Flood, A. (2009) 'Christian group sues for right to burn gay teen novel', *The Guardian*, Friday 12 June at http://www.guardian.co.uk/books/2009/jun/12/christian-group-sues-burn-gay-teen-novel/print. Last accessed 16 March 2010.

Fornas, J. and Bolin, G. (1995) *Youth Culture in Late Modernity*, London: Sage.

Fornas, J., Lindberg, U. and Sernhede, O. (1995) *In Garageland: Rock, Youth and Modernity*, London: Routledge.

Foucault, M. (1978) *The Archaeology of Knowledge*, London: Tavistock.

Frank, T. (1997) *The Conquest of Cool: Business Culture, Counterculture, and the Rise of Consumerism*, Chicago: University of Chicago Press.

Frankenberg, R. (ed.) (1997) *Displacing Whiteness: Essays in Social and Cultural Criticism*, Durham, NC and London: Duke University Press.

Freedland, J. (2006) 'If this onslaught was about Jews, I would be looking for my passport', *The Guardian*, 18 October at http://www.guardian.co.uk/commentisfree/2006/oct/18/comment. politics. Last accessed 16 March 2010.

Freud, S. (1977) *On Sexuality: Three Essays on the Theory of Sexuality and Other Works*, Harmondsworth: Penguin.

Frith, S. (1978) *The Sociology of Rock*, London: Constable.

Frith, S. (1983) *Sound Effects: Youth, Leisure, and the Politics of Rock 'n' Roll*, London: Constable.

Frith, S. (1987) 'Towards an aesthetic of popular music', in Leppert, R. and McClary, S. (eds) *Music and Society—The Politics of Composition, Performance and Reception*, Cambridge: Cambridge University Press, pp. 133–149.

Frith, S. (1996), 'Music and identity', in Hall, S. and du Gay, P. (eds) *Questions of Cultural Identity*, London: Sage, pp. 108–127.

Frow, J. (1995) *Cultural Studies and Cultural Value*, Oxford: Oxford University Press.

Gaines, D. (1998) *Teenage Wasteland: Suburbia's Dead End Kids*, Chicago: University of Chicago Press.

Gauntlett, D. (1997) *Video Critical: Children, The Environment and Media Power*, London: John Libbey.

Gauntlett, D. (ed.) (2000) *Web Studies: Rewiring Media Studies for the Digital Age*, London: Arnold.

Gauntlett, D. (2007) *Creative Explorations: New Approaches to Identities and Audiences*, London: Routledge.

Gauntlett, D. (2010) at http://www.theory.org.uk. Last accessed 16 March 2010.

Gauntlett, D. and Hill, A. (1999) *TV Living: Television, Culture and Everyday Life*, London: Routledge.

Geertz, C. (1973) *The Interpretation of Cultures*, New York: Basic Books.

Gelder, K. (ed.) (1997/2005) *The Subcultures Reader* (second edition), New York: Routledge.

Giddens, A. (1979) *Central Problems in Social Theory*, London: Macmillan.

Giddens, A. (1991) *Modernity and Self-Identity: Self and Society in the Late Modern Age*, Cambridge: Polity Press.

Gillborn, D. (1995) *Racism and Antiracism in Real Schools: Theory, Policy, Practice*, Buckingham: Open University Press.

Gillborn, D. (2008) *Racism and Education: Coincidence or Conspiracy?*, London: Routledge.

Gillespie, M. (1995) *Television, Ethnicity and Cultural Change*, London: Routledge.

Gilroy, P. (1987) *There Ain't No Black in the Union Jack: The Cultural Politics of Race and Nation*, London: Hutchinson.

Gilroy, P. (1993a) *The Black Atlantic: Modernity and Double Consciousness*, London: Verso.

Gilroy, P. (1993b) *Small Acts: Thoughts on the Politics of Black Cultures*, London: Serpent's Tail.

Gilroy, P. (2004a) *After Empire: Multiculture or Postcolonial Melancholia*, London: Routledge.

Gilroy, P. (2004b) *Between Camps: Nations, Cultures and the Allure of Race*, London: Routledge.

Gilsenan, M. (1982) *Recognizing Islam: An Anthropologist's Introduction*, London: Croom Helm.

Giroux, H. (1997) 'Is there a place for Cultural Studies in colleges of education?', in Giroux, H. and Shannon, P. (eds) *Education and Cultural Studies: Toward a Performative Practice*, New York: Routledge, pp. 231–249.

Gleeson, K. and Frith, H. (2004) 'Pretty in pink: young women presenting mature sexual identities', in Harris, A. (ed.) *All About the Girl*, New York: Routledge, pp. 103–114.

Goldstein, J., Buckingham, D. and Brougere, G. (eds) (2004) *Toys, Games, and Media*, Mahwah, NJ: Lawrence Erlbaum Associates.

Goodson, I. and Sikes, P. (eds) (2001) *Life History Research in Educational Settings: Learning from Lives*, Buckingham: Open University Press.

Grahame, J. (1999) *Making Junk: From Page to Screen*, London: English and Media Centre (in collaboration with Zenith North and BBC Education).

Gramsci, A. (1971) *Selections from the Prison Notebooks of Antonio Gramsci*, selected and translated by Hoare, Q. and Nowell-Smith, G., New York: International Publishers.

Gray, A. (2003) *Research Practice for Cultural Studies: Ethnographic Methods and Lived Cultures*, London: Sage.

Gray, A., Campbell, J., Erickson, M., Hanson, S. and Wood, H. (eds) (2007) *CCCS Selected Working Papers Volumes One and Two*, London: Routledge.

Gray, J. (2006) *Watching with the Simpsons: Television, Parody, and Intertextuality*, London: Routledge.

Green, J. and Bloome, D. (1995) 'Ethnography and ethnographers of and in education: a situated perspective', in Flood, J., Heath, S. B. and Lapp, D. (eds) *Handbook of Research on Teaching Literacy through the Communicative and Visual Arts*, New York: Macmillan, pp. 181–202.

Green, L. (1988) *Music on Deaf Ears: Musical Meaning, Ideology and Education*, Manchester: University of Manchester Press.

Green, L. (1997) *Music, Gender, Education*, Cambridge: Cambridge University Press.

Green, L. (2001) *How Popular Musicians Learn: A Way Ahead for Music Education*, London: Ashgate.

Griffin, C. (1985) *Typical Girls? Young Women from School to the Job Market*, London: Routledge and Kegan Paul.

Griffin, C. (1993) *Representations of Youth: The Study of Youth in Britain and America*, Cambridge: Polity.

Griffin, C. (2008) *Branded Consumption and Social Identification: Young People and Alcohol—Full Research Report RES-148-25-0021*, Swindon: ESRC.

Griffiths, M. (2002) 'Pink worlds and blue worlds: a portrait of intimate polarity', in Buckingham, D. (ed.) *Small Screens: Television for Children*, London: Leicester University Press, pp. 159–184.

Griffiths, M. and Troyna, B. (1995) *Antiracism, Culture and Social Justice in Education*, Stoke-on-Trent: Trentham Books.

Grossberg, L., Nelson, C. and Treichler, P. (eds) (1992) *Cultural Studies*, New York: Routledge.

Haddon, M. (2003) *The Curious Incident of the Dog in the Night-Time*, London: Cape.

Hall, A. and Bishop, M. (eds) (2007) *Pop Porn: Pornography in American Culture*, Westport, CT: Praeger.

Hall, S. (1969) 'The hippies: an American "moment"', in Nagel, J. (ed.) *Student Power*, London: Merlin Press, pp. 170–202.

Hall, S. (1969/2007) 'The hippies: an American "moment"', in Gray, A., Campbell, J., Erickson, M., Hanson, S. and Wood, H. (eds) *CCCS Selected Working Papers Volume Two*, London: Routledge, pp. 146–167.

Hall, S. (1972) 'The determinations of news photographs', in Editorial Group *Working Papers in Cultural Studies*, Number 3, Birmingham: University of Birmingham, pp. 53–88.

Hall, S. (1983a) 'Teaching race', *Early Child Development and Care*, Volume 10, Number 4, London: Routledge (Taylor and Francis Group), pp. 259–274.

Hall, S. (1983b) 'Teaching race', reprinted in *The English Curriculum: Race*, Inner London Education Authority English Centre, pp. 72–75.

Hall, S. (1992) 'Cultural studies and its theoretical legacies', in Grossberg, L., Nelson, C. and Treichler, P. (eds) *Cultural Studies*, New York: Routledge, pp. 277–294.

Hall, S. (1996a) 'For Allon White: metaphors of transformation', in Morley, D. and Chen, K.-H. (eds) *Stuart Hall: Critical Dialogues in Cultural Studies*, London: Routledge, pp. 287–305.

Hall, S. (1996b) 'Introduction: who needs "identity?"', in Hall, S. and Du Gay, P. (eds) *Questions of Cultural Identity*, London: Sage, pp. 1–17.

Hall, S. (ed.) (1997) *Representation: Cultural Representations and Signifying Practices*, London: Sage.

Hall, S. and Jefferson, T. (eds) (2006) 'Once more around', in *Resistance through Rituals: Youth Subcultures in Post-war Britain* (second edition), London: Routledge, pp. vii–xxxii.

Hall, S. and Whannel, P. (1964) *The Popular Arts*, London: Hutchinson.

Hall, S., Critcher, C., Jefferson, T., Clarke, J. and Roberts, B. (1978) *Policing the Crisis: Mugging, the State and Law and Order*, London: Macmillan.

Haraway, D. (1991) *Simians, Cyborgs and Women: The Reinvention of Nature*, London: Free Association Books.

Haraway, D. (1992) *Primate Visions: Gender, Race, and Nature in the World of Modern Science*, London and New York: Verso.

Harris, A. (ed.) (2004a) *All About the Girl*, New York: Routledge.

Harris, A. (2004b) *Future Girl: Young Women in the Twenty-First Century*, New York: Routledge.

Harris, R. (2005) *New Ethnicities and Language Use*, London: Palgrave.

Harvey, D. (1989) *The Condition of Postmodernity: An Enquiry into the Origins of Cultural Change*, Oxford: Blackwell.

Harvey, S. (1980) *May '68 and Film Culture*, London: British Film Institute.

Heath, S. B. (1983/1996) *Ways with Words: Language, Life, and Work in Communities and Classrooms,* Cambridge: Cambridge University Press.

Hebdige, D. (1975) 'Reggae, rastas and rudies', in Jefferson, T. (ed.) *Working Papers in Cultural Studies, Number 7/8: Resistance through Rituals,* Birmingham University: Centre for Contemporary Cultural Studies, pp. 135–155.

Hebdige, D. (1979) *Subculture—The Meaning of Style,* London: Methuen.

Hebdige, D. (1987) *Cut 'n' Mix: Culture, Identity and Caribbean Music,* London: Comedia.

Hedges, C. (2007) *American Fascists: The Christian Right and the War on America,* London: Jonathan Cape.

Herring, S. C. (2008) 'Questioning the generational divide: technological exoticism and adult constructions of online youth identity', in Buckingham, D. (ed.) *Youth, Identity, and Digital Media,* Boston, MA: MIT Press, pp. 71–92.

Hewitt, R. (1986) *White Talk Black Talk: Inter-racial Friendship and Communication amongst Adolescents,* Cambridge: Cambridge University Press.

Hewitt, R. (2005) *White Backlash and the Politics of Multiculturalism,* Cambridge: Cambridge University Press.

Hey, V. (1997) *The Company She Keeps: An Ethnography of Girls' Friendship,* Buckingham: Open University Press.

Himmelweit, H. T., Oppenheim, A. N. and Vince, P. (1958) *Television and the Child: An Empirical Study of the Effect of Television on the Young,* London: Oxford University Press.

Hinton, S. E. (1970) *The Outsiders,* London: Gollancz.

Hodge, R. and Kress, G. (1988) *Social Semiotics,* Cambridge: Polity.

Hodge, R. and Tripp, D. (1986) *Children and Television: A Semiotic Approach,* Cambridge: Polity.

Hodkinson, P. (2002) *Goth: Identity, Style and Subculture,* Oxford: Berg.

Hoechsmann, M. and Low, B. (2008) *Reading Youth Writing: "New" Literacies, Cultural Studies and Education,* New York: Peter Lang.

Hoggart, R. (1957) *The Uses of Literacy: Aspects of Working-Class Life with Special Reference to Publications and Entertainments,* London: Chatto and Windus.

Holland, J., Ramazanoglu, C., Sharpe, S. and Thomson, R. (1998) *The Male in the Head: Young People, Heterosexuality and Power,* London: Tufnell Press.

hooks, b. (1992) *Black Looks: Race and Representation,* Boston, MA: South End Press.

hooks, b. (1994a) *Outlaw Culture: Resisting Representations,* London: Routledge.

hooks, b. (1994b) *Teaching to Transgress: Education as the Practice of Freedom,* New York: Routledge.

Horowitz, A. (2004) *The Falcon's Malteser,* Harmondsworth: Puffin.

IOE (Institute of Education) (2010) at http://www.childrenyouthandmedia.org.uk/. Last accessed 17 March 2010.

James, A. (1993) *Childhood Identities: Self and Social Relationships in the Experience of the Child,* Edinburgh: Edinburgh University Press.

James, A. (1995) 'Talking of children and youth: language, socialization and culture', in Amit-Talai, V. and Wulff, H. (eds) *Youth Cultures: A Cross-Cultural Perspective,* London: Routledge, pp. 43–62.

James, A. (2009) 'Agency', in Qvortrup, J., Corsaro, W. and Honig, M.-S. (eds) *The Palgrave Handbook of Childhood Studies*, London: Palgrave Macmillan, pp. 34–45.

James, A. and Prout, A. (eds) (1990) *Constructing and Reconstructing Childhood*, Basingstoke: Falmer.

Jefferson, T. (ed.) (1975) *Working Papers in Cultural Studies Number 7/8: Resistance through Rituals*, Birmingham University: Centre for Contemporary Cultural Studies.

Jenkins, H. (2006) *Convergence Culture: Where Old and New Media Collide*, New York: New York University Press.

Jhally, S. (1989) *Dreamworlds*, Northampton, MA: Media Education Foundation DVD.

Jhally, S. (2009) *Dreamworlds 3: Desire, Sex and Power in Music Video*, Northampton, MA: Media Education Foundation DVD.

Johnson, R. (1979) 'Really useful knowledge—radical education and working-class culture 1790–1848', in Clarke, J., Critcher, C. and Johnson, R. (eds) *Working-Class Culture*, London: Hutchinson, pp. 75–102.

Johnson, R. (1986/1987) 'What is Cultural Studies anyway?', *Social Text*, Number 16, 38–80.

Jones, G. S. (1969) 'The meaning of the student revolt', in Cockburn, A. and Blackburn, R. (eds) *Student Power: Problems, Diagnosis, Action,* Harmondsworth: Penguin, pp. 25–56.

Jones, K. (ed.) (1992) *English and the National Curriculum: Cox's Revolution?* London: Kogan Page and the University of London Institute of Education.

Jones, K. (2003) *Education in Britain: 1944 to the Present*, Cambridge: Polity.

Jones, S. (1988) *Black Culture, White Youth: The Reggae Tradition from JA to UK*, London: Macmillan.

Jordanova, L. (1989) 'Children in history: concepts of nature and society', in Scarre, G. (ed.) *Children, Parents and Politics*, Cambridge: Cambridge University Press, pp. 3–24.

Jowett, L. (2005) *Sex and the Slayer: A Gender Studies Primer for the Buffy Fan*, Middletown, CT: Wesleyan University Press.

Kaplan, C. (1985) *Sea Changes: Culture and Feminism*, London: Verso.

Kapur, J. (1999) 'Out of control: television and the transformation of childhood in late capitalism', in Kinder, M. (ed.) *Kids' Media Culture*, Durham, NC: Duke University Press, pp. 122–138.

Kassem, D., Murphy, L. and Taylor, E. (eds) (2010) *Key Issues in Childhood and Youth Studies*, London: Routledge.

Kearney, M. C. (1998) '"Don't need you": rethinking identity politics and separatism from a girl perspective', in Epstein, J. (ed.) *Youth Culture: Identity in a Postmodern World,* Malden, MA: Blackwell, pp. 148–188.

Kearney, M. C. (2006) *Girls Make Media*, New York: Routledge.

Kedward, R. (1973) 'Beyond the constraints', in Radical Faculty Action Group (eds) *Socialist Education and the University, Focus,* Number 30, Falmer: University of Sussex Information Office, pp. 1–2.

Kenway, J. and Bullen, E. (2001) *Consuming Children: Education-Entertainment-Advertising*, Buckingham: Open University Press.

Kipnis, L. (1999) *Bound and Gagged: Pornography and the Politics of Fantasy in America*, Durham, NC: Duke University Press.

Kipnis, L. (2006) *The Female Thing: Dirt, Sex, Envy, Vulnerability*, New York: Pantheon.

Kline, S. (1993) *Out of the Garden: Toys and Children's Culture in the Age of TV Marketing*, London: Verso.

Kress, G. (2003) *Literacy in the New Media Age*, London: Routledge.

Kress, G. and van Leeuwen, T. (1996) *Reading Images*, London: Routledge.

Kress, G. and van Leeuwen, T. (2001) *Multimodal Discourse*, London: Arnold.

Kuhn, A. (1995) *Family Secrets: Acts of Memory and Imagination*, London: Verso.

Kuhn, A. and McAllister, K. E. (eds) (2006) *Locating Memory: Photographic Acts*, New York: Berghahn.

Kuhn, T. (1970) *The Structure of Scientific Revolutions*, Chicago: University of Chicago Press.

Kurosawa, A. (1954/1999) *Seven Samurai*, London: British Film Institute DVD.

Laclau, E. (1977) *Politics and Ideology in Marxist Theory*, London: New Left Books.

Lakoff, G. and Johnson, M. (1980) *Metaphors We Live By*, Chicago: University of Chicago Press.

Laplanche, J. and Pontalis, J-B. (1985) *The Language of Psycho-Analysis*, London: The Hogarth Press.

Lassiter, L. (2005) *The Chicago Guide to Collaborative Ethnography*, Chicago: Chicago University Press.

Laurie, N., Dwyer, C., Holloway, S. and Smith, F. (1999) *Geographies of New Femininities*, Harlow: Pearson Education.

Leavis, F. R. (1930) *Mass Civilization and Minority Culture*, Cambridge: Cambridge University Press.

Leavis, F. R. and Thompson, D. (1933) *Culture and Environment*, London: Chatto and Windus.

Lees, S. (1983) 'How boys slag off girls', *New Society*, pp. 51–53.

Lees, S. (1986) *Losing Out: Sexuality and Adolescent Girls*, London: Hutchinson.

Le Guin, U. K. (1993) *The Earthsea Quartet*, Harmondsworth: Penguin.

Le Guin, U. K. (1985) *The Language of the Night: Essays on Fantasy and Science Fiction*, New York: Berkley Books.

Lesko, N. (1996) 'Denaturalizing adolescence: the politics of contemporary representations', *Youth and Society*, December, Volume 28, Number 2, 139–161.

Lesko, N. (2001) *Act Your Age! A Cultural Construction of Adolescence*, London: Routledge.

Levy, A. (2005) *Female Chauvinist Pigs: Women and the Rise of Raunch Culture*, London: Simon and Schuster.

Lievrouw, L. and Livingstone, S. (eds) (2006) *The Handbook of New Media: Updated Student Edition*, London: Sage.

Lindley, R. (1989) 'Teenagers and other children', in Scarre, G. (ed.) *Children, Parents and Politics*, Cambridge: Cambridge University Press, pp. 72–93.

Livingstone, S. (1998) *Making Sense of Television: The Psychology of Audience Interpretation*, London: Routledge.

Livingstone, S. (2002) *Young People and New Media: Childhood and the Changing Media Environment*, London: Sage.

Livingstone, S. (2009) *Children and the Internet*, Cambridge: Polity.

Livingstone, S. and Haddon, L. (eds) (2009) *Kids Online: Opportunities and Risks for Children*, Bristol: Policy Press.

Loader, B. (ed.) (2007) *Young Citizens in the Digital Age: Political Engagement, Young People and New Media*, London: Routledge.

Loubert, P., Smith, C. and Hirsch, M. (1986a) *The Care Bears Family: Care-A-Lot's Birthday; Grumpy's Three Wishes*, VVD408 Virgin/Nelvana/Those characters from Cleveland Inc. Toronto: Nelvana.

Loubert, P., Smith, C. and Hirsch, M. (1986b) *The Care Bears Family: The Cloud of Uncaring; Big Star Round-Up*, VVD284 Virgin/Nelvana/Those characters from Cleveland Inc. Toronto: Nelvana.

Lowery, S. A. and DeFleur, M. L. (1988) *Milestones in Mass Communication Research*, New York: London.

Lumby, C. (1997) *Bad Girls: The Media, Sex and Feminism in the 90s*, St Leonards, NSW: Allen and Unwin.

Lushington, C. (1973) 'The idea of an open university', in Radical Faculty Action Group (eds) *Socialist Education and the University, Focus*, Number 30, Falmer: University of Sussex Information Office, pp. 34–35.

Mac An Ghaill, M. (1999) *Contemporary Racisms and Ethnicities*, Buckingham: Open University Press.

MacInnes, C. (1959) *Absolute Beginners*, London: MacGibbon and Kee.

McCallum, R. (1999) *Ideologies of Identity in Adolescent Fiction: The Dialogic Construction of Subjectivity*, New York: Garland Publishing Inc.

McCarthy, C., Hudak, G., Miklaucic, S. and Saukko, P. (eds) (1999) *Sound Identities: Popular Music and the Cultural Politics of Education*, New York: Peter Lang.

McDonell, N. (2002) *Twelve*, New York: Grove/Atlantic.

McEwan, I. (2007) *On Chesil Beach*, London: Jonathan Cape.

McNair, B. (2009) 'Teaching porn', *Sexualities*, Volume 12, Number 5, 558–67.

McRobbie, A. (1978) 'Working-class girls and the culture of femininity', in Women's Studies Group (eds) *Women Take Issue*, Birmingham and London: Centre for Contemporary Cultural Studies/ Hutchinson, pp. 96–108.

McRobbie, A. (1989) *Zoot Suits and Second-Hand Dresses: An Anthology of Fashion and Music*, Basingstoke: Macmillan.

McRobbie, A. (1991) *Feminism and Youth Culture: From Jackie to Just Seventeen*, Basingstoke: Macmillan.

McRobbie, A. (1994) *Postmodernism and Popular Culture*, London: Routledge.

McRobbie, A. (ed.) (1997) *Back to Reality? Social Experience and Cultural Studies*, Manchester: Manchester University Press.

McRobbie, A. (1999) *In the Culture Society: Art, Fashion and Popular Music*, London: Routledge.

McRobbie, A. (2005) *The Uses of Cultural Studies: A Textbook*, London: Sage.

McRobbie, A. (2007) 'Postfeminism and popular culture: Bridget Jones and the new gender regime', in Tasker, Y. and Negra, D. (eds) *Interrogating Postfeminism: Gender and the Politics of Popular Culture*, Durham, NC: Duke University Press, pp. 27–39.

McRobbie, A. (2009) *The Aftermath of Feminism*, London: Sage.

McRobbie, A. and Garber, J. (1975) 'Girls and subcultures: an exploration', in Jefferson, T. (ed.) *Working Papers in Cultural Studies Number 7/8: Resistance through Rituals*, Birmingham University: Centre for Contemporary Cultural Studies, pp. 209–222.

McRobbie, A. and McCabe, T. (1981) *Feminism for Girls: An Adventure Story*, London: Routledge and Kegan Paul.

McRobbie, A. and Nava, M. (eds) (1984) *Gender and Generation*, London: Macmillan.

Maira, S. (2002) *Desis in the House: Indian American Youth Culture in New York City*, Philadelphia, PA: Temple University Press.

Maira, S. (2009) *Missing: Youth, Citizenship, and Empire After 9/11*, Durham, NC: Duke University Press.

Maira, S. and Soep, E. (eds) (2004) *Youthscapes: The Popular, the National, the Global*, Philadelphia, PA: University of Pennsylvania Press.

Mander, J. (1998) *Four Arguments for the Elimination of Television*, Other India Press.

Marsh, J. and Millard, E. (2000) *Literacy and Popular Culture: Using Children's Culture in the Classroom*, London: Paul Chapman.

Marsh, K. (2008) *The Musical Playground: Global Tradition and Change in Children's Songs and Games*, Oxford: Oxford University Press.

Marshall, E. (2009) at http://www.springerlink.com/content/b220378188706952/. 'Girlhood, sexual violence and agency in Francesca Lia Block's "Wolf"', in *Children's Literature in Education*, Netherlands: Springer, pp. 217–234, Volume 40, Number 3. Last accessed 6 June 2010.

Masterman, L. (1980) *Teaching about Television*, London: Macmillan.

Masterman, L. (1985) *Teaching the Media*, London: Comedia.

Matheson, D. and Grosvenor, I. (eds) (1999) *An Introduction to the Study of Education*, London: David Fulton

Mayall, B. (2002) *Towards a Sociology for Childhood: Thinking from Children's Lives*, Buckingham: Open University Press.

Mayne, R. (2001) *Photographs*, London: Jonathan Cape.

Media Education Foundation (MEF) (2010) at http://www.mediaed.org/wp/about-mef. Last accessed 17 March 2010.

Mercer, K. (1994) *Welcome to the Jungle: New Positions in Black Cultural Studies*, London: Routledge.

Messenger-Davies, M. (1989/2001) *Television is Good for Your Kids*, London: Shipman.

Meyer, S. (2005) *Twilight*, New York: Little, Brown and Company.

Meyer, S. (2006) *New Moon*, New York: Little, Brown and Company.

Meyer, S. (2007) *Eclipse*, New York: Little, Brown and Company.

Meyer, S. (2008) *Breaking Dawn*, New York: Little, Brown and Company.

Middleton, D. and Edwards, D. (eds) (1990) *Collective Remembering*, London: Sage.

Mills, C. Wright (1959) *The Sociological Imagination*, Oxford: Oxford University Press.

Mills, J. (1993) *Sexwords*, Harmondsworth: Penguin.

Milne, A. A. (1928/1980) *The House at Pooh-Corner*, London: Methuen.

Mitchell, C. and Reid-Walsh, J. (2002) *Researching Children's Popular Culture: The Cultural Spaces of Childhood*, London: Routledge.

Mitchell, C. and Reid-Walsh, J. (eds) (2005) *Seven Going on Seventeen: Tween Studies in the Culture of Girlhood*, New York: Peter Lang.

Mitchell, J. (1971) *Woman's Estate*, Harmondsworth: Penguin.

Modleski, T. (1991) *Feminism without Women: Culture and Criticism in a "Postfeminist" Age*, New York: Routledge.

Morley, D. (1980) *The 'Nationwide' Audience*, London: British Film Institute.

Morley, D. (1986) *Family Television: Cultural Power and Domestic Leisure*, London: Comedia.

Morley, D. (1992) *Television, Audiences and Cultural Studies*, London: Routledge.

Morley, D. (2000) *Home Territories: Media, Mobility and Identity*, London: Routledge.

Morley, D. and Chen, H.-K. (1996) *Stuart Hall: Critical Dialogues in Cultural Studies*, London: Routledge.

Morse, D. (1971) *Motown and the Arrival of Black Music*, London: Studio Vista.

Morse, D. (1973) 'Knowledge and impotence', in Radical Faculty Action Group (eds) *Socialist Education and the University, Focus*, Number 30, Falmer: University of Sussex Information Office, pp. 13–14.

Moss, G. (1989) *Un/Popular Fictions*, London: Virago.

Moss, G. (1993) 'Girls tell the teen romance: four reading histories', in Buckingham, D. (ed.) *Reading Audiences: Young People and the Media*, Manchester: Manchester University Press, pp. 116–134.

Muggleton, D. and Weinzierl, R. (eds) (2003) *The Post-Subcultures Reader*, Oxford: Berg.

Mukarovsky, J. (1977) *Word and Verbal Art: Selected Essays*, New Haven, CT: Yale University Press.

Mulhern, F. (1979) *The Moment of 'Scrutiny'*, London: Verso.

Muller, R. (1993/2003) *The Wonderful Horrible Life of Leni Riefenstahl*, London: Eureka Entertainment, DVD.

Murdock, G. and Phelps, G. (1973) *Mass Media and the Secondary School*, London: Macmillan/Schools Council.

Muscio, I. (2002) *Cunt: A Declaration of Independence*, Emeryville, CA: Seal Press.

Muslim Hip Hop (2010) at http://www.muslimhiphop.com/. Last accessed 16 March 2010.

My Little Pony—Twinkle Wish Adventure (2009), London: Minimetro DVD.

Nagel, J. (ed.) (1969) *Student Power*, London: Merlin Press.

National Council of Teachers of English (1994) 'How to Write a Rationale' at http://www.ncte.org/library/NCTEFiles/Involved/Action/Rationale_HowtoWrite.pdf. Last accessed 17 March 2010.

Nilan, P. and Feixa, C. (2006) *Global Youth? Hybrid Identities, Plural Worlds*, London: Routledge.

Nixon, H. (2002) 'South Park: not in front of the children', in Buckingham, D. (ed.) *Small Screens: Television for Children*, London: Leicester University Press, pp. 96–119.

Opie, I. (1993) *The People in the Playground*, Oxford: Oxford University Press.

Opie, I. and Opie, P. (1959/2001) *The Lore and Language of Schoolchildren*, New York: New York Review Books.

Opie, P. and Opie, I. (1969) *Children's Games in Street and Playground*, Oxford: Oxford University Press.

Osgerby, B. (1998) *Youth in Britain Since 1945*, Oxford: Blackwell.

Osgerby, B. (2004) *Youth Media*, London: Routledge.

PABBIS (Parents Against Bad Books in Schools) (2010) at http://www.pabbis.com. Last accessed 16 March 2010.

Parker, I. (1997) *Psychoanalytic Culture: Psychoanalytic Discourse in Western Society*, London: Sage.

Perry, P. (2002) *Shades of White: White Kids and Racial Identities in High School*, Durham, NC: Duke University Press.

Peucker, B. (2004) 'The fascist choreography: Riefenstahl's tableaux', *Modernism/Modernity*, Volume 11, Number 2, 279–297.

Phillips, A. (1998) *The Beast in the Nursery*, London: Faber.

Pilkington, H. (1996) *Gender, Generation and Identity in Contemporary Russia*, London: Routledge.

Pilkington, H. (2010) *Russia's Skinheads: Exploring and Rethinking Subcultural Lives*, London: Routledge.

Pini, M. (2001) *Club Cultures and Female Subjectivity: The Move from Home to House*, Basingstoke: Palgrave.

Pink, S. (2001/2007) *Doing Visual Ethnography: Images, Media and Representation in Research* (second edition), London: Sage.

Pountain, D. and Robins, D. (2000) *Cool Rules: Anatomy of an Attitude*, London: Reaktion Books.

Postman, N. (1994) *The Disappearance of Childhood*, New York: Vintage Books.

Preston, J. (2007) *Whiteness and Class in Education*, Dordrecht: Springer.

Price, R. (1992) 'For the Family' Afterword to Mann, S., *Immediate Family*, New York: Aperture Foundation (not paginated).

Pullman, P. (2007) *His Dark Materials*, London: Scholastic.

Radway, J. (1984) *Reading the Romance: Women, Patriarchy and Popular Literature*, Chapel Hill and London: University of North Carolina Press.

Rampton, B. (2006) *Language in Late Modernity: Interaction in an Urban School*, Cambridge: Cambridge University Press.

Redhead, S., Wynne, D. and O'Connor, J. (1998) *The Subcultures Reader: Readings in Popular Cultural Studies*, Oxford: Blackwell.

Reid, S. and Hutchinson, B. (1994) 'Lanky Lizards! Francesca Lia Block is fun to read but . . .: reading multicultural literature in public schools', *ALAN Review*, Volume 21, Number 3, 60–65.

Richards, C. (1974) 'William Burroughs: language and reality', Unpublished MA dissertation M238, Sussex University Library at http://catalogue.sussex.ac.uk/ABL/. Last accessed 16 March 2010.

Richards, C. (1981) 'Review of *US Girls*', in TLK editorial group (eds) *Teaching London Kids*, Number 17, not paginated.

Richards, C. (1982) 'Topicality', in TLK editorial group (eds) *Teaching London Kids*, Number 19, pp. 20–22.

Richards, C. (1983) 'Media-Race-Riots', in TLK editorial group (eds) *Teaching London Kids*, Number 20, pp. 2–7.

Richards, C. (1990) 'Intervening in popular pleasures: media studies and the politics of subjectivity', in Buckingham, D. (ed.) *Watching Media Learning: Making Sense of Media Education*, London: Falmer Press, pp. 151–168.

Richards, C. (1992) 'Teaching popular culture', in Jones, K. (ed.) *English and the National Curriculum: Cox's Revolution?* London: Kogan Page and the University of London Institute of Education, pp. 62–94.

Richards, C. (1993) 'Taking Sides? What young girls do with television', in Buckingham, D. (ed.) *Reading Audiences: Young People and the Media* Manchester: University of Manchester Press, pp. 24–27.

Richards, C. (1995) 'Room to dance', in Bazalgette, C. and Buckingham, D. (eds) *In Front of the Children: Screen Entertainment and Young Audiences*, London: British Film Institute, pp. 141–150.

Richards, C. (1998a) 'Beyond classroom culture', in Buckingham, D. (ed.) *Teaching Popular Culture: Beyond Radical Pedagogy*, London: UCL Press, pp. 132–152.

Richards, C. (1998b) *Teen Spirits: Music and Identity in Media Education*, London: UCL Press.

Richards, C. (1999) 'Live through this: music, adolescence and autobiography', in McCarthy, C., Hudak, G., Miklaucic, S. and Saukko, P. (eds) *Sound Identities: Popular Music and the Cultural Politics of Education*, New York: Peter Lang, pp. 255–288.

Richards, C. (2004) 'What are we? adolescence, sex and intimacy in *Buffy the Vampire Slayer*', *Continuum: Journal of Media and Cultural Studies*, March, Volume 18, Number 1, 121–137.

Richards, C. (2005a) 'Securing the self: risk and aspiration in the post-16 curriculum', *British Journal of the Sociology of Education*, November, Volume 26, Number 5, 613–625.

Richards, C. (2005b) 'Translations: encounters with popular film and academic discourse', *European Journal of Cultural Studies*, February, Volume 8, Number 1, 23–43.

Richards, C. (2006) 'In the wake of Hendrix: reflections on a life after death', in Homan, S. (ed.) *Access All Eras: Tribute Bands and Global Pop Cultures*, Milton Keynes: Open University Press, pp. 103–120.

Richards, C. (2007) 'Addressing "young adults"? The case of Francesca Lia Block', in Matthews, N. and Moody, N. (eds) *Judging a Book by Its Cover: Fans, Publishers, Designers, and the Marketing of Fiction*, Aldershot and Burlington, VT: Ashgate, pp. 147–160.

Richards, C. (2008) *Forever Young: Essays on Young Adult Fictions*, New York: Peter Lang.

Riefenstahl, L. (1934/1935/2008) *Triumph of the Will*, Berlin, Germany: Universum Film AG. Demand DVD.

Riefenstahl, L. (1938/2006) *Olympia*, Pathfinder Home Entertainment DVD.

Riefenstahl, L. (1976a) *The Last of the Nuba*, London: Collins.

Riefenstahl, L. (1976b) *The People of Kau*, London: Collins.

Riefenstahl, L. (1994) *Olympia*, London: Quartet Books.

Riordan, R. (2008) *Percy Jackson and the Lightning Thief*, Harmondsworth: Puffin.

Robins, D. and Cohen, P. (1978) *Knuckle Sandwich: Growing Up in the Working-Class City*, Harmondsworth: Penguin.

Roof, J. (2007) 'Panda porn, children, google, and other fantasies', in Hall, A. and Bishop, M. (eds) *Pop Porn: Pornography in American Culture*, Westport, CT: Praeger, pp. 27–44.

Rosaldo, R. (1993) *Culture and Truth: The Remaking of Social Analysis*, London: Routledge.

Rose, J. (1984) *The Case of Peter Pan or The Impossibility of Children's Fiction*, London: Macmillan.

Rose, N. (1989/1999) *Governing the Soul: The Shaping of the Private Self*, London: Free Association Books.

Rose, S., Lewontin, R. C. and Kamin, L. J. (1984) *Not in Our Genes: Biology, Ideology and Human Nature*, Harmondsworth: Penguin.

Rosen, M. (1997) 'Junk and other realities: the tough world of children's literature', *The English and Media Magazine*, Autumn, Number 37, 4–6.

Rowbotham, S. (1973) *Woman's Consciousness, Man's World*, Harmondsworth: Penguin.

Rowbotham, S. (2000) *Promise of a Dream: Remembering the Sixties*, London: Penguin.

Said, E. (1981) *Covering Islam: How the Media and the Experts Determine How We See the Rest of the World*, London: RKP.

Samuels, T. (2009) *Hardcore Profits Parts 1 and 2* (Executive Producers: Daws, W. and Cabb, S.), London: BBC Television.

Sandikci, O. and Ger, G. (2005) 'Aesthetics, ethics and politics of the Turkish headscarf', in Kuchler, S. and Miller, D. (eds) *Clothing as Material Culture*, Oxford: Berg, pp. 61–82.

Sarland, C. (1991) *Young People Reading: Culture and Response*, Milton Keynes: Open University Press.

Savage, J. (2007) *Teenage: The Creation of Youth 1875–1945*, London: Chatto and Windus.

Savage, M. (2000) *Class Analysis and Social Transformation*, Buckingham: Open University Press.

Scarre, G. (ed.) (1989) *Children, Parents and Politics*, Cambridge: Cambridge University Press.

Schon, D. (1991) *The Reflective Practitioner: How Professionals Think in Action*, Burlington, VT: Ashgate.

Schor, J. (2006) *Born to Buy: The Commercialised Child and the New Consumer Culture*, New York: Simon and Schuster.

Schramm, W., Lyle, J. and Parker, E. (1961) *Television in the Lives of Our Children*, Palo Alto, CA: Stanford University Press.

Screen (2010). http://www.gla.ac.uk/services/screen/. Last accessed 16 March 2010.

Sefton-Green, J. (1993) 'Untidy, depressing and violent: a boy's own story', in Buckingham, D. (ed.) *Reading Audiences: Young People and the Media*, Manchester: Manchester University Press, pp. 135–158.

Sefton-Green, J. (ed.) (1998) *Digital Diversions: Youth Culture in the Age of Multimedia*, London: UCL Press.

Sefton-Green, J. and Sinker, R. (eds) (2000) *Evaluating Creativity: Making and Learning by Young People*, London: Routledge.

Seiter, E. (1993) *Sold Separately: Children and Parents in Consumer Culture*, New Brunswick, NJ: Rutgers University Press.

Sewell, T. (1997) *Black Masculinities and Schooling: How Black Boys Survive Modern Schooling*, Stoke-on-Trent: Trentham Books.

Shain, F. (2003) *The Schooling and Identity of Asian Girls*, Stoke-on-Trent: Trentham Books.

Shain, F. (2010) *The New Folk Devils: Muslim Boys and Education in England*, Stoke-on-Trent: Trentham Books.

Shakespeare, W. (1969) 'Hamlet', in Craig W. J. (ed.) *William Shakespeare: Complete Works* , London: Oxford University Press, pp. 870–907.

Shank, B. (1994) *Dissonant Identities: The Rock'n'Roll Scene in Austin, Texas*, Hanover, NH: Wesleyan University Press.

Skeggs, B. (1997a) 'Classifying practices: representations, capitals and recognitions', in Mahony, P. and Zmroczek, C. (eds) *Class Matters: 'Working-Class' Women's Perspectives on Social Class*, London: Taylor and Francis, pp. 123–139.

Skeggs, B. (1997b) *Formations of Class and Gender: Becoming Respectable*, London: Sage.

Skeggs, B. (2004) *Class, Self, Culture*, London: Routledge.

Skelton, T. and Valentine, G. (1998) *Cool Places: Geographies of Youth Cultures*, London: Routledge.

Slater, D. (1997) *Consumer Culture and Modernity*, Cambridge: Polity.

Slobin, M. (1993) *Subcultural Sounds: Micromusics of the West*, Hanover, NH: Wesleyan University Press.

Smith, C. (2009) 'Pleasure and distance: exploring sexual cultures in the classroom', *Sexualities*, Volume 12, Number 5, 568–85.

Snyder, I. (ed.) (2002) *Silicon Literacies: Communication, Innovation and Education in the Electronic Age*, London: Routledge.

Sontag, S. (1983) 'Fascinating fascism', in *Under the Sign of Saturn*, London: Writers and Readers Publishing Cooperative Society, pp. 71–105.

Sontag, S. (2003) *Regarding the Pain of Others*, New York: Penguin.

Sophocles (1962) *Sophocles: Three Tragedies*, Kitto H. D. F. (trans.), London: Oxford University Press.

Stallybrass, P. and White, A. (1986) *The Poetics and Politics of Transgression*, Ithaca, NY: Cornell University Press.

Steedman, C. (1982) *The Tidy House: Little Girls Writing*, London: Virago.

Steedman, C. (1986) *Landscape for a Good Woman: A Story of Two Lives*, London: Virago.

Steedman, C. (1990) *Childhood, Culture, and Class in Britain: Margaret McMillan, 1860–1931*, London: Virago.

Steedman, C. (1992) *Past Tenses: Essays on Writing, Autobiography and History*, London: Rivers Oram Press.

Steedman, C. (1995) *Strange Dislocations: Childhood and the Idea of Human Interiority 1780–1930*, London: Virago.

Steinberg, D., Epstein, D. and Johnson, R. (eds) (1997) *Border Patrols: Policing the Boundaries of Heterosexuality*, London: Cassell.

Steinberg, S. and Kincheloe, J. (2004) *Kinderculture: The Corporate Construction of Childhood*, Boulder, CO: Westview Press.

Stewart, S. (1988) 'Ceci tuera cela: graffiti as crime and art', in Fekete, J. (ed.) *Life After Postmodernism: Essays on Value and Culture*, London: Macmillan Education, pp. 161–180.

Stoehr, S. (1991/2003) *Crosses*, Lincoln, NE: iUniverse, Inc.

Sun, C. and Picker, M. 2008 *The Price of Pleasure*, Northampton, MA: Media Education Foundation DVD.

Sutton-Smith, B. (1997) *The Ambiguity of Play*, Cambridge, MA: Harvard University Press.

Thompson, E. P. (1963) *The Making of the English Working-Class*, Harmondsworth: Penguin.

Thorne, B. (1993) *Gender Play: Girls and Boys in School*, Buckingham: Open University Press.

Thornton, S. (1995) *Club Cultures—Music, Media and Subcultural Capital*, Cambridge: Polity Press.

Tinkham, L. (1969) 'Learning one's lesson', in Cockburn, A. and Blackburn, R. (eds) *Student Power: Problems, Diagnosis, Action*, Harmondsworth: Penguin, pp. 82–98.

Tolkien, J. R. R. (1968) *The Lord of the Rings*, London: George Allen and Unwin.

Trites, R. S. (2000) *Disturbing the Universe: Power and Repression in Adolescent Literature*, Iowa City, IA: University of Iowa Press.

Twain, M. (1884/1966) *The Adventures of Huckleberry Finn* (with an introduction by Peter Coveney) Harmondsworth: Penguin.

Volosinov, V. N. (1929/1973) *Marxism and the Philosophy of Language*, New York: Seminar Press.

Vonnegut, K. (1972) *Slaughterhouse-Five*, St. Albans: Panther.

Vonnegut, K. (1973/1975) *Breakfast of Champions*, St. Albans: Panther.

Walkerdine, V. (1986) 'Video replay: families, films and fantasy', in Burgin, V., Donald, J. and Kaplan, C. (eds) *Formations of Fantasy*, London: Routledge and Kegan Paul, pp. 167–199.

Walkerdine, V. (1990) *Schoolgirl Fictions*, London: Verso.

Walkerdine, V. (1997) *Daddy's Girl: Young Girls and Popular Culture*, Basingstoke: Macmillan Press.

Walkerdine, V. (2007) *Children, Gender, Video Games: Towards a Relational Approach to Multimedia*, London: Palgrave Macmillan.

Walkerdine, V., Lucey, H. and Melody, J. (2001) *Growing Up Girl: Psychosocial Explorations of Gender and Class*, Basingstoke: Palgrave.

Ward, S. (ed.) (2008) *A Student's Guide to Education Studies* (second edition), London: Routledge.

Waskul, D. D. (2009) 'My boyfriend loves it when I come home from this class: pedagogy, titillation, and new media technologies', *Sexualities*, Volume 12, Number 5, 654–661.

Watt, I. (1957/1979) *The Rise of the Novel: Studies in Defoe, Richardson and Fielding*, Harmondsworth: Penguin in association with Chatto and Windus.

Weedon, C. (2004) *Identity and Culture: Narratives of Difference and Belonging*, Maidenhead: Open University Press.

Wells, K. (2009) *Childhood in a Global Perspective*, Cambridge: Polity.

Wells, P. (2002) '"Tell me about your id, when you was a kid, yah!": animation and children's television culture', in Buckingham, D. (ed.) *Small Screens: Television for Children*, London: Leicester University Press, pp. 61–95.

Whelehan, I. (2000) *OverLoaded: Popular Culture and the Future of Feminism*, London: The Women's Press.

Willett, J. (ed. and trans.) (1978) *Brecht on Theatre: The Development of an Aesthetic*, London: Methuen.

Willett, R., Robinson, M. and Marsh, J. (eds) (2008) *Play, Creativity and Digital Cultures*, London: Routledge.

Williams, A. (2007) *Portable Music and Its Functions*, New York: Peter Lang.

Williams, L. (2008) *Screening Sex*, Durham, NC: Duke University Press.

Williams, R. (1958) *Culture and Society 1780–1950*, London: Chatto and Windus.

Williams, R. (1961/1965) *The Long Revolution*, London: Chatto and Windus/Penguin.

Williams, R. (1974) *Television: Technology and Cultural Form*, London: Fontana/Collins.

Williams, R. (1976) *Keywords: A Vocabulary of Culture and Society*, London: Fontana.

Williams, R. (1977) *Marxism and Literature*, Oxford: Oxford University Press.

Williams, R. (1980) *Problems in Materialism and Culture*, London: Verso.

Williamson, J. (1981/1982) 'How does girl number twenty understand ideology?' *Screen Education*, Autumn-Winter, Number 40, pp. 80–87.

Williamson, M. (2005) *The Lure of the Vampire: Gender, Fiction and Fandom from Bram Stoker to Buffy* London: Wallflower Press.

Willis, P. (1972) 'Pop Music and Youth Groups', Unpublished Ph.D., CCCS, University of Birmingham.

Willis, P. (1977) *Learning to Labour: How Working-Class Kids Get Working-Class Jobs,* London: Saxon House.

Willis, P. (1978) *Profane Culture,* London: Chatto and Windus.

Willis, P. (2000) *The Ethnographic Imagination,* Cambridge: Polity.

Willis, P., Jones, S., Canaan, J. and Hurd, G. (1990) *Common Culture: Symbolic Work at Play in the Everyday Cultures of the Young,* Buckingham: Open University Press.

Wilson, J. (1996) *Bad Girls,* London: Transworld/Doubleday.

Wilson, J. (1997) *Girls in Love,* London: Doubleday.

Wilson, J. (1998) *Girls Under Pressure,* London: Doubleday.

Wilson, J. (1999) *Girls Out Late,* London: Doubleday.

Winn, M. (2001) *The Plug-In Drug: Television, Computers and Family Life,* Harmondsworth: Penguin.

Wright, R. (1970) *Black Boy,* London: Longman.

Yon, D. A. (2000) *Elusive Culture: Schooling, Race, and Identity in Global Times,* Albany, NY: State University of New York Press.

Zipes, J. (1983) *Fairy Tales and the Art of Subversion,* London: Heinemann Educational Books.

Zipes, J. (2001) *Sticks and Stones: The Troublesome Success of Children's Literature from Slovenly Peter to Harry Potter,* New York: Routledge.

Index